C0-AUG-869
JUNIOR COLLEGE
LIBRARY

THE CHALLENGE OF LOVE

THE CHALLENGE OF LOVE

Practical Advice for Married Couples and Those Planning Marriage

José de Vinck, LL.D.
John T. Catoir, J.C.D.

HAWTHORN BOOKS, INC., NEW YORK

THE CHALLENGE OF LOVE

 All inquiries should be addressed to Hawthorn Books, Inc., 70 Fifth Avenue, New York City 10011. This book was manufactured in the United States of America and published simultaneously in Canada by Prentice-Hall of Canada, Ltd., 1870 Birchmount Road, Scarborough, Ontario. Library of Congress Catalogue Card Number: 69-17614.

First Edition: 1969

Designed by Gene Gordon

Illustrated by Sandra J. Melcher

TO CATHERINE, WITH LOVE

José and John

FOREWORD

This book is a venture in hope, like an outstretched hand or an expectant smile, both confident and reticent: confident, because the authors are offering their best; reticent, because even that is not enough. This book has two authors, but a single purpose: to encourage young people in the tremendous adventure of marriage. And so, we begin with hope, and we offer love, but there is need also of the third of the theological virtues: faith. Without faith, hope is meaningless and love has no sufficient object. Faith, then, is an essential condition of happiness: faith in self, in the intrinsic goodness of God's earth and its greatest marvel, man and woman in love; faith in God himself, Father, Son, and Holy Spirit, the Creator, the Example, and the Principle of love. May happiness in love, now and forever, come to those who seek it in this light.

JOSÉ DE VINCK
JOHN T. CATOIR

Epiphany, 1969

FOREWORD

PREFACE

In spite of the enormous amount of literature available on the subject of marriage, those who are engaged in teaching young people are often at a loss to find a book that meets modern needs adequately. There are pious books that reduce human love to a religious experience, and there are sex-oriented books that equate physical satisfaction with marital happiness. Both tendencies miss the meaning of marriage. There are also reams of printed material that focus on specific aspects of marriage, but very little that covers, in a practical way, the entire range of marital activities. The authors have combined their experience for precisely that purpose. The attempt may seem ambitious, but the need is great for a text that would appeal to our modern generation, to people in constant need of reassessing their goals and polishing up their techniques of daily living.

The entire work has been developed within the context of Christian experience and in the belief that God is Love. The pursuit of human fulfillment in marriage must be extended beyond the search for sexual harmony, and beyond the "I-Thou" relationship. The whole man needs to be considered. Not merely in an abstract way, but in a way that makes sense to those engaged in the problems of the here and now. The modern generation is facing questions that were never asked before. A study of contemporary tensions must be meaningful to those who understand what it is to be alive now, in the nuclear age—when there are rapid social evolution, protest, demonstration, revolution.

There are many aspects of modern life that affect the emotional development of everyone, and therefore the emotional harmony of every human couple. Some of these aspects are new; others are merely modifications of past experiences. Taken together, they form a new synthesis. Common sense will be the foundation of the new wisdom, as it was of the old.

While many factors in life undergo transition, human nature

remains fundamentally the same. Everything good must be preserved in the exploration of adequate training for our times. But there are significant changes taking place in society that cannot be resolved with ancient platitudes.

What makes a marriage "modern"? The most important difference between traditional and contemporary views seems to consist in the enlargement and upgrading of the concept of womanhood. Traditionally, woman had been seen as the wife and mother, the homemaker, the "heart" of the family; and her only acceptable position was thought to be one of service to husband and children. Even in Christian times, with the recognition of female rights on the spiritual level, not much progress had been made from the notion of chattel, of a "thing" owned by the male for his ease and enjoyment. Most of the manuals of ethics and spirituality addressed to women—and written by men—confirmed the prejudice of subjection, and exaggerated the Pauline attitude, overlooking the fact that St. Paul was writing, no doubt with the inspiration of the Holy Spirit, but also in the light of the sociology of his time. What St. Paul writes about a woman's dignity is far above the level of recognition—or lack of it—to which she had been used. Yet, it is also far below the full development of her potentials.

What, then, are a few of the aspects of modern woman with which she comes to marriage as a person very different from the old?

Not only does a woman have spiritual rights: she has every other human right besides. She has a right to be herself intellectually, emotionally, and physically. Undoubtedly, a woman can claim with perfect justification her independence of thought. She can work out and live by her own theology and philosophy, without any obligation to submit to her husband's position in these matters.

Intellectually, a woman has the right to be the person that she is. She may develop her own inner world of thoughts and desires, create her own ideals, and work toward them in her own way. She may determine the pattern of her life, which may take the form of a career, an art, or some kind of study that would make her a useful and creative being.

Emotionally, a modern woman cannot be restricted to spending her natural warmth on husband and children alone: she has the whole world to love, and everyone in it, and is perfectly free to lavish as much of herself as she wishes within the context of *true* love. True love is liberating, and a woman must be allowed to be herself, a loving, faithful wife with a vision wider than that of her grandmother.

Finally, in the physical order, a woman has the fullness of rights on her own body, before and after marriage. She no more "belongs" to her husband than her husband "belongs" to her. If marriage is not the coming together in love of two completely developed freedoms, it can never attain the heights to which it is called. This is true also of sex: no man has any right over his wife other than to love her. Both are equally free to seek in marriage and through each other the full satisfaction of their natural needs; both have an equal right in the choice of timing and means; and both have the freedom to express their personal desires and to expect the sexual partner to be considerate about them.

What we have, then, in modern marriage is not a timid wife submitted to the absolute power of a domineering male. This Victorian image has been replaced by a much more dignified relationship: that of two equals, each of whom is free, independent, and valuable in his or her own right, coming together for the sake of love, and expressing this love in their sexual union.

Woman is acquiring her freedom. But as with all newly acquired freedoms, there is a problem of proper use. History shows that emancipation was not the end of slavery: it was only the first step in turning a slave into a fully free man. Besides freedom, there is need for the conditions under which freedom may be used so as to flourish into a wholesome life.

A number of women are bewildered and insecure with their newly acquired freedom. This insecurity may take the form of overaggressiveness, in competition with the male in jobs and careers, or of assertions of liberty without any organized effort to do anything about it. It is not enough to be free: one must be free for something.

In fact, then, it is only an élite among the more intelligent and educated women that has attained the level of personality that has been opened to them by the recognition of their position as the equals of men. And it is only this élite that is able to bring to marriage a fully mature and integrated person, the ideal partner of a fully mature and integrated man.

Let us remember, then, in all these discussions that what is being proposed may be a distant goal for some, an ideal worth working for, but still out of reach. As far as our own lives are concerned, emphasis should be placed on realism, on the facts of "this man" and "this woman" here and now, who happen to be married. Both are necessarily imperfect—one perhaps more or less than the other. Both need to make concessions and compromises —and to improve themselves. One may be strong and the other weak, and it may be either the husband or the wife. But both should have clearly in mind the idea that *modern marriage is the equal partnership of two free individuals, living their personal lives, and meeting in their common life of love.*

CONTENTS

An artist whose motives are pure can allow himself the greater range of expression offered by dispensing with clothing, and can do so without offense.

ALPHONSUS JANSEN

Beauty, nakedness, dancing, music, love: can those be among the materials of which holiness is made?

GERALD VANN, O.P.

Christianity is not necessarily against nature, and within its tradition lie the seeds of a flowering which may some day change its atmosphere profoundly.

ALAN WATTS

The appreciation of the sensual is the mark of human rationality and not of animal instinct.

ERIC GILL

To know it is not so good as to love it. To love it is not so good as to enjoy it.

CONFUCIUS

What we really need are a few sexy saints.

ANN MARTIN

Yes!

A ZEN MASTER

PART I

ADVICE TO THE MARRIED

CHAPTER 1
HOW TO ENJOY THE HONEYMOON

Spend Your First Night Close to Home . . . Be Realistic About What to Expect . . . Put Away Your Fears and Anxieties . . . The Only Right You Have Is the Right to Love . . . Intercourse Must Be an Act of Love . . . Total Nudity Is the Natural State . . . Your New Life in Common Has Now Begun . . . The Honeymoon Is a Time for Giving . . . Pleasure Will Come if You Do Not Seek It

The last strains of the orchestra have faded away. The bouquet has been thrown. A blushing bride and groom glide down the stairs in brand-new traveling clothes, and go as fast as possible to their waiting car. Alone at last! Yes, this is it. You two are on your own.

Spend Your First Night Close to Home

Whether you plan a six-month tour of the Aegean Sea or a weekend at Niagara Falls, the most important thing is where you will spend your wedding night. Let it be close to home so as not to add the exhausting effects of a long trip to the nervous fatigue of the preparation, wedding, and reception. A wise groom will have done some exploring on his own. He will have made reservations in some cozy motel or plush hotel in the next town or close to the air terminal. If at all possible, the newlyweds should try to arrive at their room late in the afternoon, so as to have plenty of time to rest before having dinner. Planning ahead will prevent needless hurry and indecision. You may not feel like eating at all, but if you do, the meal should be relaxed and delightfully romantic in its setting. Then you will go arm in arm to your room and close the door. This was as far as old-fashioned stories and counseling dared to go. It was presumed that from here on nature could be safely left to take its course. Unfortunately, in the majority of cases, young lovers are very much in need of advice in these intimate matters, if they are to start out right on the way to happy wedded love.

A man's earlier experiences may not serve as a reliable guide to a night such as this, especially if his new wife is a virgin. Many young men come to this point with an assortment of successes and failures in the art of love, and this tends to give them the impression that they know what they are doing. Even aside from any moral consideration, their past experiences may have resulted in mental and emotional attitudes that are far from ideal as an introduction to love in marriage. For instance, the female partner may have been considered merely as a plaything, a means of obtaining self-gratification, an instrument to be used for the confirmation of male power. There may have been the fear of detection or moral guilt adding a tinge of darkness to the enjoyment. Even fully satisfying premarital sex with a willing and eager partner may have left a bitter taste if it resulted in a loss of self-respect or a feeling of having fallen into sin.

There may be need, then, of some reconditioning, of turning over a new leaf. Put your mind at ease about the past. Married love is new, wonderful, holy, and you must make yourself new, wonderful, and holy. A vivid awareness of the beauty of the present will help you to make a sincere break with anything that may have been shady in your past.

If you are inexperienced, there is a great need to adapt patiently to the new world in which you are to live. This adaptation will take many forms over the years, from the development of intimate togetherness to the growth of spiritual harmony. On the first night, it is almost impossible to be fully two-in-one flesh and spirit. Such things are achievements, summits—the final and wonderful goal of a rich life together. The first night should be an introduction to this life. But you cannot trust your instincts alone to make it so. There are some things you must learn from the experience of others.

Be Realistic About What to Expect

Take a reasonable and calm view of the situation. Considering the young husband's state of mind, this may be demanding much. Yet it is extremely important.

The goal is at hand—the triumphant groom and his willing bride now enjoy the religious and legal blessings that justify their intimate love. They have at last reached a haven of privacy where it is possible to be completely free and uninhibited. This is the expected achievement of months of build-up, hope, and fear. It must be taken realistically and handled lightly in order to avoid any letdown and possible catastrophic disappointment.

First of all, try to be realistic about what to expect. It is possible that your very first intercourse will be completely satisfying—that you will climb on clouds of bliss and count the stars. That from the very start you and your mate will strike a high level of sexual harmony. It is possible but very far from probable.

Inexperienced young people are naturally clumsy lovers. They do not know exactly what to do, how and when. They are tired, nervous, scared, often not a little disturbed by a false sense of shame, upset by the novelty of preparing for something that had been forbidden. These prohibitions have often been handed down with a negative and heavy-handed boorishness by the best-intentioned people in the world. They were trying to do good, but managed only to express their own fears and prejudices.

Then there are the specific fears of each sex—a young man might be in terror of possible impotency. Will he be manly enough to succeed? Will he prove himself? Will his advances be accepted or rejected? And the girl's fears can be most distressing to her—the horror of pain, the shrinking before bloodshed, the psychological trauma of surrendering her precious virginity. All these can be grossly exaggerated in the mind of an inexperienced bride.

Put Away Your Fears and Anxieties

Let us take these one by one. A young man has very little to fear. His potency, his power of effecting and maintaining a proper erection of his male organ, is practically automatic. The less he thinks about it, the easier it will be. It would be much preferable for him to forget about his own equipment and concentrate on the forthcoming revelation of his bride's charms. If he thinks too much about possible impotency, he will miss the pleasure of considering her body. By doubting his own powers, and failing to enjoy their most potent stimulant, he may very well end up by inducing in himself a temporary psychological impotency.

As for the girl, there is no need to fear. The loss of blood induced by a normal defloration is almost nil. The pain is comparatively slight, and quickly forgotten in the fire of emotion. Surrendering her virginity should be a joyful gift. Preservation would now be pointless, for virginity has served its purpose. It has been preserved precisely for this—to be given up in an act of love. In this act, there is not the slightest "sullying" in spite of much pious literature to the contrary; there is nothing dirty or degrading; there is no irretrievable loss of any worthwhile treasure. On the contrary, the expectant, incomplete virgin has now fully become a woman.

The folklore of virginity is endless and generally unfounded. Much has been made by nineteenth-century literature of the exceptional pleasure of deflowering a virgin, and many a rogue seems to have made of it his favorite sport. In fact, there is much less pleasure in the initial act with a scared and inexperienced girl than in intercourse consummated with a mature and knowing woman.

The Only Right You Have Is the Right to Love

The mutual bodily attraction of young male and female is an extremely strong and moving power. Most of the art of love consists in the ability to maintain breath-taking eagerness at the thought, sight, act of it—the very opposite of the bored and sophisticated attitude of those for whom it is old stuff. The emotional high-point of the relationship may generally be found at the moment when, for the first time, the free and legitimate compenetration of bodies is accomplished as a final seal to marriage. There is here an entirely new contact with an entirely different reality, a connection so deep, so intimate, as to be organic, functional, and unitive to a degree attained by no other human act. The intensity of possible pleasure arises precisely from this sense of extraordinary contact—the successful response of reality to the probing of love. It is so very great precisely because, in the consummation of love, each partner is doing to the other precisely what he *and* she most passionately desire to do, and is receiving from the other precisely what he *and* she most passionately desire to receive. Pleasure arises from the coincidence of passions that are bent on the common goal of total union and compenetration. Pleasure is a sign of access to reality, the assertion of the "I" in the presence of the other, and the corresponding reassertion received from the other. This is perfect sex; this is what to look forward to; but you have not yet reached this point.

A little more patience, and we shall get to the act itself. As a final word of advice, remember that the only right a man has over the woman he marries is the right to love her. It emphatically does not include the right of imposing upon her at any time some form of sexual activity that he alone would enjoy. It takes two to make love, and it takes two to play perfect sex. The worst possible blunder on the wedding night is for a man to use it as an occasion to assert his "sexual rights." In the worst sense of the term, this means the absolute power of the male to use and abuse the female as he pleases—it is a barbaric and subhuman distortion that has often resulted in something like a first-night rape. Needless to say, this is a severely damaging start to marriage. In the mind of the bride, sex will then be associated forever with brutal greed. There is nothing more repellent than forced sexual attentions—a violation of the most secret areas of the personality, an invasion of sacred privacy, a forced grasping of what has value only as a free gift.

Intercourse Must Be an Act of Love

The act of love is not an act of lust. This is the time to be tender and patient, to relax together as completely as possible. This is the time for gently undressing or dressing for love. No fast rule is possible here. With a timid bride, it may be better at first for both to wear whatever nightclothes they prefer—something loose and comfortable. With a completely uninformed bride, the sight of the erect male organ may produce a shock of fear and disgust. A wise groom will avoid needless risks, and gently accustom his bride to the male body.

Lovers will then pass from tender words and looks to kisses and caresses. The whole gamut of seduction does not need to be played in full. But there should be systematic courting, sweet and patient overcoming of timidity and reserve. All this will be glowing with the awareness that it is now a reality. The first night should be seen, not as the first chance for all-out sex-play, but as the first chance for all-out love-play, and it is immensely different. Love-play is exciting the other for the other's sake, out of the desire to express tenderness, to make the partner emotionally and physically happy and prepared. In love-play before the first intercourse, the young husband does all he can to appease and at the same time seduce his new wife. It may take immense patience and great control to hold her so close, to breathe her odor of life and love, and yet postpone the satisfaction of the normal male's strongest desire—to penetrate the beloved female and spend himself in the total act of love. This patience and postponement are most important, not only on this first night but also in every future intercourse. Some few wives may be eager and well prepared without drawn-out preliminaries, but the greatest majority even of mature women need considerable time before they are ready actually to surrender their bodies. This is the important point—more time and attention before they are ready and able to be transformed into cooperating, enthusiastic, passionate playmates.

On a first night, the preliminaries may need to be quite long. The husband, however, should not take every defensive movement as a refusal. He should be firm and assertive. He should know what he is doing, do it, progressing from superficial and general caressing to the gentle but deep stimulation of the sexually excitable areas. He should continue until the first signs of response appear—eyes closed, breath short and panting, heart beating faster, distillation of fluid in the female genital area, slow pelvic thrusts and gyrations—the bride is now ready. In future acts, it will be good to go beyond this point, to continue caresses in such a way that the girl is brought not only to the first signs of readiness but also to the absolute brink of orgasm. In the present instance, however, there seems to be no reason to delay the final consummation.

The only rule concerning position for the first intercourse is that the bride should be made as comfortable as possible. The position generally recommended is for her to lie in bed on her back, with knees wide open and lifted up. The young man bends over her. He may kiss her and keep his eyes reassuringly on hers. When she is ready, he takes his penis and places it exactly before the opening of her vagina. The wife, if properly excited, may want to do it herself. She should not be shy about touching the male organ. Now is the time for the man to be gentle. A few light thrusts will show how far penetration is possible. Perhaps the hymen is open. Some women have a naturally open vagina that should not be taken as a sign of nonvirginity. A progressive penetration may be obtained right away. If the hymen is tightly drawn, it will permit penetration of only the tip of the male erection. There will then be need of "defloration": the tearing of the hymen. With a few reassuring words, the young husband will ask if his bride is ready. She may nod, or murmur, or remain silent and expecting. He will then press his body in a fast, firm motion against hers. In all probability, the hymen will yield. The girl may experience momentary pain, but it is soon forgotten. If the hymen does not yield after many tries, there is no need to worry. A slight incision by a gynecologist will solve the problem without any difficulty.

Frequently, a young man who has gone through all this is in such a state of sexual disquietude that he will ejaculate instantly. He may even ejaculate before total penetration, in which case defloration will have to be postponed since the penis will probably lose its necessary rigidity. There is nothing shameful or disgraceful in premature ejaculation: on the contrary, it is a not unusual reaction of the chaste young man to his first coital experience. It will vanish as soon as better control has been obtained through repetition.

The bride may have perceived no pleasure whatsoever. Even this is completely normal. There is so much in her that has to be reconditioned—so much that needs to be unlearned, so much more that needs to be learned through practice—because of the artificial conditions of her education and the tone of her former life. Instinctive pleasure-inducing reactions are seldom released at the first try.

Hence, a first act of love may vary between complete mutual pleasure or premature ejaculation on the part of the husband without any pleasure in the wife. Even the worst experience is no cause for anxiety. Sex is an art, and it needs to be learned. Whatever way it may go, the first try is valuable and necessary —it has opened the door for further experiences.

Perhaps this is all that can be accomplished tonight, but there is no absolute reason to stop. An ardent couple may want much more. The game can go on. Soon both partners will again be in complete readiness. The right thing to do after a first try is to spend some time in tender, reassuring intimacy, maintaining a close embrace and sweet conversation, expressing gratitude for the girl's surrender and some concern and pity for her physical pain—but not too much, since it is nothing worth fussing about. The tender game may be stretched out far into the night, but, as wisdom indicates, it is better not to overdo anything. Your whole life is before you. There will be other times, better times, when you are less tense and tired. And so, good night! Sleep well! And think of the surprise of waking up with your beloved breathing peacefully next to you in bed.

Total Nudity Is the Natural State

The story is told of a British officer who was called before a military court to answer a charge of "conduct unbecoming an officer." He had been seen in a hotel corridor in Adam's garb pursuing a lady in the state of Eve. The defense quoted an article of the Military Code that read: "When practicing any sport, a British officer will wear the proper apparel." He was acquitted.

Total nudity is the most normal and natural state in which to practice the sport of love. It is only in periods of strict and pessimistic sexual mores that the opposite was ever advocated. The worst of these periods was, of course, the Victorian age in which our grandmothers were deprived of much of the freedom and fun of life. It was not uncommon in those days for a husband to see his wife's legs only by accident—and to be soundly scolded for his indecency if he did not immediately avert his eyes! A young lady's sexual upbringing was then so insanely strict that she would much rather have been caught dead than naked—even by her husband. The greatest fear in a maiden's life was to meet "a fate worse than death." This explains in part the extraordinary flourishing of houses of prostitution—where naked love-making prevailed—in the nineteenth century. Many an old lady is now sighing, "If only we had known . . ."

Traces of this state of mind may still be lingering at the present time. They should be eliminated with care, as one erases a damaging stain from a work of art. Nudity in married life is one of the foremost signs of the mutual gift, and one of the best means of mutual enjoyment besides the total union, for sexual joy may be found in many ways. Actual intercourse is all too brief, and it should be seen not as the only form of sexual expression but also as the culmination of a whole way of life. In fact, if sex is reduced to copulation, copulation itself is in danger of being reduced to impersonal physiological relief. And that is as nothing compared to what it could have been.

The total sexual life of a man and a woman consists in their manner of being together, of living together in all circumstances. It is a night-and-day conversation, a state of mutual observation and donation, an offering, a gift of much more than the organic differences. One of the most enduring and valuable of the natural offerings is the nude body at night. Away with wraps, creases, buttons, bows, ticklish lace, strangling ropes, smothering "billows of the finest lawn." Too bad for the lingerie and pajama merchants—that stuff is out, passé, fini. It may be used in the preliminary phases of love as a bird uses its brilliantly colored feathers to attract a mate. But it is definitely not part of natural, all-out, all-satisfying sex. So, except for use on those very special nights when the full scenario of love is to be played and some amount of décor may be needed, silk pajamas and transparent nighties should go out on the rubbish heap to join celluloid collars, whalebone corsets, and ankle-length skirts. We were all born naked, whether we like it or not, and it is much more fun to like it.

Your New Life in Common Has Now Begun

And so, our newlyweds wake up around noon and face a world that is entirely new. A world in which they have actually made love! The first shock comes as soon as they realize that it is still very much the same old world and that it does not pay the slightest attention to what has been, for them, the most emotionally intense event in their lives. They now live in two different worlds —the new, their own, and the old that keeps rolling along with as little concern as Ol' Man River. They are perfectly justified in developing, preserving, and defending their new world, but they cannot live in it exclusively. They are still human beings, social beings, part of the family of man. During the first days of the honeymoon, they may be so deeply absorbed in each other that they will be living almost solely on each other. Then they will slowly come down to earth, no longer acting moon-struck, but responsible newlyweds. This means that they progressively will learn about their responsibilities toward each other, their families, neighbors, and God.

No longer are they independent individuals. They are now strongly dependent upon each other, bound by a tie that may be turned either into a form of slavery or into the greatest mutual liberation. The unstable, neurotic, and security-craving will cling to their marital partner like leeches and seek to "mobilize" all the powers of this new possession for the exclusive service of their needs, real or imaginary. The free and generous, on the contrary, will accept the gift of the other's presence and love as a grace —a gratuitous and inexhaustible marvel, something to be rejoiced over in the communion of love. Their inner liberation comes from the fact that their deepest longings have ceased to roam. They now have settled on an appropriate object, and find in it a substantial fulfillment. Since the lovers are no longer anguished, tired, or upset by the insecurity of their search, they can settle down. Not to the petty enjoyment of their newly acquired comfort and pleasure, but to the much vaster task of living. This they can pursue in a deeper, more human way with the assistance of a companion at their side, and the warm awareness that they are no longer wandering about, but walking straight ahead—running, even, or dancing to the tune of timeless love.

The Honeymoon Is a Time for Giving

The honeymoon, then, is a unique time during which two nervous and inexperienced strangers begin to establish the foundations of true understanding and mutual help. *The honeymoon is much more a time for giving than a time for receiving.* It is not composed exclusively of the bliss of sexual satisfaction. There may be that, of course, but there must be much more.

For the children of light—both loving and wise—the discovery of the tremendous depth of intimacy and joy in the man-woman relationship will greatly surpass the urge toward ever-increasing pleasure. It will be a clear sign of their participation in the goodness of reality on every level—not only sex but also kindness, understanding, generosity, dedication, work, career. Beginning with sensual delight, the lovers, if they are wise, will grow in quality—intellectually, emotionally, and physically. The high level of happy functioning of their sexual power will be reflected in the high level of efficiency of whatever else they happen to be doing. The sexual glow will carry over to enlighten them in their everyday tasks. It will have been lighted and cared for during the honeymoon—it must be kept going forever after as a steady flame.

That is why the handling of first-night love and the honeymoon period is so important. The attitude you take sets a pattern of success or failure for the rest of your married life. There is no need for every moment of the honeymoon to be perfect or for every try to be a success. But what is of paramount importance is that this very special time be marred by no memory of sensual gluttony, impatience, frustration, or anger that would spoil its ethereal sheen. Some failures are inevitable: they may be surmounted with patience and humor. Sex, after all, is not so solemn an occasion that any minor imperfection would be catastrophic. On the contrary, it is something so fragile, so rare, and so heavily fraught with human frailty that the marvel is that it can ever succeed at all. It should be approached, not with pompous and lofty expectations, but very simply, as a sweet and highly rewarding game, full of variety and surprises—some of them delightful, others good, others not so good—all of which must be accepted with a kind of lighthearted unconcern. Only then, in the absence of any demand for perfection and without any preplanned program of orgiastic satisfaction, will it have a chance to yield its fruits of joy.

Pleasure Will Come if You Do Not Seek It

It is important to start out very soon during the honeymoon with a proper approach to sexual experience. If sex is believed to be an automatic procurer of pleasure, something that will give total physical satisfaction each and every time the proper procedures are followed, it will prove to be endlessly disappointing. What would be wanting here is not sex, but a right understanding of its nature and of the conditions of pleasure. As in any other form of delight, pleasure cannot be an end in itself. *Instead of being a goal, pleasure is a result.* It is the glow that follows doing well something that needs to be done. In the sexual union man and woman—two incomplete units—are fused into a whole that is greater than the sum of its parts. The parts are man and woman, and also love. In a mysterious way, this is a very close parallel to the Father, the Son, and the Holy Spirit, a deeply religious reality that far exceeds the search for emotional and physical thrills. Furthermore, if the relationship is reduced to an expression of self-seeking, it will not result in two-in-one. It will not yield fruits of pleasure, only bursts of satisfied lust—and this is subhuman.

Putting all this in precise terms related to the performance of intercourse, we could say that, instead of concentrating on the accomplishment of his or her orgasm, the partners should penetrate each other as loving persons in such a way that they allow the marvel of sexual bliss to come to them as a sign of the consummation of their love.

This is neither farfetched nor impossible. There is no need to be aware of such a high disposition of the mind in the midst of sexual play. But in the calm that precedes it there is always the possibility of making a choice between two entirely different approaches that will have entirely different results in terms of both pleasure and merit. One consists in thinking, "I will seek you sexually as an instrument of my pleasure." The other, "I will seek you sexually out of love for you, to express and feel the marvel of our oneness." There may be some pleasure derived from the first approach: the coarse satisfaction of an instinctive need. In the second, the pleasure will be both complete and holy because it will be whole—the whole man and woman coming together in the consummation of true love.

CHAPTER 2

A HAPPY MARRIAGE IS POSSIBLE

Learning How Depends on You . . . Happy Marriages Are Built on Good Communications . . . To Communicate You Must Tear Down Obstacles . . . The Heart-to-Heart Talk Overcomes Fear . . . The Most Important Thing You Have to Give Is Yourself . . . To Give Yourself You Must Love Yourself . . . Accept Yourself and You Can Accept Others . . . When You Love Others, You Love Them Just as They Are . . . You Are a Link in the Chain of Life . . . The Decisions Are Up to You

Genuine human happiness and perfection may be found in marriage, the most natural and common life condition of man and woman. Failures are due, not to any inherent defect in the institution of matrimony, but to the imperfections and lack of preparation of the partners themselves. It is encouraging to realize that these damaging causes of failure can be remedied: lack of preparation, by an organized study of the married state; imperfections, by a serious self-analysis and an attempt at improvement, first as an individual, then as a marriage partner. For the two go together: *Someone unable to live in peace and harmony with himself will never manage to live in peace and harmony with another.*

Let us then begin with a formal affirmation of optimism: A *happy marriage is possible.* It is possible in theory because marriage is the state of the majority, and God would not have planned that the majority of mankind be unhappy. It is possible in fact because vast numbers of married people have actually achieved the full and rich rewards of the happily married.

Learning How Depends on You

Many others, however, have settled for half a loaf, when they could have enjoyed the fullness of love. They married without a long-range view, and settled for the half-loaf of immediate pleasure and self-seeking when they could have had a full loaf of kindness, self-giving, and enduring love by partaking of the "bread of life," the invisible reality by which man lives.

Happiness cannot be defined; neither can it be caught as a prey. If you pursue it as a prize designed to your own specifications, it will lead you a merry chase and finally disappear in the distant world of lost illusions. There is no magic formula for happiness in marriage, as there is none for happiness in life. And no one can make you happy but yourself. What a book like this can do for you is to awaken you to the conditions required for happy love. Although every man and woman's life is personal and unique, there are many useful facts and notions that the common experience of mankind has discovered along the way. Learning such things from others is both faster and considerably easier than going through your own series of trials and errors. A number of these facts and notions are essential for a man and woman to grow into loving persons.

Let us begin by considering a happy union as already achieved. Imagine the happiest marriage you know. How did this couple make it? If you look closely at the realized promises of a wholesome love relationship, you will begin to understand the basic ingredients that make it possible to enjoy life fully in the marriage state. Happiness may be elusive and difficult to define, but it is not an accident. It is the result of dedicated self-giving.

Happy Marriages Are Built on Good Communications

The first condition of successful love is the ability to communicate. This may seem obvious, but it is not all that simple.

Communication is the most difficult art in marriage, and the lack of it is the most frequent cause of misery and divorce.

For two people to communicate well, there must be an honest and spontaneous flow of information and self-revelation that grows and expands with the development of mutual trust. Because of countless fears and anxieties, human beings are usually reserved, and often overcautious. They build a protective barrier of silence and secretiveness between their own insecurity and the outside world. In a truly effective love-relationship, this defensive armor must fall. It would be better to say it must be dropped. The defensive habit is so strong that it will be overcome only by a positive act of will impelled by a clear understanding of the need for openness.

There is a tragic story of a short man who guarded himself excessively in his relations with others. He had allowed his feelings of inferiority to consume him to the point that he had become a rather nasty and defensive person. By some beautiful miracle, a fine young lady was attracted to him, and the two fell in love. He softened and sweetened under the influence of her love, but he could never really believe that she loved him, for he was unable to accept himself as an object of love. And so he allowed his doubts about her sincerity to grow; he even suspected that she was unfaithful to him. He questioned and nagged her constantly, searching for the reassurance he so badly needed. In fact, he tormented her to the point that she could no longer live with him. And so he lost her. His great opportunity for peace, love, and joy dissolved because he was not whole enough to give and receive love—freely and joyfully. His inability to accept her love was a fatal defect in his power to communicate.

To Communicate You Must Tear Down Obstacles

A happy marriage is something you have to work at. Marriage is like a city divided by a high wall. To achieve unity the wall must be torn down piece by piece. In this parable of the divided city, two groups come together, one representing man, the other woman—to settle in a particular area with the idea of forming a single community. Not trusting each other fully, they had built a wall between them. Their exchanges were limited to the sending of envoys, formal, guarded, and well armed. Correspondingly, a man and woman who become formally married may still live their own individual lives without surrendering themselves to that life they are to have in common. They communicate as a matter of protocol, but they have not as yet seen each other's true glories or miseries.

And so, the two cities live close to each other, depending upon each other for their survival and external help: Gynepolis and Andropolis—the She-City and the He-City. Never did Gynepolis, rich and warm and ready to give, hear of the slums and miseries of Andropolis. Never did Andropolis, so true to its culture and faith, ever hear of the sighs and longings in Gynepolis for a sharing in this particular wealth. For all they knew of each other came to them through the cool, official eyes of their government delegation.

Then, one day, a few children from Gynepolis scrambled over the wall. They had been warned of all the dreadful things they would find on the other side: they were afraid to die, but their eagerness for the discovery of life was greater than their fear of losing it. They met some children from Andropolis, doubtful, retiring, afraid. Being children, they were still unprejudiced, so the two groups came together. The children of Gynepolis told of their abundance of love and of their yearning for strength. Those of Andropolis told of their abundance of strength and of their yearning for love. Then they all went home and spoke to their parents, and the parents beat their breasts, crying: "Little ones, you have done what we have not dared to do for years. You have spoken with your hearts to the people across the wall. Now we know they too have hearts. Let us go out together and pull down the wall." And so it was done. And the warmth and love of Gynepolis mingled with the power and splendor of Andropolis, and a truly complete and human community was born.

The parable may be a poetic image, but it has a point. A

married man and woman may be living in the same house but on different sides of a wall of suspicion, incomprehension, lack of communication. Their messages are formal greetings, perfunctory good-bye kisses, polite conversation across the supper table. In the beginning, communication may have been good and promising, but they allowed things to deteriorate. After years of marriage they have become impersonal. Never would you hear them say: "Do you know how much I love you? I sincerely believe. I hope. I suffered, did you?"

The Heart-to-Heart Talk Overcomes Fear

Then by some fortuitous circumstance, like the children climbing over the wall, there would be a break in the silence. An absence, an accident, or an illness would occur to make them realize that their method of ambassadorial communication had failed—that they needed a good heart-to-heart talk, expressing not only their successes but also their needs, failures, and miseries. Then they could get together on the important task of breaking down the wall—of becoming one city, one complete and human community of love.

This lack of communication is part of the ancient fear of surrendering one's life into another's hands: "Who knows what he or she will do with my pains, my longings, my failure, my true beliefs? Perhaps I put on a false front; perhaps I will be found out, and it will be the end. Our marriage will die." But a marriage built on such false premises was never alive. Only in true, childlike, honest, spontaneous communication can there be any chance for substantial happiness.

A true lover attempts to develop the gift of trust and the art of surrounding the beloved in an atmosphere of security and confidence. Since trust implies trustworthiness, the emphasis is placed immediately on the perfections of personal life. So we can repeat here, now that the need for communication is better understood—No one unable to live in peace and harmony with himself will manage to live in peace and harmony with another.

The Most Important Thing You Have to Give Is Yourself

Good communication implies not only that messages be clearly transmitted, but, most of all, that these messages be worth transmitting—that you *have* something to communicate. Something you are, know, care about, have a right to give—*yourself.* If you do not know and like yourself, you will not be any good at communicating. For, besides yourself, what do you have to give? No talent or special gift could possibly make up for your inability to make a full offering of your very person.

To Give Yourself You Must Love Yourself

Before you can give yourself, can fully accept and love another person, you must first accept and love yourself. Does that seem strange? It shouldn't. The destructive results of self-distrust and self-contempt are obvious. These defects poison many potentially good people who fill their own lives and the lives of others with bitterness and sorrow. They get used to their unhappiness, become addicted to a spirit of self-rejection that closes them to love. Eventually they seem to cultivate unhappiness as if self-imposed misery were a condition of salvation.

To understand is to forgive. Coming to terms with yourself is the beginning of understanding. The opening of negotiations is the first step to peace. So, begin by asking a few vital questions of this "self" you may be afraid to face: *Who am I? What do I plan to do with my life? Where am I going?* In some of the following chapters, you will have a chance to explore the highways and byways of self-discovery that eventually lead to a noble self-love that will color your life with peace and joy.

By God's design, that is precisely what you are: a creature of peace and joy, made for love. One day you will be totally confirmed in this state, which is your true destiny as a person. It is not unnatural or unrealistic to begin working your way to this goal right at this very minute, for it is your home country, your fatherland, and you will never be completely at peace until you have crossed its border.

Accept Yourself and You Can Accept Another

Now, to return to our successful couple. It is a joy to live with them as an observant guest. Each thinks automatically of the well-being of the other; they are eagerly trying to understand each other; they honestly explain themselves to each other. Each one of the partners, knowing his or her own mistakes, easily forgives those of the other. Faults and weaknesses are embraced together with strength and virtue: faults and weaknesses, in the name of charity and in the hope of change; strength and virtue, in the name of faith and love. Both spouses are left free to be themselves, free to discover who they are, because true love is liberating. Love is also creative and bountiful: it gives and gives, and keeps giving to the point of complete self-sacrifice. And the more it gives, the more it increases joy.

Such joy can belong only to men and women who are at peace —with themselves, with each other, with the world around them, and with God. That is why it is both sad and frightening to see people approach marriage with deep insecurity and unresolved conflicts. They seek in it nothing but their own healing, what they can "get" out of it for themselves. This offsets from the very start the balance of give-and-take—the eager offering and the grateful receiving, to each and from each, that are conditions of true love.

People cannot assume the burden of marriage if they are unable to carry the weight of their own lives, if they cannot bear inevitable imperfections in themselves and others. Young lovers who come to marriage in the right spirit, at the right pace and with the right dispositions, should not be prejudiced about what the partner should be or how he or she should behave. It is folly to preplan every detail of the other's behavior and habits. There are reasons why a person acts the way he or she does. Understanding these reasons is the key to genuine acceptance of the person. Major traits or important personal characteristics should be discovered during the engagement period. Sinful or grave and irreversible character defects should steer you away from marrying a particular person. But once you are married, it is with an unavoidably imperfect partner.

When You Love Others, You Love Them Just as They Are

"I love you" does not mean "I will love you only if you overcome your annoying faults." For how is a normal person to overcome a personal defect, except by the power of being loved unconditionally, just as he or she is? Love withheld for the sake of some imperfection is not true love but a form of bargaining. It is a sign of rejection rather than of approval. Many married people who have pledged undying love to each other destroy their union with this game of holding back, of never entering into the uncalculating mystery of love. And they never get more than half a loaf because from the very beginning they set limits and conditions to their offering. They are more concerned with what they will receive than with what they will give.

Your vocation as a person demands that you learn the meaning of unconditional love:

> "Love is patient and kind; love is not jealous or boastful; it is not arrogant or rude. Love does not insist on its own way; it is not irritable or resentful; it does not rejoice at wrong, but rejoices in the right. Love bears all things, believes all things, endures all things. Love never ends." [I Cor. 13: 1,4]

To arrive at this freedom and power, this liberation from self, you must learn to love yourself properly.

Love of self is not wrong. Only pride is wrong, and pride is defined as excessive love of self. The unconditional love of yourself simply means that you have attained a degree of maturity where you can accept yourself as you are, for better, for worse, in weakness and in strength, until death, while at the same time doing your best to improve.

You Are a Link in the Chain of Life

There is much more to marriage than experimenting by trial and error. You must first understand its essence as a holy institution of love and as the appointed source of life.

To be is to be loved. To be is to have been created by a loving God, to have been conceived in the act of love between a man and a woman, the highest symbol of the divine creative act of love out of which all things are made.

You, in turn, if such is your vocation, may become the source of life continuing the chain of generations, linking the first man to the last through Christ. You have saints in heaven among your ancestors—a great number of them, although you probably do not know anything about them. You have a chance to give life to many saints by becoming parents to others who will become parents to others again, and so on. You are not lost, alone, isolated, abandoned: on the contrary, you are part of a tremendous, immense, utterly breathtaking picture of life emerging out of God's loving hands and returning to him in its most glorious form. You are, in the present state of the world, the most glorious form of life, because you are alive here and now.

Place yourself in God's hands and entrust your future to his providence. This is a positive act of confidence that is most pleasing to God. Once you have done that, take every reasonable precaution, learning, listening, observing; and then, when you know that you love well and are well loved in return, abandon yourself to the impulses of life in holy marriage.

The Decisions Are Up to You

Good people are attractive. It is only by trying to be good yourself that you will be able to attract a good spouse. To be "good" does not mean goody-goody; it is not pietistic sop. To be good is to be fully the man or fully the woman you were created to be. And that is how you will recognize each other: in the measure in which you can each be as fully, frankly, delightfully what each one of you is supposed to be. To be such a man and a woman implies some lofty virtues: faith, hope, and charity first, but also integrity, honesty, courage, objectivity, purposefulness, awareness, social responsibility, and many others not found in any catechism. Such perfections, however, are never fully present in any one man or woman on earth; they never existed in any individual besides Christ. Part of wisdom, of the art of growing up, of progressing toward adulthood, is the capacity to accept human limitations in yourself and in others while aspiring to develop your more lofty characteristics. The important thing is to be able to discern who you are and who you should be. You alone must decide what is essential for your success. The only thing a counselor can do for you is to point in the general direction. Ultimately, you alone will be responsible for your failure or success.

A happy marriage is possible for you, but all happiness is a gift from God. Humbly pray for this gift while you strive to attain it.

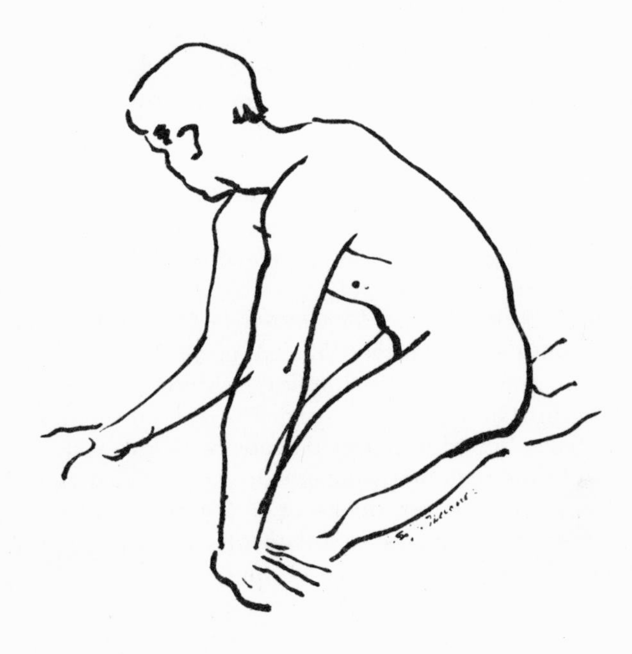

CHAPTER 3

LEARN TO TALK TO EACH OTHER

"I Love You" Has Many Meanings . . . Only One Meaning Is Fully True . . . Communication Is Sharing Your Life with Another . . . Be Wise When You Disagree . . . The Pure of Heart Are Free to Talk . . . Be Able to Laugh at Yourselves . . . Children Should Not Hamper Conjugal Life . . . The Sharing of Silence Is an Expression of Love . . . Guard Against Outside Distractions . . . Common Sense and Courage Can Save You

We have already mentioned the art of communication as a condition of happy marriage. The subject is so important that it is worth expanding into a full chapter, with particular emphasis on verbal communication. The ability to talk to each other means that you have the ability to conceive and express meaningful messages that will be mutually revealing and helpful toward unity and love.

The Vatican II document *The Church in the Modern World* points out obviously enough that the core of marriage is conjugal love. Such love needs to be communicated, since it is a two-way relationship. Christian joy for the married is realized through conjugal love. Hence the often repeated sentence "I love you." What does it mean to the men and women who say it? What should it mean to you? How can you make of it a soothing, reassuring, nourishing message, a soul-to-soul, heart-to-heart, body-to-body signal that all is well with the two of you?

"I Love You" Has Many Meanings

"I love you" may mean a number of different things. Beginning from the bottom, it signifies: "You excite me sexually. I wish we could do something about it right away!" In that sense, it is devoid of foundation other than physical attraction. It is the expression of physiological, sensorial reaction to the image of a desirable member of the opposite sex. It is a lie, because although it may express a true desire, it is totally lacking in the ingredients of true love. It means "I wish I could have you, and care nothing about the consequences." It is used as a means of seduction, more generally by the male, since he knows very well that the way to a woman's surrender is through her emotions. Except in the cases of overly experienced and oversexed women, no true female will surrender her body without at least an illusion of love.

One step higher, "I love you" means "I am emotionally attracted to you. You make my stomach muscles tighten when I see you. You even take my breath away from time to time. You are definitely different from the others. I would like to play with you, cat-and-mouse style—have fun, then let you go. I may get a kick out of it, and perhaps you will too. But I am not promising anything or giving myself to you. This is strictly a sophisticated game in which I don't want to get caught. If you lack a sense of humor and play it straight—too bad for you. You won't make me suffer because I am not engaged. And if you get in trouble, emotionally or otherwise, I just don't care."

A little higher still, "I love you" means "I appreciate you as a person. I would love to change you into a lover. You have what it takes. You satisfy me in all ways. Your promises are so rich I just can't wait to taste what you have to offer. I will give you myself when we are together, in exchange for the gift of you. I hope to have marvelous sex with you. Why not give it a whirl? But don't imagine I am stuck on you. There are dozens around who would do just as well. And, frankly, I want to be free to play the field."

Again, "I love you" may mean "I have a tender, whimsical fancy for your funny face, for the way you walk or dress, for your voice and your laughter. You are an elf, an inspiration, a delight. I am attracted to you with every fiber of my heart and soul. Life with you would be marvelous—forever and ever. I would love to take you as a baby doll to have and to hold in some castle in Spain, where we would enjoy fresh air, fun, and laughter. Will you marry me?" This is butterfly love—real, but lacking in any stable foundation.

Only One Meaning Is Fully True

Finally, "I love you" may mean something earth-shattering, solemn, hopeful, final, and marvelous—with a wild expectation of human and divine joy. It may mean "In full consciousness of what I am doing, I declare with absolute sincerity, in the name of the Father and the Son and the Holy Spirit, that having known you for some time and having seen what you do, think, hope, dream, I am now willing to offer you forever everything I am and ever will be in the hope that you will give me yourself—not as an exchange, but as freely and spontaneously as I give myself to you. I love you also for fun and pleasure; I love your funny face, the way you walk, dress, your voice and laughter. I love all this, but what I really love is *you*."

Now, this should not be said once for all. It must be repeated over and again, in different circumstances of pain or joy, relaxation or tiredness, boisterous health or depressing disease. It can be enriched constantly from within with new meaning, expressing a more perfect union, more shared joys and sorrows, more victories and defeats, more of the infinite variables of human life, the total of which makes a destiny.

The "I love you" of a married couple may be compared to the Sign of the Cross. It is the symbol of the married as the Sign of the Cross is the symbol of the Christian. Some make it shamefully and fast, a flutter of the hand before the nose and breast—some people are afraid to be caught being Christians. Some couples are afraid to be caught loving—to be caught by their own partner. So they mumble "I love you," coldly and routinely. Other people make a careful Sign of the Cross, placing their fingers accurately and attentively on forehead and heart and shoulders. They probably say "I love you" to each other with dutiful warmth and conviction—because that is what they are supposed to do, and so, who can complain? But there are other people, the marvelous people, whose Sign of the Cross is a whole crucifixion of themselves—ample, simple, and all out, a broad gesture of faith and love, unafraid, in the eye of the sun! When these people say "I love you" to each other, they mean something immense, timeless, and eternal, a total gift.

As you see, the words "I love you" mean many different things to different people, and so the question before you and your beloved is this: What do you mean when you say "I love you" to each other? Once you grasp the depth of the question, and begin to answer it as fully as you can, you will understand the meaning of true communication.

There must be a time in the week set apart for serious interpersonal communion. You must try to explore intimate questions together in a spirit of love. Don't be afraid to ask penetrating questions of each other. "What can I do as a husband or as a wife to improve the sexual act as an expression of my love for you?" "In what ways do I help you realize that I love you?" "What can we do to help the children better understand our love for them?"

Communication Is Sharing Your Life with Another

Communicating love is not mere reporting. You do not owe your husband or wife a copy of the minutes of your daily life. You are not a secretary, even less an accountant. Do not bother to keep detailed records of your actions, good, bad, or indifferent. Not of the good actions, or else you will thin out your merit to nothing by gloating over them. Not of your bad actions, or else they will make you sad and you will live under a pall of remorse. Not of your indifferent actions, for who needs them?

What, then, will you tell each other after a day's work? What will remain of it? Keep score of what was *alive* in your day. Of what was new, surprising, spontaneous. It doesn't even have to be real—speak of a thought, a dream, a glimpse of humor. Tell what the children said that made you smile. Tell of the cabbie who told you the story of his life. Or of the road sign—Smile! You are on radar. Speed limit 35. Be human, share the lovely, miraculous, endless joy and pain of coming across different flashes of life.

Never be ashamed to speak of your sorrows, burdens, pains, disappointments, for they belong to both of you. The marvelous thing about a true marriage is that it does away with the tiring obligation of putting up a false front. Be your frail, mistake-making, bumbling self. Be also the self-confident hero exulting over victories great and small. If a marriage is good, you will see through each other, so why hide anything or have any pretense? Simply be yourself, and hope and dream together.

Be Wise When You Disagree

Even if conflicts come up within a home, face them with simplicity. Have a good, lively argument if you must, but be careful never to say anything wounding that you may later regret. And don't try to win at all costs. Be in the habit of giving in to unreasonable arguments rather than starting a fight. It is surprising how fast the hot air cools off when you do not fight back.

The same happens when you drive a car. If you hog the road, travel at maximum speed, carry a chip on your shoulder, and never give the other guy a break, you may get there a few seconds faster, but so what? On the other hand, you may risk an accident, provoke other drivers to fury and dangerous retaliation, build up your aggressive and disagreeable ego. Try an experiment next time you come to a busy crossroad. Just bow the other car through even if you were there first. Enjoy the wave of thanks, the look of utter amazement. If the driver happens to be a pretty girl, the fun will be more than doubled for the courteous male.

The same applies to a family squabble. Do not stand on your legal rights. Give in before the assault—and the assault may not even materialize. If you had held on, you would perhaps still be bitter about it. Bitterness is the result of carefully cultivated anger and frustration. If you don't give anger a chance to build up, it won't grow sour and turn into resentment.

There may be occasions for anger between man and wife. Neither of you has to take everything lying down, when, for instance, the other has made a serious mistake. But take it as a mistake, not a crime, and think of rehabilitation rather than punishment. Find a way by which the other can make up, without hating himself or herself for the slip. A good fight is necessary from time to time, and a good fight is one that comes to a definite resolution. The point is made, and understood—a conciliatory gesture is offered, maybe with an apology thrown in. A bad argument is one that just lets off steam, heading nowhere, serving no purpose except emotional release.

This may seem valuable in itself, but it really is not. Letting off steam is merely a way of coddling yourself, a way of engaging in emotional self-indulgence. Sometimes you may not be able to help yourself, but if you fail to apply restraint you will develop the nasty habit of fighting and grumbling over everything. Try to resolve the conflict with a definite remedy. A decision should be arrived at as a result of the emotional outburst. Otherwise if you leave the issues unresolved, the two of you will merely set the stage for a future battle.

By learning to talk things out together, you will avoid the danger of estrangement—of the progressive splitting of your fundamental unity into two hostile elements. Be allies, not adversaries, in all things—even in your imperfections and failures.

You should learn to talk together not only about what goes wrong but also about what goes right. About your dreams, successes, most personal hopes and desires. The habit of reticence and restraint should not be continued in marriage. The state here should be one of openness, not of hiding. There may also be a need to undo a lot of old ideas about what is a proper subject of conversation and what is not.

The Pure of Heart Are Free to Talk

Among the subjects most strongly tainted with negative prejudice are those related to the very essence of your marriage. You have been told a hundred times in a hundred different ways to be pure, avoid dirty words or thoughts—meaning that you should never enjoy thinking or talking about anything related to sex. Yet, as you know from experience, any attempt at suppressing sexual thoughts only brings them back stronger than before, because of the very attention focused upon the conscious effort of suppression.

The thing to realize is that man and woman are sexual through and through. The sexual instinct is so much a pattern of daily life and ordinary constitution that it expresses itself automatically in the thinking process, imagination, reactions to daily circumstances of life. In our present world sexual provocations are greatly multiplied by a number of artificial stimuli that add fuel to the natural fire of instinctive interest. There are sexy ads everywhere, sexy magazines, shows, books, so that to keep the mind "clean"—meaning sexless—is impossible. Those who keep trying keep failing. And they blame themselves for failures that result from trying the impossible.

You must realize by now that "purity" does not consist in living as if sex did not exist, or, worse, as if it were something dangerous, dirty, and generally despicable. Purity consists in avoiding dirt. There is much dirt in the filthy, degrading, pessimistic mind of the prude. For the married it is quite natural and wholesome to enjoy sexual thoughts. Since the days of Christ, there is no longer anything "impure" in nature. As St. Paul explains, impurity comes, not from natural objects, but from the slime that is smeared upon them by an unclean heart.

Sexual thoughts were condemned in a dark age of false perfection. They came under the beautifully expressive term of *delectatio morosa*—which is scholastic Latin for lovingly dwelling upon the thought of an erotic situation. That was said to be a sin. That was believed to be "dirty." You certainly have been told over and over not to harbor such a thing in your mind. The words may have been different, but the meaning was the same.

Now here are the newlyweds. The sexual union, deep compenetration of bodies, heart, and soul, is their vocation, that which they are called upon to perform as well and enthusiastically as they can. It is perfectly good to rejoice in the thought of sex.

Do not build it up to the proportions of an extravaganza, an impossible vision of superhuman bliss, which it cannot possibly be. But do not believe there is any guilt in thinking and dreaming of the most precise and graphic sex with your beloved.

Get to agree on what you will and will not do. It is too much to say that in marriage anything goes, but you may safely assume that there is a world of discovery, mutual joy, and perfectly natural happiness well beyond what is acceptable to the conservative moralist or the United States Post Office! More will be said of this later. What we are concerned with here is communication. Talk about things, openly, hopefully, joyfully. Get to the point of spontaneous honesty where both of you feel perfectly free to ask for a particular caress, a special form of erotic excitation—free to experiment and progress in the art of love.

Be Able to Laugh at Yourselves

Some things are much too important to be taken seriously. Sexual love is one of them. It must be taken in a spirit of playfulness, lightheartedness, spontaneous joy. Speak about your past performances with your beloved; increase your present joy by communicating in the very act of love, speaking, guiding, thanking, laughing. Do not hold back information out of the fear of upsetting your lover—communicate, feel, be together as rational, expressive, vocal beings.

You may, if you like, create your own vocabulary, a secret language you share with your beloved alone, so that even in the midst of a crowd, at a party, or anywhere, you may offer the delightful gift of an unexpected sharing of some warm memory that could not have been expressed in ordinary words. In this way, you will be creating your own world, or rather, re-creating it at will wherever you happen to be.

Talk together of what you will do together as a means of increasing your mutual love. Express the delight of offering, of being what the other desires. Of being together what both desire, in order to increase in mutual union through the best possible use of your compenetrating bodies.

Children Should Not Hamper Conjugal Life

Keep at this conversation of love all the way into the depth of your married life. Preserve your moments of communication; keep the channels open with care so that nothing happens that can obscure each to the other. When children come, when pain and tiredness strike, preserve some time for intimate communication, for a heart-to-heart sharing of ideas. Do not be afraid of being strict in this—sometimes you have a duty of keeping the children out of your life. Many a marriage was wrecked because a husband suddenly lost his wife to his children. Many a mother has the false notion that her duty is to her children first, and to her husband next. It is not so. She is married to her husband, not to her children. By giving priority to husband over children, she will not be depriving the children of any right, since they have no first claim. On the contrary, by giving priority to children over husband, she may ruin both her own happiness and that of her children by turning her husband into an enemy, and the father of her children into a stranger to them.

A happy, rich, and harmonious married life between parents reflects on the children, because the home will be free of major tensions and frustrations. The children's own future married life will be deeply affected by their parents' ability or inability to communicate. Where there are closeness, simplicity, open talk, there will be for the children a much better prospect of happy love.

The Sharing of Silence Is an Expression of Love

Keep talking, then, but do not chatter. Speak when you have something worth sharing, and when the other is in a mood to listen. For there are two conditions to a valuable conversation—the message must be worth conveying, and the participants must be attuned to each other. Otherwise there is a monologue, or worse still, preaching in the wilderness. Sometimes a better communication is established through the sharing of silence.

In moments of peace or relaxation, or at the summit of sexual harmony, there may be no need for verbal communication, but only for the mutual awareness of a tender, loving presence. There are experiences better said with a pressure of the hand, a caress, a glance, a smile, than with the all-too-imperfect stringing of words and sentences. There are times when being is much more important than manifesting, when feeling takes precedence over doing, when a wordless receiving of the other becomes a much deeper form of communication than trying too hard to understand, give, or do.

This is particularly true in the sexual relationship in which a joyful erotic response never arises from trying too hard. You cannot work at sex; you cannot pursue it with any chance of success; you can never force it in any way, for it is not the result of any systematic labor or the goal of any charted course. It is a purely spontaneous happening of your natural self.

One of the most difficult things for "civilized" people to do is to return to the spontaneity of natural communication without a sense of guilt. You probably have been so much impressed by the primacy of the intellect that a condition of earthy happiness in which the intellect has almost nothing to do may seem degrading, unworthy of your noble nature. But this utter simplicity of communication on the level of your sexual selves is precisely one of the richest characteristics of your noble nature, and one of the elements of its nobility.

Guard Against Outside Distractions

There is very little possibility of happiness in marriage without sexual harmony, and there is no truly human sexual harmony without communication. But the keeping in contact with the beloved is no simple, automatic thing: it is the result of careful attention and a great measure of awareness. It may require a certain effort, for the constant distractions received from the world around us are a powerful force for division. They distract us; in the etymological sense of the word, they tear us apart. And since we have only a limited supply of physical and nervous energy, the constant answering to the solicitations of radio, TV, advertising, and noise in general taps so great an amount of our strength that we do not have enough left for living.

We need physical and nervous strength in order to communicate. In the stress of the contemporary rat race, most of our energies are consumed by tasks that are valuable only by the standard of an artificially distorted way of life. We let ourselves be influenced by advertising to the point that false "needs" are created in us and that false compulsions are developed in our minds. We get to believe that it is unthinkable for a modern middle-class American not to have a new car, a color TV, a membership in an expensive social club. The damage is not only in the silly things we feel obliged to do. It is also in the strenuous work entailed by the necessity of paying for them. And so we kill ourselves twice —in conforming with the Joneses and in trying to pay for it. No wonder, then, that little energy is left for real living, for communicating with each other on a plane of love and truth.

And it is not even enough to do this during our working day. As soon as we get home, most of us continue under pressure, by submitting to the completely unnecessary tensions displayed on the TV screen.

When our appointed supply of energy has been consumed by activities that are generally useless, we can no longer live as human beings. We no longer have the strength to speak. We grunt in monosyllables, so that what should have been a supreme form of communication between man and wife turns into an impersonal cat-and-dog fight.

Common Sense and Courage Can Save You

Can anything be done about ? Of course. All it takes is a little common sense and a powerful dose of courage and perseverance. Only a fool would be unable to see that the modern way of pretense and conventions can only lead to unhappiness. But it takes a strong and persevering man and woman to stand in the stream and buck the current. Try it, anyway. Do not bend to class standards, status symbols, outward signs of success. Do not rush to buy every new gadget. They generally break down before the last installment of the easy-payment plan. Slow down! Don't get excited! Save your breath and your strength and your money for the deeply human development of yourself. Become a garden of peace where things are allowed to grow their natural way—instead of being rushed to tasteless "jumbo" size, and gobbled up before they are ripe! See to it that in the newly acquired peace the real values of beauty, love, art, imagination, creativity are properly sown so that you will have something of worth to reap, to communicate, to exchange spontaneously with another human person, another peaceful garden—your own beloved.

Living together will be infinitely more than the pitiful search for compensation that it so often is. It will be the natural and holy exchange of the true values of life in an authentic communion and communication of love.

CHAPTER 4

HOW TO PERFECT THE ACT OF LOVE

The Act of Love Is Positively Virtuous . . . Imaginative Preparation Deepens the Experience . . . Freedom and Desire Must Be Mutual . . . Variety Is the Spice of Life . . . Pleasurable Love Develops Slowly . . . There Is More to Love Than Orgasm . . . Perfect Sex Is a Myth . . . The Problem of Tiredness Can Be Overcome . . . Tenderness Reduces Sexual Disparity . . . There Are Natural Limitations to Sexual Pleasure . . . Love Life Is Broader Than Sex Life . . . The Desire of Love Is Infinite . . . Love Is God in Us

We have seen that communicating love is essential for the survival of a deep interpersonal relationship. It is most desirable that this verbal communication be developed. There is nothing harmful or shameful—on the contrary—in talking about sex, before, during, and after the actual performance. We now come to the point of what lovers do. There are a number of questions that may be raised here. What are the possibilities of married love? What are its principal obstacles, and how can they be overcome? What is complete happiness, and how close can lovers get to it?

The Act of Love Is Positively Virtuous

If you are elated by the most deeply physiological contacts with the erotically attractive parts of your beloved partner, this is no sign of animality: an animal can never know the height of emotional and spiritual bliss that can be attained by lovers flowing into each other in the vital spasm of love. This is not an animal act. It is a truly human communication that affects your whole being concentrated on this most human of all activities. The "going into" each other, the biblical "knowing" each other.

There should be no shame in the verbal expression of sexual love. Neither should there be any shame in the wordless communication that goes with its performance. True lovers never cease to speak of their love, in words or silently. They begin with mental caresses long before any physical contact. They need this time of peace, this distant preparation, this slow pacifying and relaxation before love. Periods of silence, of contemplation, will come and go. Glances, smiles will be exchanged. Hand will seek hand, bodies will come closer, exchanging their warmth and slowly kindling their inner fires. All this is a quite indispensable approach to love.

The situation in marriage is different from that before marriage only in that now all acts leading to the warmest and most perfect performance of the sexual union are not only permissible but positively virtuous.

In order to be good, a sexual act must meet some basic conditons:

1. It must contribute to mutual love, either in itself or with an added procreative intent.
2. It must be respectful of the freedom and desires of both partners.
3. It must conform to the physical constitution of man and woman.
4. It must not involve the inflicting of excessive pain. (sadism).
5. It must not be founded on abject submission (masochism).
6. It must not be opposed to the procreative end, when there is an obligation to procreate.

It is impossible to list individual human acts considered in the abstract, and to attach to them any moral rating. This is particularly true of sexual acts in marriage. We shall, however, try to explain here the legitimacy of a number of activities condemned without sufficient reason. Certain negative and erroneous traditions that still find supporters are so strong that if they are not carefully and systematically demolished by an objective and rational study, many good people would be led to by-pass a number of natural joys because of the very refinement of their consciences and their desire to do the best.

Let us consider in turn the means of preparation and the means of consummation of love.

Imaginative Preparation Deepens the Experience

There are many delightful and permissible means of preparation for love besides those universally permitted, such as the usual kissing and caressing. Some have been dramatically condemned, even by public laws, with no other justification than a total misunderstanding of sex and a total ignorance of what is natural and what is not. Others have been omitted because of faintheartedness and lack of imagination. Others, again, are by-passed because they seem to be the stock in trade of "bad" people.

For instance, is there anything wrong when husband and wife undress before each other as a preliminary means of sexual excitement? We have already spoken of nakedness as the natural state for total love. This is the object of much prejudice and false shame, and no wonder. When a girl has been told all her life to dress modestly, not to provoke boys, and never, under any circumstance, to let a male have a glimpse of her sacrosanct nipples, how can she be expected to do with gusto the very thing she has been conditioned to regard as absolutely forbidden? Great patience may be necessary here, on the part of the male; much tenderness and understanding must be shown, leading first to timid consent, then to loving compliance, and finally to enthusiastic cooperation.

Freedom and Desire Must Be Mutual

Then there is the more immediate preparation—caressing and kissing. Here also there is in many cases a residue of fear, restricting both the means and the areas of permissible contact. In fact, there is no part of the clean and fresh human body that is not naturally excitable and naturally accessible to love caresses and love kisses. Once again, no objective rules apply here; the matter rests entirely in the field of personal acceptance as expressed in Rule 2: *In order to be morally acceptable, a sexual act must be respectful of the freedom and desires of both partners.*

This does not mean that each partner is limited once for all by the pattern established by the other: on the contrary, there is much need of education, of a mutual development of the areas of acceptance, and of the kind and patient encouragement of the slower partner in order to bring the couple up to the full potential of a rich sex life.

Such an education applies, for instance, to the genital kiss—which still makes the participants liable to arrest in certain puritanical states. It is now recognized as perfectly healthy, normal, and natural, and is even recommended as a method by which the slower partner may be brought to a state of readiness. It is acceptable when practiced by husband and wife individually, and also as a means of mutual excitement by which lovers may bring each other to the verge of climax—which is then consummated in any of the copulatory positions.

In ancient manuals, only one position was recognized as natural: that of the wife lying on her back with the husband over her. Such a narrow teaching was based on the false concept of the "dominant" role of the male. There is, of course, no such thing as a "natural" position: any position in which the sexual organs meet is as natural as any other. Some positions, however, are more convenient in given circumstances, for instance, when the wife is pregnant or when one partner is obese. Some positions have advantages over others as regards proper contact with the clitoris, but generally speaking, the attitude in which intercourse will take place may be determined by personal preference.

Perhaps one of the greatest errors in earlier religious teachings on marriage and sexuality was the almost constant refusal to accept the human value of full sensual satisfaction. With so much emphasis on the spiritual aspect of the union of man and wife, religious teachers have generally taken for granted that the sensual and erotic aspects of the marriage relationship were inferior, material, that they needed to be downgraded rather than developed. With the procreative end of marriage in the forefront, it was easy to bypass the personal function, and even to scorn it. This attitude disregards the deeply human and almost universal need for perfective and dynamic sexual relations. What happens, then, is that a considerable number among the best and holiest of couples, conforming to rules of negative discipline rather than positive development, live in a narrow and somewhat fearful way. Obeying fully the commands and counsels of conservative Church authorities, they feel cramped and limited.

Is there any answer to this growing anguish, to this so common frustration, to this envy at the sight of a lighthearted, topless world passing by with giggling scorn?

If Christian couples happen to have this particular feeling of not being "with it," perhaps it would be better to help them join the world of the living than to protect them against it. Does this mean that they should reject sexual discipline, become swingers, mate-swappers, free-love addicts? Not in the least. Those who do so are not among the living. Freedom is not license. But between traditional rigidity and contemporary license, there is a whole field of true freedom that has not been sufficiently cultivated.

What we mean is that young married people should not be overwhelmed with negative views on the dangers of sex. Yes, sex is sometimes ambiguous, repulsive, even criminal. On the other hand, it has an endless potential of good, of healthy, dynamic and sporting fun that may be developed within the rich relationship of a truly loving couple. The best protection against the inroads of immorality and the temptation of outside adventures consists in showing the possibility of more complete happiness and sexual fulfillment within monogamous marriage than without.

If the basic man-and-wife couple is to remain the building block of civilized society, then this living of two together must be made to satisfy the natural hungers, hopes and dreams of both partners. There must be enough of the spice of variety to avoid boredom, enough mutual concern to avoid hedonism, and enough freedom to allow the male and female bodies the full range of their natural games.

Whole books have been written on the play value of sex. This aspect seems never to be stressed, or even mentioned, in morally oriented manuals. Yet, while work is a necessity imposed upon man, play is the supreme form of rational activity. It is in play that man and woman are themselves, creative, new, uninhibited. It is in play that they can sufficiently let go to be totally themselves. No other human activity lends itself so naturally as sex to this freedom of being oneself, resulting in humor, laughter and fun.

Variety Is the Spice of Life

Many couples seem to fall into a monotonous routine. They fail to take advantage of the possible variations that may add liveliness and interest to the union. These variations have been numbered in the hundreds by Far Eastern and Near Eastern experts, Chinese, Japanese, Indian, and Arabic. The actual choice is not that wide. Since this matter is explained extensively in any manual on the "how-to" of sex, there is no need to go over it here. Besides, you should be able to discover all this by yourselves and to experiment without the use of books. The printing press was not invented until the fifteenth century, and human beings managed to make love very nicely without printed instructions. The important thing right here is to impress upon you the fact that *the warmest and most erotic sexual performances between husband and wife are not only morally acceptable but even virtuously good.*

You know that men and women increase in sanctifying grace by performing well the duties proper to their state of life. A husband and wife actually increase in holiness as they develop the perfection of their love-making. Everything truly human is truly beautiful in the eyes of the Lord—and it is truly human and truly beautiful to enjoy sexual love to the limit of your liveliness, generosity, and imagination.

The natural effect of this realization is to lead you to seek the means of improvement of your relationship. That improvement is necessary seems obvious enough: remember the clumsiness, perhaps even the misery, of your first experiments in intercourse. Love-making, in a sense, resembles dancing in that it is very much a matter of coordination, muscular and emotional. It is not enough for two dancers to be automatically attuned: all they would do in such a case is perform like two perfect robots. There must also be a sense of emotional harmony, a happiness together that expresses itself in spontaneous beauty. In sex-play, as in dancing, one must lead and the other follow. The leader must know exactly where he is going and what he wants, and the follower must respond instantly, meeting and matching advances and retreat, adding from time to time inspired moves. In love-making, however, there is no reason why the woman should not assume from time to time the leading role: instead of being humiliating for the husband, it will, on the contrary, be a very special delight for him to know that she is fully as eager and "with it" as he is. Harmonious coordination comes with experience: only mature lovers make love really well.

Pleasurable Love Develops Slowly

One of the most frequent mistakes is haste. In love-making, the most important and delightful phase is rarely the final climax; it is, rather, the state that immediately precedes it. So much emphasis has been placed by sexologists and psychiatrists on achieving orgasm that it is often considered the supreme and only goal. While it is indeed the summit and consummation of love, it is only a short flash when compared to the pleasure of the preliminaries.

The pursuit of sensual and sexual pleasure as a supreme goal is a cause of certain disappointment, for sex is not merely a toy to be exploited for the sake of physical ecstasy: it is fully valid only as a means of human communication, as the tangible expression of the union of love. The pursuit of sex in itself, with no consideration for the person of the partner, any sexual pleasure attainable with no regard to the "other," even the highest exaltation procured by the most expert and gorgeous professional playgirl, all have something intrinsically degrading—the teaching of well-known authors to the contrary. *The difference between sex-for-itself and sex-for-love is that the former worships sex as a god, while the latter worships God through sex.* The attitude of lovers, then, will depend entirely on the object of their adoration.

The most exquisite forms of sexual preliminaries and consummation are compatible with love for the Living God when they are received and returned as gracious gifts, gratuitous favors lavished on us, offered to our intelligence and free will by the Author of all pleasure, who is himself the source and achievement —the *only* source and the *only* achievement—of total beatitude.

There Is More to Love Than Orgasm

With this in mind, let us get back to a comparison between the preliminaries and the consummation of love. While the preliminary phases of love may be turned into the most delicious and reverent sharing of extremely conscious joy, orgasm itself contains nothing that is consciously personal. It is neither tender nor subtle. In the final burst of sexual energy, there is something overwhelming that obscures the personal relationship. It is precisely this that made the scholastic philosophers so wary of it. Their fear was definitely exaggerated, but let us follow them at least in this, in admitting that concentration on orgasm alone is a form of clumsy greed that deprives lovers of their richest exchanges. Refined lovers can transform the preludes into the highest and most personal form of human bliss. And so, do not hurry! Play lightly, joyfully, spontaneously, as long as the game can possibly last, without concentrating with desperate energy on the goal to be attained. Enjoy what you are doing now as a thing delightful in itself. Only then will it serve as a means toward what is to come.

For both man and woman, orgasm is almost automatic. If it seems to occur with less regularity in woman, this is generally due to her different psychological make-up that requires a much longer preparation and more definite conditions of right mood and circumstances. In both husband and wife, the fullness of orgasm will be very much dependent on the duration and quality of preparation, the ideal being the progressive development of a state in which the culmination blossoms spontaneously as the most urgent and only possible solution to the tension of love.

"The orgasm is spontaneous when it happens of itself and when the rest of the body moves in response to it. Active or forced sexual intercourse is the deliberate imitation of movements which should ordinarily come about of themselves. Given the open attitude of the mind and senses, sexual love in this spirit is a revelation.

"Long before the male orgasm begins, the sexual impulse manifests itself as what can only be described, psychologically, as a melting warmth between the partners so that they seem veritably to flow into each other. To put it in another way, 'physical lust' transforms itself into the most considerate and tender form of love imaginable." [1]

Perfect Sex Is a Myth

Now to come down from Cloud Nine. The fully satisfying sexual joy of simultaneous orgasm cannot be obtained as a matter of course. It results occasionally from an extraordinary combination of circumstances. Everything must be right, and so many things can be wrong. Let us then sober up long enough to consider some of the difficulties of love.

First, there are the inevitable hardships of life. How seldom, indeed, do lovers come together with that rosy, healthy, glowing vitality that is conducive to perfect sex! The more usual state is rather one of tiredness, anguish, perhaps even exhaustion. In such circumstances, the sexual game cannot possibly result in the joyful explosion of lively bliss that it should be in its ideal form. The only things attainable at such times may be the compenetration of bodies, mutual reassurance, quiet togetherness without any consummation. Even this is of high value. It is still very much a manifestation of sexual love: no one else but the loving partners would ever be allowed that level of intimacy. When you or your partner are not in sufficient physical shape to go sucessfully all the way, instead of bemoaning what you miss, try to concentrate on the privilege of being that intimate with the one

[1] Alan Watts, *Nature, Man and Woman* (Mentor Book, New York, 1958), p. 165.

you love. Do not try, by a desperate effort, to bring about any more than is physically possible at the time.

The Problem of Tiredness Can Be Overcome

When both partners are in poor shape, there is not much difficulty in reaching an agreement on what to do and how far to go. Nature eliminates any excess by the simple method of refusing to "produce." But what can be done when one partner is exhausted and the other is eager and hungry? When the active one is the husband, there is no great difficulty for the wife to let herself be comfortably passive. It will require some effort from her good will, but almost none from her body. Although the highest point of sexual pleasure cannot be attained without a sense of mutual enjoyment, the normal male can receive sufficient satisfaction and relief from intercourse with a totally inactive female.

But when the husband is tired and the wife alert, there may be quite a problem, since tiredness in the male will generally result in the loss of erection. It seems that the eager wife of a tired husband has as much right to satisfaction as the eager husband of a tired wife. If her desire is genuine and strong, meaning that she would be nervously and emotionally upset if she could not be appeased, there appears to be no reason why she could not be satisfied by methods other than coition. Any caressing or kissing acceptable to both partners that would bring her the needed relief would be an act of conjugal love that should not be considered in the least immoral.

Sexual sinfulness should be seen not in the procuring of pleasure but in the misuse of the powers of love. If the major principle of justification of sexual activity is the fostering of mutual love within marriage, it must certainly apply here. There is nothing sinful in this act. Not the slightest damage is being done to anyone: on the contrary, very definite good. Even the old taboo against placing an obstacle between male and female genetic cells is not broken, since in such circumstances the male genetic cells would not be produced at all.

Perhaps it would be meritorious for the wife not to appease her sexual hunger this one time. But if the same situation occurs at frequent intervals or during extended periods, the build-up of frustrations and privations would do more damage than restraint and self-control would do good. This is merely a matter of fact, of simple logic, of common sense. For those in whom there lingers some kind of doubt as to the legitimacy of orgasm induced by anything but the complete sex act, a reasonable estimate of the good and evil effects will convince them that the advantages are obvious, while the inconveniences are purely imaginary. Mutual love can be fostered and the intimate bond strengthened through this form of conjugal charity.

Tenderness Reduces Sexual Disparity

Now to come to another difficulty—besides the lack of harmony due to temporary circumstances, and the element of tiredness, there may be a permanent difference in the intensity of sexual drive in husband and wife. The husband may be a sexual athlete, while the wife is satisfied with a once-a-month performance—or it may be the other way around.

This is a serious problem. It must be handled by a combination of methods. The first is to do everything possible to increase the sexual interest of the slower partner. Through progressive development and systematic cultivation, surprising results may be obtained. But it is all too easy to go overboard and obtain the exact opposite—an increase, not in enthusiasm for sex, but in disgust. So the going is extremely delicate. Do not give up too soon, but realize that even after everything possible has been done, and well done, in the hope of awakening interest, there still may be a wide difference in the frequency of desire. There seems always to be a ceiling, a terminal point beyond which no further progress is possible.

The second method consists in compromise. When something cannot be changed, the best thing to do is to learn to live with it. The active partner should then make the most of those few occasions when all is well, while the slow one should try to make such occasions as satisfying as possible for the mate. There may be great merit in this effort toward harmony. It should not be pushed to the level of a sacrificial offering, for such a thing would be totally destructive of the sexual appeal, but it should imply the greatest possible good will and the fullest possible cooperation on both sides. Such things can come about only in a marriage founded on true love, tenderness, and mutual respect.

The third method consists in applying what has been explained above concerning temporarily exhausted partners: whenever the challenge becomes unbearable and the hunger too strong, it is a matter of kindness and charity to satisfy the eager partner. Sexuality is a means of giving love.

There Are Natural Limitations to Sexual Pleasure

Besides the accidental obstacles to perfect sexual fulfillment, there are a number of built-in imperfections that will always keep marital love and sexual delight well below the level of total happiness. The first consists in the fact that the partner, the sexual object, is no more perfect than the subject. In youthful love dreams, the beloved damsel or Prince Charming is imaginatively endowed with every natural and supernatural attribute of perfect love. But in the reality of the sexual union in marriage, there is the meeting of an imperfect human being with another imperfect human being—and much unhappiness has been created by the so frequent demand for an impossible perfection. Both partners may aspire to perfection and infinity; their very nature holds them down to imperfection and temporality.

Again, in the sexual ecstasy, pleasure is nothing but a fleeting and accidental occurrence. It is not a state; it has no enduring effect. It is merely a "happening"—and almost as soon as it has happened, it vanishes into the past. "Venus came, and went," as Vladimir Nabokov writes in *Lolita*: this is probably the shortest description of intercourse in literature.

The normal state of sexual desire is a tendency toward absolute satisfaction, total mutual compenetration and absorption, perfect communication and happiness. In the pleasures of foreplay and in the flash of orgasm, there is often an illusion of all this. But as the mystic must weep after his return to earth from the cloud of his vision of God, so must lovers cling to each other in mutual consolation after love for not having given each other the full perfection of all. They should not be sad to excess, for all was not theirs to give, and they have given each other everything they have and are. This should be enough for now, enough as a timely solace on the way toward the promise of all.

The wider the scope of the love relationship, the more lovers will be able to give to each other. If they remain essentially on the level of sex alone, if their efforts and experiments are limited to the techniques concerned with the best possible use of their genitals, they will remain below the level of their *essential* limitations, and their mutual gift will be less than what it could have been.

Love Life Is Broader Than Sex Life

While love life is broader than sex life, sex life is broader than copulation. Although limited in its essence, the husband-and-wife relationship should never be despised on account of such limitation. Our natural boundaries are not punishments imposed upon us by some peevish God. They are, in a positive sense, those signposts within which we are to exercise the freedom of our will. Outside them there is nothing we can do, no true kingdom, but only the domain of prideful fantasies. Trying to escape from our own humanity is a game as fraught with illusions as that of seeking some physical reality outside space or before time: there is none.

It is clearly within this frail humanity of ours—and not beyond, besides, above, or below it—that we will find our greatest happiness and be able to reach the highest level of relative perfection. Nothing on earth can ever be absolutely perfect.

Perhaps the greatest illusion of all is the possibility of absolute delight in the consummation of erotic love with a perfectly conformed and eagerly participating mate. It is this very illusion that is being constantly exploited in commercial advertising, literature, art—in every form of expression of man's desire. It seems to be what keeps most of us going—like the unattainable lump of sugar dangling from a stick before the donkey's nose. This illusion may help to provide in part an explanation of the constant unrest, the sexual starvation, the compulsive mate-switching of our times. How many believe that the next woman will be different—the all-perfect mate, the giver of total delight! But it always turns out that the latest lover-girl or the latest wife is far from matching what the great illusion had built her up to be. And so the search goes on and on.

There is here something very touching, immensely naïve, but also quite moving. The search for the perfect God. The yearning for the perfect Spirit of Life. The desire for a perfect fulfillment of love. But it is immature, childish, misguided, a form of idolatry that is bound to fail when the idol is found out to be nothing but flesh and blood. God is not there.

The error is to have identified the absolute with the object of sexual love, to have sought this object as an end in itself, to have made a god of erotic pleasure. When this fails, the normal reaction is to rush to the opposite extreme and to deny that anything of God can be found in sex. This is the aberration of ascetical extremists.

The Desire of Love Is Infinite

Is there any hope, then, of finding perfection—relative, human, and yet highly satisfying perfection—in the man-woman relationship? There certainly is. Let us begin by considering the possibilities offered to us in the natural order:

> "Sexual love is the most intense and dramatic of the common ways in which a human being comes into conscious relationship with something outside himself. It is, furthermore, the most vivid of man's customary expressions of his organic spontaneity, the most positive and creative occasion of his being transported by something beyond his conscious will." [2]

[2] Watts, *op. cit.*, p. 19.

Sexual love may be immensely high and immensely deep because it is related first of all to the very heights and depths of the forces of living nature.

> "If human love is never totally fulfilled, it is because human nature offers unlimited life." [3]

Now, this offering of unlimited life can be understood only of the life of eternity. The goal of love is the infinite perfection of infinite life, while the means available to us are the finite perfections of temporal life. There will, then, always be some tension, some tending, some effort, and some measure of failure—none of which should cause despair, since they are the natural consequences of our human nature. The more perfect a love, the more clearly will the lovers become aware of a certain absence of the all.

Perhaps the artist can penetrate the depth and tenderness of love even better than the philosopher. Boris Pasternak has expressed them exquisitely:

> "How he loved her! How beautiful she was! In exactly the way he had always thought and dreamed and wanted! Yet, what was it that made her so lovely? Was it something that could be named or analyzed? No, a thousand times no! She was lovely by virtue of the matchlessly simple and swift line that the Creator had, at a single stroke, drawn all around her, and in this divine form she had been handed over, like a child tightly wrapped in a sheet after its bath, into the keeping of his soul." [4]

A love of such quality extends infinitely beyond the created limits of the beloved object:

> "Often since then I have tried to define and give a name to the enchantment that you communicated to me that night, the faint glow, the distant echo, which later permeated my whole being and gave me a key to the understanding of everything in the world." [5]

[3] Louis J. M. Sahuc, *Homme et femme* (Bloud & Gay, Paris, 1960), p. 253.

[4] Boris Pasternak, *Doctor Zhivago* (Signet Book, The New American Library, Inc., New York, 1957), p. 306.

[5] *Ibid.*, p. 355.

And Pasternak concludes:

"Ah, that was just what had united them and had made them so akin! Never, never, even in their moments of richest and wildest happiness, were they unaware of a sublime joy in the total design of the universe, a feeling that they themselves were a part of that whole, an element in the beauty of the cosmos." [6]

The love of man and woman are in the order of the infinite, but they will never reach infinite perfection. There will always remain an intense yearning for more, for something higher and less fragile, with no risk of disillusion, fading, or loss. The highest love relationship on earth is the closest symbol of the perfect love relationship fulfilled in the direct vision of God, and it is the greatest incentive toward acquiring it. If, indeed, human love can be that high and that good, God's love is inconceivably delightful, since it is most certainly better than the lovers' highest bliss. Having known from experience such peaks of happiness, successful lovers will be much more strongly attracted than others to this promise of still greater delights.

Love Is God in Us

Perhaps we are now in a better position to understand where God is to be found in the human love relationship. Between the two extreme aberrations—that God is found only in the total denial of sexual pleasure or that sexual pleasure itself is a god—there is another way, a middle way of truly divine joy. It consists in seeing sex and the sexual partner, not as God, but as a gift and as a child of God, and in seeking sexual pleasure, not as an end, but as a means of love. If we address the totality of our adoration to the only One who is worthy of it, and discover reflections and signs of this perfect One in the loving and lovable creature with whom we are bound for life, the personal object of our human love may then be seen in its divine origin and its divine end—as coming from God and returning to Him. Then the full richness of love, spiritual,

[6] *Ibid.*, p. 417.

emotional and, yes, even its spontaneous and wildly erotic forms, may be addressed to the human beloved in the name of the Father and of the Son and of the Holy Spirit.

> "What lovers feel for each other in this moment is no other than adoration in its full religious sense, and its climax is almost literally the pouring of their lives into each other. Such adoration, which is due only to God, would indeed be idolatrous were it not that in that moment love takes away illusion and shows the beloved for what he or she in truth is—not the socially pretended person but the naturally divine." [7]

[7] Watts, *op. cit.*, p. 173.

CHAPTER 5
BIRTH CONTROL AND FAMILY PLANNING

You Certainly Do Have the Right to Plan Your Family . . . What Are the Methods of Birth Control? . . . The Moral Problem of Contraception Is Not Solved by the Encyclical . . . Bishops Have Not Approved the Encyclical Unconditionally . . . Sexual Love Is Good in Itself . . . When Is Birth Control Legitimate? . . . Your Marriage Is a True Christian Calling

Sexuality is but a limited aspect of conjugal life. The birth-control question, in turn, covers only a limited aspect of sexuality. The topic has received so much attention and notoriety that it has been magnified out of all proportion. In order to approach it in an orderly manner, let us consider the issues one by one.

A preliminary question needs to be solved: Does a married couple have a moral right to limit the size of their family? There actually are some people who scrupulously believe that any such intentional control would be an unjustified interference with God's plan. This, of course, goes beyond even the strictest conservative position of the Church.

You Certainly Do Have the Right to Plan Your Family

Not only do you have an absolute right to plan your family; you even have a strict duty to do so, since responsible parenthood is a Christian obligation. The duty for a married couple to have children is not absolute, but relative. The command to "increase and multiply" does not apply in the same way to everyone. The degree of obligation is vastly different in a family with seven children or in a family that has only one. The true Church doctrine has never interpreted the biblical text in the sense that parents should have as many children as physically possible. Each couple must assess the particular circumstances of their lives, and come to a responsible decision.

In a simple agrarian society, a very large family is perfectly compatible with human dignity both for parents and children. A great number of children means greater production, greater wealth because of the number of hands available to plow, to sow, and to reap. By contrast, in overcrowded urban centers, the task of raising many children is very often well beyond the means and strength of some parents. Obviously, circumstances differ from age to age and from family to family. This has been very well expressed by the Fathers of the Second Vatican Council:

> "Parents should regard as their proper mission the task of transmitting human life and educating those to whom it has been transmitted. They should realize that they are thereby cooperators with the love of God the Creator, and are so to speak the interpreters of that love. Thus they will fulfill their task with human and Christian responsibility, and with docile reverence toward God, will make decisions by common council and effort. Let them thoughtfully take into account both their own welfare and that of their children, those already born and those which the future may bring. For this accounting they need to reckon with both the material and the spiritual conditions of the times as well as their state of life." [*The Church in the Modern World,* II:1]

The circumstances determining the number of children will be entirely personal. They will include, for instances, the relative wealth of the parents, their degree of health and physical strength, their capacity for giving, their courage and generosity, and, most of all, their personal style of life.

Generosity will consist, not in bringing forth as many children as possible, but in loving well those brought to life. The style of life is the most difficult element to define, but perhaps also the most important. It coincides with your personal calling, that which you were made to become or to do. It consists in the encounter between your desire for children and everything else that you are and that you hope to be.

It is quite evident, then, that you do have the right to plan your family through the use of reason and foresight. This right is founded both on common sense and on the teaching of the Church. The next question will then be, "How?" And the answer, "By some means of birth regulation acceptable to both parties and compatible with the rules of moral good."

What Are the Methods of Birth Control?

Before approaching the question of morality, let us try to analyze objectively the different possible methods.

The only method of birth control presently permitted by the official magisterium of the Catholic Church is the so-called "Rhythm Method." It consists in limiting intercourse to those times during which fecundation of the ovum is impossible—or at least highly improbable. It has been approved on the grounds that it does not oppose "nature" but takes advantage of "natural" periods of sterility.

Theoretically, this is the method that should work to the satisfaction of the married partners. However, for many couples, the arguments against it are so overwhelming that these couples look upon it as the most unnatural of all. A summary listing of the reasons why rhythm is generally unsatisfactory would include the following points:

1. It is basically defective as a reliable method of birth control since pregnancies do occur even when couples conform scrupulously to all the rules.
2. Because of this unreliability, the peace and harmony of the couple may be completely disrupted.
3. In the great number of cases of irregular menstrual periods,

the time for love will be reduced to such a severely limited number of days that no reasonable frequency of intercourse will be possible for any truly loving husband and wife.

4. The permissible time for love will coincide by physiological necessity with those days when a wife is most nervous and upset by the forthcoming menstrual flow, and has the least chance of being in the proper mood for happy and relaxed intercourse.

5. Even when the menstrual periods are perfectly regular, the rhythm of fertility can be completely disturbed by some unrelated physical or emotional shock, thus resulting in unanticipated ovulation and unwanted pregnancy.

6. The fact that intercourse is forced into narrow time limits is incompatible with the variations of natural sexual desire. The appointed time for love will seldom coincide with the peaks of sexual capacity.

7. Since the permissible time may be calculated in advance, anguished expectation and anticipation may inhibit the magic of sexual love, which is then liable to be replaced by a pretimed and unsatisfactory routine.

8. Because the safe period is often too short, there is a natural tendency to crowd too much sex within too narrow time limits. This added defect may damage the communication of love.

9. When rhythm is used in conjunction with a thermometer, litmus paper, or smear test, the artificial and unnatural character of the method becomes even more apparent.

10. Since constantly renewed frustration may build up to an intolerable level, the temptation of infidelity can become very serious, and can also increase the tendency to have recourse to escape through alcohol or drugs.

11. According to a recent article in *Time* magazine, an unusually high incidence of abnormal babies may result when couples use the rhythm method, because pregnancies may then more often be produced by a stale spermatozoid at the beginning of the cycle or a stale ovum at the end, both resulting in deteriorated chromosomes and fetal abnormalities.[1]

It seems that rhythm could be acceptable in the case of parents living a most stable life, and having a relatively low sexual urge,

[1] August 30, 1968, pp. 61–62.

and only when the wife has extremely regular periods. Obviously, then, it cannot be accepted as a general solution to the problem of birth control.

Among the other methods of birth control, the most widely used at present in countries of Western culture seems to be the estrogen pills, the different forms of oral contraceptives. At the present state of development, however, oral contraceptives are contraindicated for patients with heart or kidney diseases, breast or genital cancer, or hypertension. Their use is not recommended before a thorough testing of endocrine functions. Caution is recommended in cases of patients with metabolic disorder (including diabetes), migraine, epilepsy, and asthma. Thromboembolism, with some fatalities, has been noted and confirmed by recent research in England. Mention has been made of additional growth of the mother's body hair, showing a modification in secondary sexual characteristics. There also seem to have been some cases of inversion effects on the sexual characteristics of the female embryo. To this list, culled from current medical literature, there must be added the findings of independent physicians who noticed mental depression, nasal irritation, shrinking of the uterus, skin disease, and even possible brain damage.

One advertisement of a commercial brand frankly states, "The use of [X] for more than three years must await the results of continuing studies"—a clear confession that the long-range effects of oral contraceptives are not yet fully known.

Even an improved pill with less numerous and dangerous side effects would have to wait for final medical approval until it is sufficiently established that a repeated disturbance of the female hormonal balance is not damaging in the long run either to mother or offspring. At the present time, there seems to exist no other pill with such a variety of potential adverse reactions. Its use implies a serious gamble.

The intrauterine device (I.U.D.), better known as the "loop," "ring," or "coil," widely used in underdeveloped countries, seems to have obtained disappointing results. There have been many instances of infection, expulsion of the device, and even rupture of the uterine wall. A young woman who has never given birth could not use an I.U.D. without danger. Furthermore, there is a strong suspicion that it works, not as a contraceptive that prevents fecundation, but as an abortifacient that prevents implantation of the fecundated ovum—which makes the moral problem more serious.

A new pill is being developed for use after intercourse. The moral arguments against it are the same as those against the I.U.D. —its action seems to be abortifacient.

The condom is awkward. Its application interrupts the natural crescendo of the act of love. It tends to dull the male's physical sensitivity, and thus hampers ejaculation.

Spermicidal suppositories, foams, and jellies are insufficiently effective. So are douches, even taken immediately after intercourse. There is a high incidence of unwanted pregnancies with these techniques.

Withdrawal before ejaculation is not safe at all. Besides disrupting the sexual act, it brings about a high risk of impregnation because ejaculation, being a reflex act, cannot be accurately controlled or timed. Furthermore, there may be some live spermatozoa in the preejaculation fluids.

The diaphragm has a relatively high rate of reliability, and no damaging side effect. It seems to be psychologically acceptable in most cases because it does not interfere in the least with the act of love. In order to be effective, however, it requires a certain amount of care and attention: proper fitting, periodical checking for size, careful examination of the rubber, and the combined use of a spermicidal jelly. Even then, it does not enjoy the same security as the pill.

Clearly, then, none of these methods is perfect. Much research and experimentation needs to be done before any really satisfying means are developed. An ideal would be, for instance, a method establishing with certainty the period of possible fecundity. It would entail a certain amount of abstention. Something like a week or less would be acceptable to the majority of couples. As of now, most married people have a difficult time determining precisely what is best for them in the light of practical medical results. They would prefer not to use any of the current methods, but because of the urgent need of limiting their families and the disastrous results of excessive and unnatural abstention, they must in conscience make a choice of the least objectionable means, considering their own personal circumstances.

The Moral Problem of Contraception Is Not Solved by the Encyclical

Withdrawal before ejaculation is often referred to as onanism. It seems to be the most ancient method of birth control. Much effort has been made to establish the immorality of all methods on the basis of Onan's condemnation, as recounted in Chapter 38 of the Book of Genesis—the only text in the whole Bible that has any connection with the subject. Scriptural scholars now generally agree that this text in no way supports the general condemnation of contraceptive intercourse. If the argument from divine revelation used in 1931 by Pope Pius XI in the encyclical *Casti connubii* had had any real value, it would have been repeated in the most recent document on birth control, Pope Paul VI's encyclical *Humanae vitae*. The argument from divine revelation was deliberately omitted because the official Church has had to admit the complete lack of scriptural backing for any sweeping condemnation of birth control. The only arguments used are those of authority, tradition and the "natural law."

The encyclical *Humanae vitae*, coming after four years of consultation and hesitation, exploded like a bombshell in the midst of a startled world. There had been great hope for an *aggiornamento*, a "bringing up to date," on moral teachings about the proper use of sex, fostered mostly by objective considerations and recent theological studies, and boosted in April 1967 by the revelation of the Majority Opinion of the Papal Commission on Birth Limitation. By contrast, every sign from the Vatican—including the celebrated statement of October 1966 that the Church's teaching on birth control was not "in doubt"—had been pointing to a confirmation of the traditional position. For many, the encyclical came as a terrible shock, even inducing a crisis of conscience. It was greeted with an unprecedented explosion of disappointment, sorrow, and dissent that more than offset the expressions of gladness and approval.

In the encyclical, Pope Paul showed himself to be a man concerned with the preservation of the faith and the constancy of doctrine, a man deeply and lovingly interested in the welfare of the Church and of its people. But he seemed to have been closed to the vast amount of evidence laid before him, not the least of which is the witness of other Christian churches. What we are discussing here, however, is not the encyclical itself, but the impact it will have upon the married. Now that the Pope has spoken, what are we to do?

There have been two main schools of thought in reaction to *Humanae vitae*. One stresses confidence in the Holy Father, and total obedience based on the commanding nature of the pronouncement. For its adherents, now that the Pope has spoken, the question is solved once for all. The followers of the other school hold that the encyclical is a fallible statement of the magisterium, and as such is subject to error and possible future reform.

The adherents of the first school of thought agree with the encyclical as a whole, not only with its beautiful exposition of marriage in the preliminary sections but even with the dogmatic views concerning the necessity of leaving each and every sexual act open to procreation. Many virtues may be seen in such a position: love and respect for the Pope, self-discipline and obedience at a high cost to personal satisfaction. The question, however, is not personal virtue but objective truth.

The followers of the second school of thought include members of the hierarchy and the clergy and laymen who generally insist on their fundamental loyalty to the Church as instituted by Jesus Christ. Among the dissenters, however, there are a few who lack proper respect for the magisterium.

Respectful dissent is widespread even in our own country, in spite of the original declaration of the American bishops. Theological justification for this dissent may be found in documents of the Second Vatican Council, which help to illuminate the important role of conscience in such difficult matters:

"... every man has the duty, and therefore the right, to seek the truth in matters religious in order that he may with prudence form for himself right and true judgment of conscience. ... The enquiry is to be free, carried on with the aid of teaching or instruction, communication and dialogue. On his part, man perceives and acknowledges the imperatives of the divine law through the mediation of conscience. In all his activity a man is bound to follow his conscience faithfully, in order that he may come to God, for whom he was created. It follows that he is not to be forced to act in a manner contrary to his conscience. Nor, on the other hand, is he to be restrained from acting in accordance with his conscience especially in matters religious."

[*Declaration on Religious Freedom,* 3]

"Conscience is the most sacred core and sanctuary of man. There he is alone with God, whose voice echoes in his depth."

[*The Church in the Modern World,* 16]

It clearly follows from these authoritative statements that everyone is always obliged to follow the dictates of his conscience, even if that conscience is in disagreement with the pronouncements of legitimate authority. This is not merely a right, but a duty. A considerable number of people have exercised this incontestable right of respectful dissent because the arguments supporting the encyclical's conclusions appeared to them of insufficient weight. These people are not rebels, but deeply involved and faithful members of the Church, often highly qualified in their own fields of work, and enjoying a depth of pastoral or experiential knowledge that may very well have been lacking or ignored within the Vatican walls. For them, dissent is not insubordination or a privilege of freedom: it is rather a matter of clear duty to a truth that supersedes obedience. In earlier days such an attitude would have caused a suspicion of heresy. In our time loyal opposition is understood as the mark of an individual responsible for his conscientious decisions. *A well-formed conscience is not necessarily a conformed conscience.*

The question still remains: How can a Catholic exercise an independent conscience in a matter that seems to have been settled so definitely by the Holy Father?

In spite of the fact that the Pope clearly intended to make a definitive pronouncement closing the issue once for all, the incontrovertible fact is that the issue remains open. The encyclical *Humanae vitae* is not an infallible document. Whatever is not infallible is fallible. Traditionally in the Church a noninfallible pronouncement is regarded as reformable, open to modification. Therefore we have no guarantee that a future Pope will not alter the present disciplinary teaching of the magisterium. In fact, there is a strong body of opinion that suggests that there will be a quick repeal of this same teaching.

It has always been part of the teaching of the Church that the individual conscience is the proximate norm of morality, while the law is a remote norm. Therefore in any individual act implying a moral judgment, it is the individual conscience, enlightened but not determined by the law, that is the final judge before God.

No law can ever be so precise, complete, and absolute as to cover adequately every possible instance of its application. The more sweeping the law, the more numerous will be its exceptions and qualifications. A moral law that tends to regulate the most minute and intimate details of life cannot possibly have universal validity because of the infinity of personal circumstances the lawgiver could not have foreseen. Every law legitimately promulgated by a competent authority obliges only insofar as it is not contradicted by another and higher principle the lawmaker may have overlooked. A more open conversation between the Vatican and the world would have avoided embarrassingly one-sided and absolute conclusions that necessarily fail to be relevant in a great number of cases.

In the exercise of private conscience as applied to the matter of birth control, there is then a rational and human approach that consists in weighing all the factors of our own personal case, while giving respectful and sincere attention to the norms presented by the Pope, and hoping that law and conscience will coincide. If they do not, conscience has the stronger claim. Unquestioning obedience to a noninfallible papal command is not the only way open to a conscientious Catholic.

Surprisingly, *Humanae vitae* makes no distinction between the use of contraceptives as the means of selfish pleasure and their use as a reasonable method by which love could be maintained in a family generously endowed with children. The reason is probably that once contraception has been placed in the absolute category of "intrinsic evil" because allegedly "against the natural law," there is no possibility of admitting its use as a relative good. This is precisely one of the points most in need of research and development, so that the confusion would cease between what pertains to man's essential and unchangeable "nature" and what is of the domain of physical and contingent "nature" and thus subject to man's dominion.[2]

Bishops Have Not Approved the Encyclical Unconditionally

From the writing of some diocesan journals and the Pope's references to his own pronouncement, it would seem that it has been endorsed universally and unconditionally by the bishops of the world. The depth of Pope Paul's unawareness, at the time, of what was really going on may be judged by a news item from Essen, Germany, related to the Katholikentag, the 120th Catholic Day Congress (September 4–8, 1968). The more than 100,000 participants, members of the hierarchy, priests, nuns and laymen, heard a message from him telling them that "an overwhelming majority" of Catholics had accepted the encyclical "with assent and obedience." Earlier, however, in the very same Congress, the participants in a Marriage and Family Workshop had voted about 3,000 to 80 in favor of a resolution that rejected the encyclical, called for a revision of its teaching, and asserted that freedom of conscience must be respected in the field of family planning.

Among the national hierarchies to have strongly endorsed the encyclical are those of the United States, Ireland, India, Ceylon,

[2] For a much more complete philosophical and theological study of contraception, natural law, intrinsic evil, and the moral importance of the male seed, cf. José de Vinck, *The Virtue of Sex* (Hawthorn Books, 1966), pp. 49–69 and 102–133.

Spain and Portugal. Other national hierarchies and prominent bishops, while stressing the obligation of obedience, very clearly leave the door open to freedom of conscience, sometimes in a manner that comes very close to double-talk.

BELGIUM

On August 30, 1968, the Belgian Bishops issued a statement which supports the authority of the encyclical, but includes the following paragraph:

"Someone, however, who is competent in the matter under consideration and capable of forming a personal and well-founded judgment—which necessarily presupposes a sufficient amount of knowledge—may, after a serious examination before God, come to other conclusions on certain points. In such a case he has the right to follow his conviction provided that he remains sincerely disposed to continue his inquiry."

HOLLAND

Before issuing definitive pastoral instructions, the Bishops of Holland have decided to consult representative organizations of laymen. With this in mind, they issued an Interim Statement which reads in part:

"In this critical hour we realize that many Catholics are feeling uneasy. Many people feel disappointed by the papal encyclical, particularly by the declaration on contraceptives. These Catholics are being tested in their faith, that is, the Church: the work of God in human appearances in the midst of us.

". . . The consequences of the encyclical have world-wide meaning and only after a long time and deep thinking can one understand its scope. You will understand that your bishops will be able to offer the guidance you need only after serious consultation with theologians and other experts. This guidance will undoubtedly be offered to you; but probably it will take time. A Catholic owes respect to the word and authority of the Pope. The individual conscience cannot ignore such an authoritative declaration as this encyclical. For that matter, many factors that determine the individual conscience with regard to the conjugal act are already clear: for example, mutual love, relations in the family and social circumstances. We Catholics believe in papal infallibility. Though this encyclical is no infallible dogmatic declaration, it is still a true plea for the dignity of life and an appeal for responsibility in sexuality and marriage that is of very great importance in our society. May the discussion about this encyclical contribute to a more pure evaluation and functioning of authority inside the Church. Let us pray in these days for our Holy Father and for each other.

WEST GERMANY

At a meeting which ended on August 30, 1968, a gathering of twenty-two heads of dioceses and over forty auxiliary bishops worked out a declaration which was published on September 11.

"He who thinks that it is permissible for him to deviate in his private theory and practice from a non-infallible teaching of the Church authority—such a case is conceivable in principle —must question his conscience soberly and critically whether he can justify this before God. . . .

"It has to be maintained, as expressed by the Second Vatican Council (see *Constitution on the Church in the Modern World*, No. 51), that the question of whether and under what circumstances birth control is permissible cannot be left to the arbitrary will of the spouses. The answer must be sought and found by them through conscientious examination based on objective norms and criteria. The concrete way to responsible parenthood should not offend the dignity of the human person or endanger the harmonious fruitful love of marriage. . . .

"Pastors will respect in their work, especially in the administration of sacraments, the decisions of conscience of the believers made in the awareness of their responsibility. We will endeavor, working together with priests and lay people, to seek practical ways for the pastoral care of the married. In the spirit of collegiality, we the bishops will carry on conversations with the Holy Father and with the episcopates of other countries."

AUSTRIA

On September 23, 1968, the Austrian hierarchy declared: "Because the encyclical is not an infallible judgment, it is conceivable that some Catholics will believe that they cannot accept this ruling.

Whoever is an expert in this field and came to a conviction different from that of the encyclical after serious self-examination and not because of an emotional reaction is allowed to follow his conviction. Such a person does not sin if he is ready to continue examining the situation and otherwise shows respect and loyalty to the Church."

ENGLAND

The hierarchy of England and Wales issued their statement on September 25, 1968. It reads in part:

"A particular difficulty faces those who, after serious thought and prayer, cannot as yet understand or be fully convinced of the doctrines as laid down. This is not surprising, in view of the discussions of recent years which have resulted in the present controversy.

"The Holy Father realizes what difficulties face married people. . . . The encyclical makes no sweeping condemnations. There is no threat of damnation.

"Far from being excluded from the sacraments those in difficulties are invited to receive them more frequently."

In terms of traditional theology, this means that such people are not in a state of serious sin.

JAPAN

In spite of a request by the Apostolic Delegate, the Japanese bishops refused to send a message of thanks to the Vatican. One of them commented privately: "The encyclical would mean many difficulties for the younger Catholic and also make the Church an object of ridicule." No pastoral comment was made until December of 1968, when the Japanese Conference expressed the awareness that the observance of *Humanae vitae* would create difficulties for many married people.

"In such cases, if, while exerting all goodwill to be obedient to the encyclical, one is unable to follow it in some point on account of unavoidable actual and objective circumstances, the faithful should not think they have been separated from the love of God."

ITALY

In the statement of the presidential council of the Italian Bishops' Conference, addressed to Pope Paul VI, and published in *L'Osservatore Romano* on September 15, 1968, there is a strong and apparently unconditional endorsement of *Humanae vitae*. Two points, however, constitute definite qualifications.

The first is a distinction clearly made between those who use contraception for selfish motives only, and others who do so because of the "difficulty, at times very serious, in which they find themselves, that of reconciling the demands of responsible parenthood with those of their mutual love." The text continues:

> "In such a case, in fact, their behavior, although not in conformity with the Christian norm, cannot surely be equated in its serious importance with that which might spring solely from motives vitiated by egotism and hedonism."

A better translation would read: ". . . cannot surely be equated, in terms of gravity, with the same behavior brought about solely by motives debased by egotism and hedonism."

The second point is a declaration in no veiled terms that the encyclical is but one of the elements of judgment in the case.

> "May they know how to put into practice and evaluate the directives and exhortations of the Pope on the whole of their conjugal life, in reference to the totality, faithfulness, fecundity of their love and the 'unitive meaning' of the conjugal acts, the Christian characteristics of responsible parenthood.
>
> "May they accept with a spirit of faith the teaching of the Vicar of Christ in regard to the different moral values of birth control methods. This teaching is an essential element for the formation of their conscience, in order that their responsible judgment may conform to God's will."

The last sentence leaves the door open to respectful dissent, since there is a great difference between an essential element of responsible judgment and a determining factor of behavior.

Canada

The Canadian hierarchy, in its declaration of September 27, 1968, made no official endorsement of the doctrinal paragraph 14. It upheld the right of dissent, allowing Catholics who follow their consciences in the use of contraceptives to receive Holy Communion without going to confession, thus implying, as did the bishops of England and Wales, that such people are not in a state of serious sin.

> "We must appreciate the difficulty experienced by contemporary man in understanding and appropriating some of the points of this encyclical and we must make every effort to learn from the insights of Catholic scientists and intellectuals who are of undoubted loyalty to Christian truth, to the Church, and to the authority of the Holy See.
>
> "Since they are not denying any point of divine and Catholic faith or rejecting the teaching authority of the Church, these Catholics should not be considered, or consider themselves, shut off from the body of the faithful.
>
> "But they should remember that their good faith will be dependent on a sincere self-examination to determine the true motives and grounds for such suspension of assent and on continued effort to understand and deepen their knowledge of the teaching of the Church.
>
> ". . . In accord with the accepted principles of moral theology, if these persons (who are involved in conflicts of duties) have tried sincerely but without success to pursue a line of conduct in keeping with the given directives, they may be safely assured that whoever honestly chooses that course which seems right to him does so in good conscience."

Surprisingly, Pope Paul seems to have approved this declaration. In a letter, quoted in the November 13, 1968, issue of *The National Catholic Reporter*, Archbishop Emmanuele Clarizio, Apostolic Delegate to Canada, told Bishop Alexander Carter, President of the Canadian Bishops Conference:

"Now I am happy to notify your excellency that his eminence Cardinal Amleto Cicognani, secretary of state to his holiness, has just communicated to the delegation that the Holy Father Pope Paul VI has taken cognizance of the document with satisfaction."

SCANDINAVIA

In a statement issued October 17, 1968, the six bishops of Denmark, Finland, Norway, and Sweden noted that the encyclical *Humanae vitae* is not infallible and that such non-infallible pronouncements have been revised or supplemented in the past. They continue:

"Therefore it is self-evident that no one should doubt the content of the encyclical without entering into its way of thinking and intention thoroughly, honestly, and with consciousness of his responsibility before God.

"However, if someone, from weighty and well-considered reasons, cannot become convinced by the argumentation of the encyclical, it has always been conceded that he is allowed to have a different view from that presented in a non-infallible statement of the Church. No one should be considered a bad Catholic because he is of such a dissenting opinion."

SOUTH AFRICA

Archbishop Denis Eugène Hurley, Primate of South Africa, said recently:

"My acceptance of the Holy See and my loyalty to Pope Paul are absolutely unquestioned. But I am convinced that there must be an increase in the scope and openness of consultations in the Church in matters of such importance as the birth control issue."

And Bishop Gerard van Nelsen, O.P., Presiding Vicar Apostolic, expressed the following opinion in Kroonstad:

"I think it is not the wish, or for that matter the right, of Pope Paul to overrule the supremacy of the Christian conscience to make moral decisions in the concrete situations of life."

FRANCE

The French bishops' pastoral note on *Humanae vitae* was issued at their plenary assembly in Lourdes (November 2–9, 1968). Like all the other declarations of national hierarchies, it supports the encyclical in principle. However, it asserts:

"Contraception can never be a good. It is always a disorder, but this disorder is not always culpable. It happens, indeed, that spouses see themselves confronted by veritable conflicts of duties.

"No one is unaware of the spiritual agonies in which sincere husbands and wives struggle, particularly when the observance of natural rhythms does not succeed 'in providing a sufficiently secure basis for the regulation of birth.' (*Humanae vitae,* No. 24)

"On the one hand, they are aware of the duty of respecting the openness to life of every conjugal act; they also judge in conscience that they have to avoid or put off till later a new birth, and they are deprived of the resource of relying on biological rhythms. On the other hand, in what concerns them, they do not see how to renounce at present the physical expression of their love without menacing the stability of their home (*Pastoral Constitution on the Church in the Modern World,* No. 51).

"On this subject, we shall simply recall the constant teaching of morality: when one has an alternative choice of duties and, whatever may be the decision, evil cannot be avoided, traditional wisdom makes provision for seeking before God which duty, in the circumstances, is the greater. Husband and wife will decide at the end of a common reflection carried out with all the care that the greatness of their conjugal vocation requires."

The door is left open to practical dissent.

UNITED STATES

After an early and almost unconditional endorsement of *Humanae vitae* which resulted in extremely strong opposition from some members of both clergy and laity, particularly from a considerable number of professional theologians, the American bishops published their Pastoral Letter on "Human Life in Our Day," on November 15, 1968. Its general intent was the defense of life and the condemnation of the use of sexuality for selfish motives. In spite of strenuous denials from members of the hierarchy, *this letter departs from the earlier declaration* by emphasizing the principle of licit dissent in matters concerned with the non-infallible teachings of the Church. It also contains a surprising statement that rejects the principle of biological necessity, which had been invoked in the encyclical as the foundation of the "natural law" argument:

> "In its emphasis on the virtues of fidelity and hope, so essential to the prophetic witness of the family, Christian sexual morality derives therefore, not from the inviolability of generative biology, but ultimately from the sanctity of life itself and the nobility of human sexuality."

The principle of licit dissent from a non-infallible papal document is admitted by the bishops themselves:

> "There exists in the Church a lawful freedom of inquiry and of thought and also general norms of licit dissent."

Cardinal Newman is then quoted in support of that basic principle:

> ". . . I have to say again, lest I should be misunderstood, that when I speak of conscience, I mean conscience truly so called. When it has the right of opposing the supreme, though not infallible Authority of the Pope, it must be something more than that miserable counterfeit which, as I have said above, now goes by the name. If in a particular case it is to be taken as a sacred and sovereign monitor, its dictate, in order to prevail against the voice of the Pope, must follow upon serious thought, prayer, and all available means of arriving at a right judgment on the matter in question. And further, obedience to the Pope is what is called 'in possession'; that is, the *onus probandi* (burden of proof) of establishing a case against him lies, as in all cases of exception, on the side of conscience.

> Unless a man is able to say to himself, as in the presence of God, that he must not, and dare not, act upon the papal injunction, he is bound to obey it and would commit a great sin in disobeying it."

This admirable passage very clearly indicates both the weighty prejudice in favor of any papal statement, and the absolute right of dissent of a well-informed conscience. After prayerful and objective study of the question, any Catholic, acting from non-selfish motives, may declare, "as in the presence of God, that he must not, and dare not, act upon [a] papal injunction. . . ."

All these declarations have in common a deep respect for the authority and intentions of the Holy Father, together with the firm expression of the primacy of conscience in the practical decisions of actual life. The general conclusions coincide very closely with a surprising document revealed in the *National Catholic Reporter* of September 25, 1968, in an article entitled "The Encyclical That Wasn't Issued." It is presented as being a preliminary text composed by Archbishop Claudius Dupuy, of Albi, France, dated June 26, 1966, and approved by a majority of bishops of the Papal Commission on Birth Limitation. The most relevant passages read as follows:

> "What has been condemned in the past and remains so today is the unjustifiable refusal of life, arbitrary human intervention for the sake of moments of egoistic pleasure; in short, the rejection of procreation as a specific task of marriage. In the past, the Church could not speak otherwise than she did because the problem of birth control did not confront human consciousness in the same way. Today, having clearly recognized the legitimacy and even the duty of regulating births, she recognizes too that human intervention in the process of the marriage act for reasons drawn from the finality of marriage itself should not always be excluded provided that the criteria of morality are always safeguarded.
>
> "If an arbitrarily contraceptive mentality is to be condemned, as has always been the Church's view, an intervention to regulate conception in a spirit of true, reasonable and generous charity (Cf. Matt. 7:12; John 13:34, 35; 15:12–17; Rom.

> 13:8–10) does not deserve to be, because if it were, other goods of marriage might be endangered. . . .
>
> "As for the means that husband and wife can legitimately employ, it is their task to decide these together, without drifting into arbitrary decisions, but always taking account of the objective criteria of morality. These criteria are in the first place those that relate to the totality of married life and sexuality. . . ."

Would that this text had been accepted! The whole document is excellent.

Sexual Love Is Good in Itself

Is there any reason to believe, as the ancients did, that any sexual intercourse that is not directly intended as a procreative means is necessarily immoral? Do we have to believe, with these same ancients, that intercourse for pleasure alone is sinful?

In the history of Church teachings on sexual morality, one of the most drastic reversals came about in the encyclical *Casti connubi,* in which Pope Pius XI permitted the use of the rhythm system under certain carefully worded conditions. The reversal consisted in this: For the first time, the performance of the sex act for its own sake, with the formal intent of avoiding procreation, was declared good. Such a change conformed with a better understanding of sexuality. As soon as the beneficial effect of sexual union in terms of mutual love, mutual support, mutual peace, came to be accepted, the old taboo against nonprocreative sex had to fall. Another taboo also came crashing down: the condemnation of pleasure. When the sexual act is considered as a highly valuable means of human communication, a mutual gift between the spouses, and when it is seen that sexual pleasure is a strong element of marital union and stability, the natural consequence is to accept as morally good those sexual acts whose sole intention and effect is to procure mutual enjoyment of husband and wife.

Common sense, expressed in common language, had long anticipated the reversal of professional moralists. People do not refer to sexual intercourse as "making children": they call it "making love"—a remarkably accurate expression of the great dignity of the function. Young people do not "fall into child-making"; they "fall in love." They do not marry because they want to make children; they marry because they want to make love. *The first effect of the sexual instinct is not an urge toward procreation, but an urge toward copulation*—the act of love. Even the most virtuous couples, those who sincerely wish to have children, may have very little awareness of "making" them while they are in the very act of doing so. In fact, children may come as a complete surprise, as an added bonus to the pleasure of love.

When Is Birth Control Legitimate?

Let us now see how a permissible method of birth limitation could be reasonably used. In the case of an early marriage, when, for instance, both partners are still in college, the coming of a child nine months after the wedding may be disruptive and disastrous. The young people would be obliged to change their plans. At least one of them would be forced to drop out. There would probably be the need of finding larger quarters. The expenses of raising a child could not be carried by a scholarship or some other minimum means of support that is generally the norm for students. Quite possibly, both parents would have to forego their college education: the mother, to take care of the child; the father, to earn a living. In such a case, it would be perfectly logical and moral to use intercourse solely in a nonprocreative way until the establishment of a true home became practically and financially possible.

Nonprocreative sex seems perfectly justified on many occasions when there is not the slightest need or desire to conceive, but only an urge to express conjugal love. This would cover by far the greatest number of sexual acts. There should, then, be two different approaches to sex: the normal, most frequent use of it as a means of love; the extraordinary and specially generous use of it as a means of procreation. Normally, the relationship would be nonprocreative. But when husband and wife agree that the time is right to have a child, the same act is then performed under fertile conditions without losing any of its value as an act of love. The child, then, will really and truly be a fruit of love.

Your Marriage Is a True Christian Calling

Christ is calling you to work out your salvation in each other's arms. You are to answer this calling with every one of your deeds, every day and night of your life. The answer must be positive, vital, enthusiastic, optimistic, and realistic. You must have faith, hope, and love—for God, most certainly, but for each other, too, since you were both made in his image and resemblance. If you seek in each other that which is divine, you will have no reason to fret that you are not yet in a state of perfect bliss. *The unavoidable imperfections of being human will be burned away by the all-powerful perfection of being made for love.*

A Zen Buddhist monk was asked what was the most important word. "Yes!" he answered. Yes to life, love, to anything that can happen to you. For with God's strength, nothing is too much. You will receive this strength in abundance because your whole way of life is founded on a promise you have made in his name.

The proper planning of your life, then, should take into consideration the two levels on which you are living simultaneously: the level of the here and now, with its pains, fatigues, imperfections, hopes, disappointments, highs and lows that make up the weaving of an individual destiny; and the level of the ever-present reality of divine beatitude. The summit of wisdom, the best chance of happiness now and hereafter, is not attained by sacrificing the "now" for the "hereafter" as if everything in this world of time and space were futile and worthless when compared to eternity. The summit of wisdom consists in seeing and living the transparency and unity of things. There are not two realities—the world and heaven. There is only one reality—*now*—and only one response to it—*yes*. Yes to the vision of God in things and to the vision of things in God—for they are the same. *Yes* to our sexual partner, for he or she is love for us, God for us in an incarnate form, a constant proposition to answer "Yes, Lord: I am here!"

Now, please don't take this to mean that there is no heaven or that heaven is on earth. What it does mean is that your heaven is being made on earth, that nothing you do here and now is irrelevant to what you will be in the state of beatitude. It is here and now that you are determining the style of your eternity, and the better you are aware of the transparent unity of things—in spite of their superficial horror, in spite of hatred and injustice and wars—the better chance you will have to organize your life along the ways of reality, along the ways of love.

This is no fancy dream, no imaginary vision: it is more realistic than the material view that takes things flatly for what they appear to be. In the long run, the view of the believer, the man of desire, the man of faith, the mystic, is infinitely more practical than that of anybody else. Believe, hope, and love *together*, and together you will enjoy "what eye has not seen, nor ear heard, nor has it entered the heart of man."

CHAPTER 6

THE MOST IMPORTANT THING YOU CAN DO FOR YOUR CHILDREN

Teach Them How to Love . . . Parents Can Teach Love Only if They Love Each Other . . . Children Should Be Taught That They Are Lovable . . . Teach Them to Use Their Freedom Responsibly . . . Love or Perish . . . Help Children to Recognize the Signs of Love . . . Feeding, Clothing, and Educating Are Expressions of Your Love . . . Teach Them to Love, and You Will Be Eternally Successful . . . With the Power to Love They Will Go Out and Heal the World

---

Many families are raised haphazardly, with little forethought and no discussion of the problems that lie ahead. This may be due either to neglect or to an unjustified optimism that everything will work out all right. Many well-intended couples fail to realize that without forethought even their best efforts in loving each other and in loving their children will necessarily bring forth results that are far from perfect. Human beings give extremely little love to one another. Even when they do attempt to give, they often do so clumsily and erratically. That is why it is important to use every reasonable means to make up for such deficiencies.

One of the important things for parents to do is to think through a master plan that will help them bring their daily actions into conformity with some long-range goals, goals that need to be reappraised occasionally so as to include the changing conditions of life. It would probably be wise to write this plan out, keep it on file, and check it from time to time against the way things are actually being handled.

A family plan should cover, for instance, your common intentions as regards children, what you believe to be the most important thing you can do for them; how many you wish to have and how soon; and how you intend to educate them. Your relationship with them should be predetermined at least in some measure, so that later you will not be anguished at the thought of what you could have done, and failed to do because you never gave it much thought.

Teach Them How to Love

The most important thing you can do for your children is teach them how to love. You know without having to be told that you should love your children, take care of them, and provide for their material, emotional, intellectual, and spiritual well-being. But in providing for them you may not be actually teaching them. There are many parents who do little, if anything, beyond providing for immediate material needs. The father brings in the money, the mother does the shopping and cooking, and that is that. How many have you heard saying, "I gave my child everything; I poured out my life for that boy, and that is how he repays me!"

Parents are very much aware of what they are giving, but are they giving what their children really need? The love addressed to children should not be limited to the providing of material comforts, nor should it be given as if children were extensions of the parents' pride. Children must be treated as rational and spiritual individuals in the making. The major consideration, the reason for love, is not that they are what *you* have brought to life but that they are children of God and persons in their own right.

To teach children how to love, you must love them well. The way to love them well is not to do so in the manner most flattering to your ego so that you can boast of their appearance, but to love them in the manner most beneficial to *them*. The program and planning of their education should be based, not on what *you* would prefer, but on what *they* should achieve as their proper destiny.

There is great egoism in spoiling children. What you are doing is lavishing favors on yourself in a vicarious way, because the children are *your* pride and joy. You want them to have the best in order to show how good and generous and powerful and rich *you are,* without any consideration for their true needs, the control and orientation of their natural instincts, or that measure of discipline and restraint that is a condition of harmonious development. Loving your children does not consist in giving them "everything." It consists rather in giving them what is truly good for them. Love does not consist in giving so many "things"; it is much more a question of giving of yourself, of your time and attention and of your loving presence.

It is certainly not a matter of giving expensive toys and gadgets. Giving a car to a teen-ager at graduation will not make up for years of neglect. He or she will be deeply resentful to you for having been absent when you were most needed. The car will be considered, not gratefully as a gift, but scornfully as a bribe, atonement, or belated peace offering. It is much better to give children nothing but your active and attentive love, for that alone is their essential food. Let them work for the rest. If you have loved them well, they will be able to provide for themselves without any trouble at all.

This may sound strange, but the important thing is not really *loving* your children. Most people are under the impression that they do love their children. The important thing for you to remember is that *they must realize that you love them.* When this happens, they will be able to love in return. In order to help them realize that it is love that is your primary gift to them, you must set about creating an atmosphere of emotional comfort and well-being for them. The security of assured love will enable them to flourish and grow. Your subjective belief about how much you are giving and sacrificing does not contribute to this atmosphere of security: on the contrary, the more loudly you remind your children about all you are doing for them, the less chances you have of creating it.

Teach your children how to love. Let your children know you love them, not through talk or material gifts, but through your daily acts and the nature of your relations with them. Teach them how to love by loving them well. For many people this is not something that can be taken for granted; it takes understanding and continued effort, and this effort is yours to make. You alone can develop and put into effect that particular style you wish to set for your family. Before offering any food for thought along these general lines, it may be good to find out if you really accept the premise: Do you agree that *the most important thing you can do for your children is to teach them how to love?* It is essential that this point be made well. Perhaps if you consider the effects of inadequate love, you will come to some firm conclusions of your own.

There are many tragic examples of marriage between fine young people who were given everything, the best of care, clothing, and education, and whose lives were filled with the promise of happiness. They started out with a big, beautiful wedding, and yet they ended up in a state of personal misery, filing for divorce and expressing bitter disenchantment with their former beloved. The reason is that one of the partners, or both, did not know how to love, were not taught how to love. Yes, they were given many costly things and lived in comfortable homes. They may even have had parents who believed that they were "loving" parents, but they were not trained in the power of love.

Parents very often do not know how to communicate love because they mistake coddling and pampering for genuine love in justice and truth. Generalizations are never wise: all divorced men and women should not be covered with a blanket condemnation. Because one crippled spouse is enough to destroy a marriage, many good and loving people end up as innocent victims. This happens, not because they themselves were incapable of love, but because they fell in love and married someone else who could not give or receive love. The defect was not discovered until it was too late.

Parents Can Teach Love Only if They Love Each Other

The best and most powerful means of learning is the example of truly loving parents. Parents can create an atmosphere of love only if they themselves communicate well with each other. As sexually adjusted and happy parents will probably give birth to children who in turn will be sexually adjusted and happy, so it is with the wider areas of love. If you provide the example of a harmonious home, children will develop in it naturally, like straight green olive shoots.

The peace of a home is felt almost materially. In a good home, there is no tenseness. There may be occasional outbursts and difficulties, but the screaming and disorder are at a minimum. Difficulties are met soberly and dealt with in proportion to their relative importance. Conflicts are resolved in the light of charitable compromise, whenever compromise is possible, and kindly firmness when it is not. But a peaceful home is always a good place to live in, and a pleasant place to visit. Parents are neither lax nor authoritarian, children are neither insolent nor fawning.

Full and ample freedom should be given to the children in unimportant matters, so that when important issues come up, everyone knows exactly where Father and Mother stand. Obedience is then a must. It is foolish to make an issue about the length of a boy's hair when no issue is made about his driving home late at night with drink on his breath. The same principle is true when the children are very young. It is quite a different thing whether your little daughter takes candy before dinner and spoils her appetite or goes to the medicine cabinet and plays with dangerous drugs. One ought not to treat each violation with the same emotional response. There may be a happy-go-lucky informality in all nonessentials, and enough sense of humor to prevent tempests from arising in teapots. But in the background there must be a substantial awareness of the daily presence of love, the reality of real concern.

Children Should Be Taught That They Are Lovable

When children are the living objects of love in action, when they are well loved, they will very soon and very simply realize that they themselves are lovable, which is the all-important message to convey. Thus they will be conditioned not only to offer love but also to receive it, something quite essential and often lacking in the emotionally disturbed. They will learn to love and accept themselves. No one unable to receive love is able to offer it. And those unable to receive love have become that way because love had not been given to them in their times of greatest need. Once again, the right kind of love is that which seeks the good, not of the lover, but of the beloved—and in doing so, finds the good of both.

And so children will become the natural fountains of love they were intended to be. But they must have received the right kind of love: warm, generous, unconditional, and yet tempered with the control of emotions and concern for their actual welfare. They will grow in the awareness of the wisdom of loving. They will also discover the proper measure of loving, and that, according to St. Bernard, is to love without measure, without counting or accounting.

As regards our children, then, there should be no measure, no restraint in the intensity and quality of our love for them, but definite measure and wise restraint in our manner of expressing that love.

Teach Them to Use Their Freedom Responsibly

It is all well and good to provide children with comfort and security, but it is totally unwise and damaging to give them so much comfort and security that they will go out in the world with the false belief that they are automatically entitled to receive out there as much as they had had at home. Not having been trained to fend for themselves, they may turn into useless and disgruntled parasites, whimpering and cringing before the demands of life, and perhaps tempted to seek painless and illegitimate short cuts to restore their threatened ease.

Love or Perish

Love is no longer a luxury, as it may have been in ancient times when the lack of it could lead to nothing worse than tribal disaster. We now live in a planetary era in which our failures to love affect mankind as a whole and may lead to global disaster. *Love is the absolutely essential ingredient of contemporary life.* Either we love today or we perish tomorrow—and we begin to perish today, since without love there is no life but the beginning of death. And the time to learn about it, and to be trained in it, and to practice it, is from early childhood to the instant of your last breath. Love for parents, brothers and sisters, neighbors and friends of all races and nationalities should be constantly in the forefront of the process of growing up. A breakdown on any level threatens the foundations of your home.

The handing down of the spirit of love is God's work, and we partake in it by teaching our children to love their neighbors and to turn to God both in their needs and in their joys. The language we use in communicating such things to them must be adapted to their need. It is useless to foist on them summaries of abstract theology in the style of classical catechisms, but it is equally wrong to reduce the whole economy of salvation to infantile stories about "sweet little Jesus." The language used to convey the truths of faith to children should be simple, but never simplistic or platitudinous. They have an uncanny sense of the real; their minds are fresh and open, unstained as yet by the commonplace and the vulgar. Young children who so readily respond to images and receive knowledge through direct vision and feeling should be given from the start the right image and sense of Christ.

Love is a mystery. This should be stressed. God is mystery, and although Jesus Christ is open to scrutiny because of the historical facts of his incarnation and life on earth, he is yet enfolded in mystery, a mystery of love too deep to be fathomed by the human mind. Children will ask questions: "Where is God?" "Why did Jesus die?" "Who is the Holy Spirit?" But facile answers that seem to provide complete and reasonable answers simply will not do. Parents should admit honestly that even the best adult minds cannot grasp fully the mystery of God, the mystery of Christ, the mystery of the Eucharist. We should be able at a certain point to say, "We don't know," without feeling that the child will be frustrated, and turn away. It would be much worse to make up a seemingly knowing answer—only to be found out later by an intelligent child. As soon as he realizes that some of your answers collapse into absurdity, he will be tempted to reject all your teachings, the true together with the false and the approximate.

An error of a different order in the teaching of love is to give a child the impression that God is his chum or that he is a partner with whom it is possible to bargain, to trade, to exchange gifts in a mercantile spirit. A child's relation with God should not be formal and severe, but neither should it be lowered to the level of familiarity that "breeds contempt." God is immanent, within, but he is also transcendent, immensely "other" and absolutely beyond anything imaginable. It is only in Christ that he has made himself accessible to us, and through Christ that he should be shown to children.

Help Children to Recognize the Signs of Love

Education in love should not be something taught, as if it were just one more study subject, but something lived; and it can be handed down only by the living through the act of life. If you wish to know how well you are succeeding, and what the range of your children's understanding and of your ability to communicate is, ask each one of them individually, at a time when they are in a mood of confidence and closeness, "Do I love you?" and then, when they answer, "Yes," ask them, "How do you know I love you?" You may very well be amazed by the answers. Remember that they reflect the child's vision of what love does and means for him in his own life. The child will have to articulate what has been recognized as an act of love.

The child will learn to see toys and clothes and movies not merely as "things" but as signs of a hidden reality, love. The best signs of success in this effort are given when the child answers with some understanding concerning the meaning behind the things you give and the things you do. This understanding will establish an atmosphere of inner security.

Recently, a happy father spent a day in New York City with his twelve-year-old daughter, as a special Christmas gift. They took the Staten Island Ferry, bought fortune cookies in Chinatown, visited the Christmas displays in the department stores, and gazed together at the giant tree that had just been lit in Rockefeller Center. The weather had been abominable—a cold, rainy, windy day—but the child's spirit was undaunted. On the way back, the car radio sputtered its usual quota of commercials. "Buy Brand X! Increase your happiness!"—"How could I?" said the child.

Another good father did his best to love his children—and he had seven of them to love. While they were small, and even when they grew up, he would go to their beds at night and sit with each of them for a few minutes. Each one had his "little time" with Daddy. This was sometimes very tiring for a man exhausted by a full day's work, but he persevered, and the routine became a much-loved family tradition. On one particular night, he was sitting at the bedside of his seven-year-old daughter, and they had talked for a while. When he was ready to kiss her good night, he drew her to him and held her tight. She seemed to hug him with greater intensity than usual, and he remained with her this way a little longer than he normally would. She eventually lifted her head from his chest and looked up at him, asking: "Daddy, is this what heaven will be like?"

Those moments were glowing experiences of love fully realized. No theologian could have improved on those children's understanding of the meaning of love, the meaning of man's destiny.

Feeding, Clothing, and Educating Are Expressions of Your Love

Let us now consider a few down-to-earth matters that will enable you to put the spirit of love and understanding into concrete action. Since love begins with serving the immediate needs of the beloved, in the case of children, the first questions to consider are food, clothing, and education.

FOOD. There are here three fundamental rules that will be found helpful:

Don't fuss. Do not be overconcerned or overeager to do everything with utter perfection. Do not get overexcited if the new baby does not get its meals on the dot, if the temperature of the food is not accurate to a tenth of a degree, or the formula to a tenth of an ounce; children are tough, and undoubtedly they do survive. If a baby needs more food, it will tell you so, loudly. If it needs less, it will throw up. Nature is that simple. You will probably notice that the second or third child is so much easier to feed than the first, because feeding will no longer be the traumatic experience it had been before.

Be pliable. Do not set up absolute rules; otherwise every meal turns into a battle of wills and wits. A baby will outwill, outwit, and outyell you anytime. Do not be a martinet, but be firm and consistent. "This is your food: take it or leave it." Unless the child is sick, it will very soon learn to take it. Do not make an issue out of eating the last scrap. Be willing, also, to admit that there are some things children really do not like. You may have disgusted them by making them eat too much of something in the past, or they may have loved it and become sick from eating too much. Food for small children does not have to be strongly spiced or particularly tasty: they may very well be happy with the blandest of mixes, provided it contains the essential elements required for proper growth. A well-balanced diet is an absolute necessity, but gourmet food is generally wasted on the very young.

There does not seem to be much reason for drastically forbidding any eating between meals—although a piece of candy or a cookie immediately before what is to be a substantial meal may decrease the appetite to the point where a child will not eat enough of what its body needs.

Stick to natural foods. Avoid overprocessed and overpreserved foods: they are too often filled with chemicals that serve the good of the producer rather than that of the consumer. Make a lavish use of milk and milk-products that contain most of the important elements of growth. Cut down severely on sweets: candy, artificial desserts, and soda drinks. Instead of candy, give the children fruit, either fresh or dry. All fruit that is not peeled must be carefully washed in order to remove dangerous insecticides that are often used by growers.

CLOTHING. Here also there are a few important points to remember:

Dress children sensibly. In older days, newborn babies were so tightly swaddled that it is a marvel they ever managed to grow. Very young children should be dressed as lightly as the climate permits. In warm and safe climates, don't be afraid to let them romp around completely nude. The freedom of movements, the natural breathing through the skin procured by the state of nature are much preferable to the restriction of airtight clothes.

Dress a child according to sex. A mother may be tempted to bring up a curly-haired boy as a Little Lord Fauntleroy, with long locks and lace collar, and a father may want to turn his young and lively daughter into a tomboy. Complete and early sex identification has such a great importance in the psychological development of young males and young females that any form of transvestism initiated by the parents may have seriously damaging effects. Homosexual tendencies may result from the seemingly innocent action of an amused parent who thought it cute to have a pretty boy in buttons and bows or a tough young lady in cowboy shirt and dungarees.

Such a thing happens when parents have ardently desired a boy, and the first child is a girl: she may be brought up as a boy, and even be given a boy's name. The reverse happens when the parents had strongly desired a girl. This is not only stupid but criminal, because it is a source of major disturbance in the child's sexual identity.

EDUCATION. Once again, there are fundamental rules:

Provide a good example. Children naturally identify themselves with the grownups around them, aping gestures, learning speech, copying intonations and reactions. They are perfectly aware of the atmosphere of peace or of the lack of it. That is why parental harmony, the presence of Father and Mother loving each other, will be the best form of preparation for life. Children will then grow up in a state of order in which everything is proportionately and properly placed, and energy can be devoted to the tremendous tasks of learning and growing, instead of being wasted on the effort of surviving in a hostile and insecure milieu.

Avoid indoctrination. As soon as children are able to learn, their natural sense of curiosity should be fed and developed by the revelation of the world as a possible object of observation and personal relation. Much too often, the goal of professional educators has been to produce well-integrated citizens, "regular guys," by the simple process of stuffing them with facts acceptable to the adult powers-that-be, and expecting children to parrot these facts in a form as close as possible to the official textbook. *This is not education but indoctrination.* Unfortunately, it is found on every level, from kindergarten to postgraduate studies, and most damagingly in the teaching of religion through passive memorization of catechisms.

Encourage creativity. The one thing most feared by an official educational "system" seems to be the production of free, thinking, creative, and critical individuals. Critical does not mean criticizing, but endowed with the power of rational independent judgment. Freedom, creativity, and a critical mind are by definition a danger to the Establishment—both Church and State—because they are always liable to make trouble by upsetting a carefully balanced applecart that was creaking along on crooked wheels. The spirit of independent thought, however, is not dangerous as such: it is an indispensable condition of progress. No great man was ever produced through an education of conformity or a personal life of bandwagon-jumping. There is always something revolutionary in genius. Revolution need not be violent. It must stay with us if we are to remain alive.

Conformity, with its general aim of leveling, will result in eliminating those very sparks of genius that may be present, and should be developed, in every individual, since every man and woman is personally different from every other. What is worthy of careful education—drawing out and cultivating—is precisely this difference.

Be observant of what your children like to do or of what they do well and naturally. Provide the tools and the means, and most of all the encouragement and freedom to develop in their own way. Remember that it is considerably better to leave children alone to their own initiatives than to push them into preplanned activities. Children are not extensions of you, nor are they the carriers of your dreams: they are persons in their own right and are not under the slightest obligation to live as incarnations of parental ambition.

Teach Them to Love and You Will Be Eternally Successful

Food, clothing and education are important, of course, but are they the most important thing as far as your children are concerned? No! The matter is so vital that it is worth repeating again and again: The most important thing you can do for your children is to teach them how to love. And so, in conclusion to the present chapter, this same all-important matter will be summarized in the light of the preceding remarks.

It is all too clear to psychiatrists that most, if not all, of the disturbed and antisocial individuals they are called upon to treat became that way because of love-starvation. In the long run, love is more necessary than food and drink: if food and drink are lacking, a man will die after having lived some time. If love is lacking, he really never will have lived at all. Perhaps the unloved may be compared to the bud that never opens into a flower, the promise that is never kept, the spring that never rises to the surface, the cloud that never turns into a beneficent shower. The unloved are self-enclosed, uselessly churning within themselves sentiments of frustration, resentment, and guilt, unable to communicate because they can neither give nor receive.

Every child is born with an immense potential of love, an unformulated hope of love. A child is, in a sense, nothing but expectation. It sends out feelers to the limits of its sense perception. It looks in the hope of recognition, feels in the hope of sensual response, cries in the hope of comforting attention. Its whole being exists as an effort toward participation.

What the child is craving is the warm expression of human affection, the response of tenderness and love. Each of these favorable responses will then be followed by a further extension, a further groping, a further hope, so that the senses and intellectual faculties develop in an increasing circle of action and reaction that reveal the surrounding world as real and good.

Once a certain level of security has been attained by means of the stored experiences of a sufficient proportion of favorable responses, disappointment, pain, and sorrow become tolerable. They may even be good in that they show by contrast the positive quality of pleasure and satisfaction.

But when a child is abandoned from the very beginning in a cold and uncomfortable world, or even in a world that is cozy and warm but lacking in personal care and attention, and in the responses of love, it is not encouraged to develop its feelers, to grow and progress physically and emotionally. If every time it tries something new, it is slapped or turned down or, worse still simply ignored, it will retract its feelers and cease to try, and thus also cease to grow. It will then turn into a man or woman who has created an inner world, less real in fact but more comfortable, and will refuse to face the outer world of reality.

Such is the usual pattern of development of the mentally disturbed and antisocial patient of the psychiatric ward.

With the Power to Love They Will Go Out and Heal the World

Let us see what happens to the child who has learned how to love and how to give love. It has grown up in a world sufficiently good to enable the toleration of evil. It will develop into an adolescent and an adult fully aware of the existence of evil without being overwhelmed by a sense of its prevalence, living in a world of active hope instead of one of passive despair. A loving man or woman will seek to do something about the miseries of the world. Encouraged by early experience of successful response to attempts at communication, such persons will try to do good around them, and not be discouraged by occasional setbacks or even by a total lack of results. They will be concerned not merely about themselves but about everyone. Once the pattern of faith, hope, and love has been well established, it is capable of enduring against any trial.

It is strength of this kind that supported Charles de Foucauld, who toiled for twenty years as a missionary of love in the torrid sands of the Sahara. He never obtained a single conversion, but died a martyr, murdered by those very people for whom he was sacrificing his life. It was only long after his death that his apostolate began to bear fruit.

As a loving man and woman, you are here and now participating in the communion of saints, in the Ecclesia, the Church, the Gathering of Christ. If you teach your offspring how to love, they will bear rich fruit, and you will be honored by them generation after generation, in this life and forever in the next.

CHAPTER 7

PRACTICAL ADVICE ON RUNNING YOUR HOME

Patience and Common Sense Provide Most of the Answers . . . The First Few Years May Require Great Flexibility . . . Live Within Your Means . . . Delegate Your Responsibilities . . . Consider Things Carefully Before Buying a Home . . . Be Sensible When You Buy a Car . . . Your Home Is Not Your Master . . . Together You Must Create Emotional Comfort . . . Children Will Widen Your Goal

Let us return to daily life, to the world of reality—in the form of an unfamiliar apartment, with most of your things still packed and a number of essential items missing. The days of ease and unconcern are over. Now you must cook, commute, work, pay your bills. There will be an inevitable letdown, particularly for the young bride. No longer do beds and meals come ready-made, nor do kitchens and living rooms get cleaned automatically: there is now considerable labor attached to all that.

With the normal feeling of disorganization that comes with every major change of life pattern, the task of housekeeping, even in a small apartment, assumes staggering proportions because time- and effort-saving routines are not yet established. Doing the simplest thing in unfamiliar surroundings takes ten times the usual effort. Instead of being semiconscious, almost instinctive, the preparing of a cup of coffee or the setting of a simple table takes on the frightening responsibility of a free human act. The slightest thing now demands a complete process of planning and deliberation, a free choice of the will, a frantic search for ingredients that always seem to be hiding on purpose. No wonder the result may sometimes be far from satisfactory.

The coffee may have a taste of soap because the new coffeepot had been thoroughly washed but not rinsed; and the table setting may look like a stall in some charity bazaar, with Aunt Jane's lace napkins and Uncle Ed's Renaissance stemware! And so, what happens? The young husband, fresh from the ribbing he got at the office, may come home to find a red-eyed, droopy, and desperate wife! The best thing to do is to laugh it off together —but resist the temptation to go to a restaurant!

Patience and Common Sense Provide Most of the Answers

The minor practical adjustments of marriage are just that —minor practical adjustments. In order to establish an acceptable routine that will take care of the daily chores, all that is needed is a little logic and plenty of good humor. There must be routine in the unimportant but unavoidable activities of life that must be relegated to the domain of almost reflex action so as not to take up too large a share of mental, nervous, and physical energy. Most of your strength should be saved for true, original, and personal living, for those times when routine must be avoided absolutely, and this applies particularly to your moments of intimacy.

Reality has a way of forcing attention when it is neglected, and the sooner you two realize it, the better, for the awakening may be extremely painful. While they sleep, the Lord works wonders for those he loves—provided they take full advantage of their waking hours. Otherwise, reality can play a number of disastrous tricks—for instance, make all your cash disappear after a binge of thoughtless spending or lead you to the sudden realization that a college education has by-passed the art of boiling an egg.

The story is told of a young man who came home to his very

young wife and discovered that their supper was burned. "What happened, dear?" With eyes lowered, she replied, "There was a fire at the delicatessen!"

The First Few Years May Require Great Flexibility

There are, then, a number of prosaic, down-to-earth matters that are of immediate urgency for the running of a home. The first is money. You really should not start your marriage without some of it in the bank. Getting married on hope or the promise of support, or depending exclusively on your parents, may be extremely risky in our society. You are going to have to be on your own, and that means financially self-supporting.

There are many ways of making a living, but whatever the manner in which money will be earned, there are a few pieces of general advice that may be valuable to you.

Any young man would prefer to be the breadwinner from the start, and to provide enough for the couple so that the young woman would not have to take a job. However, it may be good sometimes for her to do so, for keeping house in a small apartment will not be sufficient to keep her happily busy.

Also, in the early years, and particularly if the husband is still studying, there will probably not be enough money to make ends meet. Serious study is generally incompatible with a well-remunerated job, since both require full-time attention and effort. Grants and scholarships are usually extremely meager means of support. And so it may sometimes be necessary for both young people to work, at least part-time. In some circumstances, for instance, when the husband alone continues very demanding studies, it may be necessary for the wife to take a full-time job to support them both temporarily. This is far from ideal, but reality may demand sacrifice. The division of labor between husband and wife is not so absolute as always to place the burden of finances on the husband. As a temporary plan, it will probably work. After all, the newlyweds are married for better, for worse: they constitute a closely fitted unit, and both of them should combine their talents to solve their problems.

Live Within Your Means

Even a perfect budget with reasonable allowances, well proportioned to a complete and accurate list of needs, will be useful only to those who lack spending discipline. If the only way not to waste money is to force yourself to remain within the limits of a budget, what you need is not a budget, but training in personal restraint.

What is much more important than a budget is to develop good spending habits. These are acquired through reason and practice. Even if money is no problem for you, lackadaisical spending will be much less satisfying than a careful use of your resources. You will obtain much better results through reasonable spending, and you may also do some additional good by saving enough to give to those in need. For one of the most imperative duties of those who have is sharing with those who have not. Ignorance of this duty has led to violence and revolution.

It is so very easy, each time you get your pay envelope, to go out on a spree and spend everything on immediate pleasures and whims. Restraining your spending to what you really need takes a strong will and considerable discipline. It is also a sure sign of maturity. If you are reasonably well off, lack of restraint will diminish the returns you get from your money. If you are not, it may lead to disaster. What, then, are a few of the rules of prudent spending?

Delegate Your Responsibilities

First, as a matter of principle, you should reach an agreement about decisions involving money. Perhaps it would be good to leave the last word to the husband in major affairs, while letting the wife decide in matters of detail. It is she who should generally be in full charge of household purchases, with no questions asked and no accounts rendered. This can be achieved only after a progressive education in the arts of buying and spending, and not before a truly efficient performance has been attained. Start out by doing your buying together, learning together; then let her take over.

How much of the pay check should a wife receive? Should she be on a "household allowance"? Or should she control most of the money while the husband retains only what he requires for his immediate needs? This again is a matter of personal choice, but it should be clearly settled in an atmosphere of cooperation and mutual good will. It seems reasonable to let the wife have full control of at least the amount estimated by experience to be necessary to run the house for a week.

A wife should preferably have her own checking account, unless the husband insists on paying all the bills himself. Even if he does, every wife fully deserves regular sums and occasional gifts that she is completely free to spend as she pleases. On the part of the husband, this is not a matter of charity or kindness, but an absolute obligation of justice.

Before deciding on suppliers, the lady of the house should investigate the town and the neighborhood for the best quality at the lowest price, and disregard completely the snobbery of the "right label" or "right store." Only a fool will pay more to get nothing but the approval of other fools.

Do not be overimpressed by advertising: the most heavily advertised goods will always be the most expensive, for you will be paying for the merchandise and for the advertising. It has been said that a tubful of the most popular soft drink costs about a nickel. Do not rush to the nearest store that carries what you need, but shop around. The wise buyer is as good as the professional "comparison shopper." Special attention should be given to items that you will be needing every day. A nickel a day saved on bread will build up to almost $20 a year. Saving a few pennies on several items every day may amount to much more than saving on a large item once a year.

When shopping for food, take advantage of sales and seasonal produce. Wise buying in quantity of bargain-priced food that is then frozen may lead to substantial savings. But beware of the frozen-food-with-freezer contract. The proposition may seem attractive, but carefully read all the small print before signing, and remember that you may become disgusted before long with a frozen-food diet, mostly because of the monotony of standardized flavors.

Do not disregard staples: with the help of seasoning and inspiration, staples may be made to taste even better than rare, exotic, and expensive dishes. Do not be so lazy that your only cooking consists in heating cans. That kind of menu can turn into a bad habit. Beware also of the TV-dinner: it is one of the surest ways to disenchant a hard-working husband. All these modern developments may be useful to cope with emergencies. They should not serve as basic food.

When buying clothes, look for good taste and quality. The same dress or suit is often available in one store at one-half or one-third of what it costs in another. One of the worst buying habits is to settle on high-class furnishers and never to "debase" yourself by looking elsewhere. If your own sense of "class" depends on such things, you have none!

Consider Things Carefully Before Buying a Home

The most important of all purchases, and the greatest investment you will ever make in your life, will probably be a home. The financial aspects of buying a house may be extremely complex. Generally speaking, there are two contradictory schools of thought. The first is that no young family is really settled and at peace until they own their own home. The other is that anyone who owns a house deserves all the headaches it brings. Deciding between the two is a matter of mental attitude.

If you seek security and happiness, and consider them more important than having immediate maximum returns on every penny you possess, it may be better to start right away by investing cash in a solidly built home that is close to a shopping center, church, and school and has convenient transportation facilities, preferably in a developing neighborhood. The mortgage payment will be a method of forced saving, and although about half of what you pay will be lost in the form of interest, the usual increase in real-estate values could make up in part for the expenses of ownership. Before buying a house, be certain to obtain a reliable report, preferably in writing, on yearly taxes and heating expenses, which are generally the heaviest.

It is reasonable to assume that, in spite of the convenience, renting a house will be more expensive in the long run than owning one, since in addition to the charges you will also be paying your landlord's profit. This is not to say that you should never rent: it may be the best thing to do for the first few years if you do not have sufficient funds to invest in the purchase of a house, if you are not settled in any place, or if you are not yet certain what kind of house you would like to own. Buying too soon may be a costly mistake.

On the other hand, if you are a genius at investing, you may possibly think you can make much more money by gambling on the stock exchange with the capital another man would have sunk in his home. You may also use this same capital in a thousand other ways, but most of these have one point in common: the risk of partial or total loss. You may lose a good share of what you have or everything you have or even more than what you have, and be saddled with debts for years.

When taking out a mortgage, be careful not to assume a charge that is too heavy for your income. There is nothing wrong in looking forward to improved financial conditions and to reasonable salary raises, but do not go overboard. For instance, do not count on your wife's salary to pay your mortgage, otherwise you will be putting a heavy strain on your early years together, besides compelling her to continue working. These matters differ so much with circumstances and are so personal that no simple rule can serve in all cases.

One very happily married couple immediately purchased a beautiful home with a heavy mortgage. After five years of forced labor, during which the husband had to hold two jobs, he had a nervous breakdown and his emotional imbalance almost ruined their relationship. They had had little time for themselves or for each other or for their children. They never had acquired a sense of achievement, since all their energies were devoted to paying off the mortgage—and that would have taken twenty years. Something drastic had to be done in a hurry. And so they wisely sold their equity in the beautiful home and moved to a garden apartment. The young husband could then give up his extra job. He was free from the burdens of mowing a lawn, shoveling snow, repairing leaky roofs and plumbing, working at two jobs in order to pay interests he could not afford. He soon became more relaxed, and settled peacefully into a much less hectic and more natural family pattern. For this particular couple, the change was definitely a success. Each family has a different drive, a different set of standards and ideals, a different threshold of tolerance; but, generally speaking, it is never wise to assume burdens that could have been avoided.

Another question related to the home is to decide whether to buy a ready-made house or to have your own built especially for you. It should be clearly understood that the latter is only for the rich. The major reason is that the final bill will always be considerably higher than even the most precise and cautious estimate.

Some enterprising people have specialized in buying a rundown home, renovating it with their own hands, selling it at a profit, and then moving on to the next. But this takes time, money to invest, and a considerable amount of technical skills, not to mention an immense amount of hard work. It may be fun—but only for the specialist. You may want to do some renovating, but do not buy a house that needs to be rebuilt!

Be Sensible When You Buy a Car

Buying a car also involves a major expense. The usual thing is to buy the flashiest, sportiest, most powerful machine you can afford. After all, the monthly payment is only $79.99. But there are a considerable number of things to do before buying, and the first is a little elementary arithmetic. The most basic is to multiply the monthly premium by the number of months it is to run—you will then have an idea of the cash cost. It will be considerably more than the price at which you had agreed to buy. The difference is represented by the carrying charges, that is, the profit of the lending organization. Bank financing is generally the most reasonable, amounting to a true 5 per cent or

6 per cent. Through private financing institutions or through the trade, the rates of interest may be considerably more. The usual gimmick consists in indicating a rate of interest that may not seem excessive at first sight, but then in applying it to the whole amount of the loan from inception to the date of final payment. This results in your paying interest on the amounts already refunded, and in boosting actual interest rate to almost exactly double what had been agreed upon. The actual interest rate in such instances may at times amount to 25 per cent or even more. A recent law has taken care of this by forcing lenders to reveal the true yearly rate of interest.

Instead of buying the best new car you think you can afford, and getting stuck with a high interest, what should you do? The usual financial situation of a young married couple can be summarized in one word: tight! And so, the first thing to do is to select a reasonable make and model that is not expensive to keep going. Then, instead of buying the latest and newest style, and throwing away at least $500 in resale value the minute you drive it off the showroom floor, why not make it a double saving by getting last year's brand-new unsold model at a considerable discount? You will make an even greater saving by obtaining a new used car in very good condition.

A final thought: Never be so unenlightened as to pay the asking price. Car traders seem to have replaced the traditional horsetraders. Haggling is a gentle and worthwhile art, particularly when large amounts are concerned. Make a firm offer at 10 per cent or even 20 per cent below asking price—and walk out with finality if you do not get it. The same thing holds for any major appliance. With the exception of a few staunchly defended fair-traded brands that you are under no obligation to buy, almost everything can be obtained at a discount. Only a sucker pays the full price unquestioningly. Even if you can fully afford it—don't! You will find a number of ways to spend your surplus. If, however, you obtain a psychological boost from the act of lavishing large bills on needy merchants, please feel free: these are only suggestions.

But how about status? How about the neighbors? Even if your neighbor does have a brand-new car, you should be smart enough to realize that within two months it will be "used," and within a year or so, yours may be in much better shape.

Many people use cars and appliances and clothes and furniture as props to support their insecure personalities. Since they are not quite sure of their own worth, they must constantly prove it to themselves and their neighbors by a display of the latest and most expensive possessions.

The fake "beautiful people" of society, fashion or show business generally indulge lavishly in this sort of thing: they can afford it. But when people of modest means do the same, the financial drain may be destructive and the final result leads to increased tension and unhappiness.

Overdoing anything is a sure sign of bad taste. The overdressy clothes, the overflashy car, the overelaborate menu, the overrich rugs and furnishings betray middle-class pretense more clearly than anything else.

By contrast, the true "quality people," even when abundantly provided with wealth, have a tendency to live in homes conspicuously uncluttered, to dress with comfort and extreme simplicity, and to pay only reasonable attention to food, liquor, or wine. Sometimes they even drive around in slightly battered station wagons. The reason is that they do not need to prove anything. They know how to use things to enhance life. Being secure and happy, they can afford to be simply themselves without having to display their success through status symbols. They can devote their full energy to creative and personal living.

Your Home Is Not Your Master

As for housekeeping, it is far better for a wife to be sparkling in a slightly bedraggled home than to be slightly bedraggled in a sparkling home. Your home is not your master, lady: don't let it push you around! Treat it lightly, with organized attention, but without overly heavy care and concern. There are more important things to do than continual dusting and polishing of floors. How about catching up on creative cooking? Is it inconceivable that an extra language could be studied during some of your free time or that a musical instrument could be practiced or that your skill at gardening could be developed if you have both the taste and the land? Or even better, how about helping someone else? There are always plenty of people around who may need your comfort and help. All this would be considerably better than devoting your whole time and energy to housework. Do in a dash what needs to be done—then start living it up on your own. An occasional thorough cleaning will overcome a multitude of negligences.

Don't ever forget to be kind to your chosen one. When you were engaged, you spent hours dressing and making yourself up. Spend at least a few minutes at it before he comes home in the evening. The results may be surprising! Do not get into the habit of making yourself beautiful only when you are expecting guests; give yourself the full treatment once in a while just for him.

Together You Must Create Emotional Comfort

All this is offered to you not as practical tips that will save you money or help you keep house properly. There are rafts of books and periodicals that can do the job more completely and effectively.

Too often marriage counseling is up in the air, catering to imaginary and incorporeal beings that do not seem to belong properly on this earth. Abstract solutions apply in the abstract only, and never seem to fit any truly existing man and woman. That is why some of the simpler questions of material life have been raised here—not that they could be solved in a few pages but that you may understand how closely intertwined are all the aspects of your life in common. If you do not live in peace and harmony on the level of daily chores, how can you ever achieve peace and harmony on higher levels? So these things are important.

It is on the simplest level of life together that you must begin to build your total harmony. There are some common-sense rules that must guide your discussions and decisions in these matters, and help you understand the other's viewpoint. What is most important for you to keep in mind as you pick and choose your way through the tangle of complicated steps in the planning of your home is the actual goal, the purpose, the reason of it all. Basically, you are both eager for a happy life, for a successful marriage. If that was not on your mind, you would not be reading this book.

Hopefully, you will not remain so self-centered that the whole world revolves around your own private set of feelings. As you mature in life and love, you will become more and more aware of the personal otherness of your partner.

Perhaps in the early days you were overwhelmed by the notion of oneness, so that you truly believed that the supreme goal of a happy marriage was the fusion of two persons into a single unit. Little by little you come to realize that the nature of a human person is much too strong to lend itself to total fusion. If you insist on the impossible goal, if you fret at every self-assertion of your lover that does not coincide precisely with what you expected of him or her, you have not quite grown up, nor have you completely understood the true nature of marriage.

The saying "They will be two in one flesh" does not mean that there will be total fusion and confusion. Indeed, "they will be *two*," different, independent, individual human beings. And the fullness of marriage will be achived only if these two come together in a state, not of fusion, but of conscious union, in the free encounter of dedicated love. Emotional comfort will be assured, not by coincidence or confusion, not by staying so close together that there is no breathing space for either one. The closeness, the unicity, is in the sexual order only, in the relationship of love. Otherwise, both partners are free to act *together* toward the same goal. They cannot possibly act *as one*. They can put up a common front, but the action of each one is different and personal. Emotional comfort, then, consists in a proper balance of freedom and unity.

Children Will Widen Your Goal

Children definitely should be included in your projections of personal happiness, both in the material and the emotional order.

Your home should be ready to receive them, and so should your hearts. Let us leave the home problem to the nursery specialist, and concentrate on the heart. The birth of a child may be seen by a loving couple as a catastrophe or as a grace. It will be a catastrophe to the egoistic people who are concerned only with their ease and pleasure, and see in the new baby only a restricting and hampering burden. Once babies begin to come, there are much less time, energy, and money left for fun and sports and travel. On the other hand, for true lovers, the birth of a child is the visible proof, the living consecration, the incredibly marvelous fruit of their love.

Here too a continued atmosphere of emotional comfort is essential. Children will grow up peacefully and beautifully only if they live in a peaceful and beautiful home. It does not have to be rich, but clean and gay and full of sunshine, and, most of all, full of the visible expression of the parents' mutual love in which the children bask and are included.

CHAPTER 8

HOW TO SETTLE DIFFERENCES

Resolve Your Conflicts by Yourselves . . . Respect Your Partner's Otherness . . . A Woman Is First of All a Person . . . Husband and Wife Should Have Moments of Privacy . . . Freedom Brings Added Responsibility . . . Respect Your Parents but Set Them Straight . . . Your Spouse Is Number One in Your House . . . You May Learn from Your Parents' Mistakes . . . Respect the Children as Free Human Persons . . . Agree to Live on Your Own . . . A Love Child Should Not Be Postponed Too Long . . . Sufficient unto the Day

Every marriage has its own difficulties. Every individual, in fact, lives with a unique set of environmental factors, family relationships, and personal virtues and defects that, because of their very uniqueness, militate against the utopian harmony young lovers expect. Automatic compatibility in marriage is a myth. It takes constant work and attention to reach even a moderately successful level of peace. The vast majority of couples are naturally incompatible in some way or other. Those who struggle long and well are called the happily married. The others give up the fight before they come to discover the joy of self-surrender.

Resolve Your Conflicts by Yourselves

Of course there will be problems, very serious problems, long before your partnership has had time to ripen. There is only one safe way of handling them: an honest frontal attack. *You must learn to settle differences yourselves, without outside arbitration.* Failure to realize this may cost you your self-respect, your happiness, or even your marriage.

Often, one party is to blame, and at a given moment reconciliation seems impossible—but even the most hardened criminal has moments of softening. If you are to survive as two-in-one-flesh, as marriage partners, you must settle your differences on your own during your interludes of peace.

In order to reach this all-important goal, you would do well to analyze each problem separately, and come together to an agreement on some sensible solution. It may even be put in writing, for the seriousness of a written contract and the irreversibility of the written word have a bracing psychological effect. A written contract may seem comical for minor conflicts, but not for major battles that may cause untold pain if they are carried on year after year. Keeping up such battles is a sign of prolonged immaturity, a demonstration of boyhood and girlhood, rather than manhood and womanhood. The parties seem to be waiting for some grownup to come on the scene to help them to make up. Behavior of this kind may turn into a painful and even deadly game.

Respect Your Partner's Otherness

One of the easiest things to forget in a marriage is that he is a man and she is a woman. Because of a very real psychological and physical difference—which has nothing to do with absolute values—the reactions of both partners to situations, even to each other, may be completely at variance. A wife may react emotionally, even tragically, to a personal event her husband considers trifling. A husband may show what appears to his wife as callous indifference in matters that are of prime importance for her.

A man may be busily at work at some important (to him) and all-absorbing project. His wife rushes in with the shattering news that her best friend is expecting a baby. He will make the effort to understand what it is all about, but his mind will not register much interest because he cannot switch instantly from total absorption to ready communication. His work is stopped, his concentration ruined. His reaction may even be an explosion that will completely startle the poor girl: "For heaven's sake! Why bother me with *that!* She's married, isn't she?"

And so it goes, every day; irritations occur perhaps several times a day if husband and wife live constantly together. What can be done about it? The first thing to do is to prepare yourselves for this very thing: be thoroughly forewarned as to the differences between the natural reactions of the male and the female, and be ready to cope with them. Any such situation can be handled with lightheartedness and humor, not of the bitter "Here we go again!" variety, but of the kind that smiles at the old dear for being so normal.

It is quite indispensable for a married couple not to be tripping over each other at every moment of the day. The usual pattern is for the husband to go out to work. This leaves some freedom for the wife, so she can be on her own at least part of the day. When the husband's job is at home, there must be a clear understanding that some moments of aloneness are indispensable to both husband and wife.

There must be space in your togetherness, enough space for love and sex-play to grow naturally and spontaneously. Each of you must develop as a person, and help the other do just that. Both husband and wife should have their own secret time and their own secret place, not to hide anything from each other, but merely to be themselves.

A Woman Is First of All a Person

A woman especially should learn to develop her own personal interests. There is no stereotype of wifehood that neatly fits every married woman. She is under no obligation to regulate her life exclusively in view of a romanticized notion of motherhood. Of course she is going to be a good mother, but that is not the whole thing. A woman must learn to be free from within, to be fully herself, exploring her talents whenever she can, developing her own distinct style of life. This does not mean that she is to concentrate less on the home and more on herself; it means merely that she is not limited to the role of a housewife. Even if she does nothing positive about it, at least she should know that she *can* be herself. Before marriage, she was a person in her own right, and she remains so after marriage.

When a woman is liberated internally from needless conflicts arising out of her efforts to live up to a predetermined role, she is much more natural at home. It is natural for a woman to be dedicated and devoted to a family, but it is so much more helpful to her psychologically when her husband helps to create an atmosphere where she can feel free to pursue some private aspiration, ideal, or project. This brings refreshment to the spirit, and lightens the burden of responsibility.

The solutions to problems of personality development will vary from year to year, according to the circumstances. At times, a woman may be pursuing a very worthwhile venture with moderation and balance. At others, she may be so deeply involved in secondary matters as to risk drowning. When tensions arise owing to her "independent" life, there is no need to panic. A woman should be free to discover her own limits of endurance and to make her own prudential judgments, but a wise woman will work out such problems calmly and objectively with her husband's help. At times, it may be necessary for the husband to assert his will in order to correct any serious imbalance. But this should be done in a spirit of love, not of tyranny.

Husband and Wife Should Have Moments of Privacy

If your husband seems not to want to be with you all the time, it does not mean that he loves you less: it may mean that he loves you more, and is doing right now something more important for your love than being together—or it may be simply that he is "busy" in one of the mysterious ways of men, and this is perfectly honorable and good. Likewise, the fact that a wife finds interests outside her home should not be interpreted immediately as treason: she may be growing in liveliness, expanding her mind, preparing herself to be a better wife and lover than the shut-in *Hausfrau* of earlier times. All this takes a high degree of maturity on the part of both wife and husband, but modern life requires that such an adjustment be made. Love shall make you free; it should not make your mate a prisoner.

Freedom Brings Added Responsibility

The woman may very well assert her freedom and independence only to realize that she has created serious tensions and disagreements. Part of the pain of marriage consists in the awareness that total independence has been freely surrendered. Even the most liberal husband and the most understanding wife will resent too much free flight on the part of the spouse. Each has the duty to please the other, and so they should curtail at least some of their escapist dreams for the sake of conjugal happiness. Yet, so much has been demanded of woman in the past, and so little liberty granted to her, that there is need to emphasize with new vigor her rights to a reasonable freedom.

Modern life is different from life in the days of our parents and grandparents. Their value system, when applied to our times, may not fit properly. Uncompromising insistence on the husband's authority in all matters is a thing of the past. It is normal for the father to be the family leader, but it is not indispensable. Authority has different domains, and should be delegated. Both should agree that certain areas of authority should be placed in the hands of the better qualified of the marriage partners. Symbolically, the father is king, but the mother is queen, with a natural right to her own dignity and mission. She is entitled to the freedom she needs to live this mission well and to shoulder her responsibilities with dignity and grace.

Respect Your Parents but Set Them Straight

Another major difficulty that may arise in modern marriage is the problem of parents. In older days, under more patriarchal or matriarchal systems, it was the children who were problems, not the parents. Now the roles seem to be reversed because of the high degree of independence the young couple enjoys in our world. This independence is good and necessary, but it may take parents steeped in a different tradition quite some time and effort to find their proper place without being hurt or without hurting their children.

What happens when one parent or both refuse to let go? What happens when a parent dominates the young couple with intrusive tactics, making them fully aware that they are still under supervision? Resentment builds up pressure. You begin to seethe in restrained silence, which eventually leads to bitter thoughts and may explode in bitter words. As soon as you feel that you are having these negative feelings for your parents or in-laws, you begin to perceive a painful and all-pervading guilt. As a compensation, you do your best to be extra sweet to the offending parties—and yet you resent doing nice things for them while actually wanting to scream out in protest against their unjustified intrusion.

Why do *you* feel guilty? Because you *believe* that no decent person would ever feel this way about his or her parent. The fact is that you are under no obligation whatsoever to tolerate the intrusion of an immature parent into your lives. Honoring your father and mother does not consist in always *feeling* good about them. The absence of good feelings does not negate your love, any more than the presence of good feelings is sufficient proof of it. Love is not a matter of feeling, but of *intentions*. While feeling resentful, you do not hate your parent: you simply react with loathing to the juvenile possessiveness he or she is imposing upon you. As long as you put up with it, you will suffer untold grief. The blood descendant is the one responsible for stopping this situation. It is his or her duty to tell Mom or Dad exactly where to get off.

A top executive in a large industrial company sent his only son to a very good college. The boy failed miserably. Most of the time he was meek, but occasionally he would explode into extremely violent temper tantrums. Emotionally, he was about ten years old, insecure, peevish, and full of buried hostility. This boy was the victim of a classic mother-in-law situation. His father had been in the habit of resolving conflicts between his own mother and his wife in a manner that was both weak and stupid. To his wife he would say, "Remember, dear, she's my mother;" and to his mother, "Now remember, Mother, she's my wife." Like a scorekeeper at a tennis match, he would keep track of the points, sweetly placating each woman in turn, believing that politeness could resolve any conflict. He knew how to control thousands of men, but he was unable to realize how much electricity passes between two women competing for the same man. His wife's distress turned into bitterness and resentment, and destroyed her personality to the point of disturbing the peace of the home and making a nervous wreck of her son.

Your Spouse Is Number One in Your House

The wife in our story eventually came to the only conclusion possible for her: that she was living with a man who did *not* consider her "Number One." She began to lose her self-respect and gradually fell into a state of deep contempt for her mother-in-law, for herself, and for her weak husband. The young boy grew up in a torture chamber of suppressed conflicts. Obviously enough, *you owe your first allegiance to your spouse, and everyone else must know exactly where you stand.* Even if it causes a parent great pain, you must convey the idea that your spouse comes first. In the example given above, the guilty party was the mother. There are also meddling fathers, but fathers are generally able to take a hint long before swords need to be drawn. If this is not done, then the blood descendant must put him in his place.

There are times when settling disagreements requires ingenuity. When both parties sit down and discuss their problems intelligently, they may come up with a clear set of firm resolutions that should be put into writing. This technique fixes attention on the seriousness of the matter, and evokes the necessary sense of binding obligation to abide by the decisions made together.

You May Learn from Your Parents' Mistakes

In the early years of childhood, parental duty consists in providing everything for the child, because the child is totally unable to provide anything for itself. But if this total providing is extended to a time when the growing boy or girl should assume some responsibility, the assurance of receiving everything without any personal effort will take away any desire to even try. Ambition and self-determination may be stifled as a result. Children, then, remain on an infantile level of total dependence, even in matters that are well within the possibilities of their own personal action. The result will be the "Gimme, gimme" attitude of those who believe that the world owes them a comfortable living simply because they have always received everything gratuitously. Such individuals become grabbers. They turn sour and indignant as soon as they cease to receive from an indifferent world all the comforts they had been getting from their overindulgent parents. They are utterly unprepared for real life. In such cases the good and natural instincts of parents—to give their children "everything" —turns out to be destructive in the long run. Such a background is a poor preparation for marriage.

The difficult things for parents to do is to let go, to realize that their children, far from being younger duplicates of themselves, may be so different, so distant, so utterly "other" as to be practically unreachable. The generation gap is never bridged by indulgence; it produces hatred more often than love. Even when there is an immense distance between the rational or emotional make-up of parents and children, there may still be some channels of communication that remain open for mutual respect and understanding. These channels are fragile and easily cut. Any excessive disciplining, any imposed conformism to some established and over-rigid pattern of life may produce a final break that changes the stranger-in-the-house into a violent enemy. All children are inevitably strangers to their parents, and the more they grow up, the stranger they seem to become! The only true means of communication, then, is through mutually respectful love.

After the umbilical cord of excessive protection has been severed, the pain will disappear, and a freer and better relationship can be developed.

What parents must do is to provide what is indispensable during the early years, and then imperceptibly slacken the reins. Let the yearling discover the joy of open fields. Teach the filly to be careful, but respect the fact that she needs freedom to graze or gallop as her nature dictates.

Another mistake parents may be making is the reverse of the coin: instead of giving too much, they expect too much. *They count on their children's eternal and total gratitude.* The reasoning in such cases seems to be: "We have given you life; we have given you everything you have. Now you owe us everything you are and have." Where is the fallacy? There never was any contractual obligation. Children do not come into the world holding a signed document by which they promise to return every ounce of food, every spark of life, and every cent of money they received. They are simply born, without any previous consultation or agreement. They are born free. They are not slaves or machines subject to their parents' every whim and fancy. They are independent, rational beings whose lives and destinies are different from those of their parents. They are not chattel, possessions, things, but persons endowed with equal rights in all essentials. Their position of weakness and dependence is only accidental.

Respect the Children as Free Human Persons

Because the parents are the originators of life, and its indispensable supporters during the early years, there is an obligation of gratitude and respect on the part of the children. It must be paralleled with an obligation of liberation and respect on the part of the parents. Children must be grateful to their parents for the gifts of life, food, care, education, home, and love. But parents have an equally strong obligation toward their children to respect them as individuals, to help them become self-sustaining, responsible, free human beings; to launch them into life as well-equipped and well-provisioned ships that will be able to cut their own path and leave their own wake on the ocean of life.

In other times and other places, parents could control things absolutely. Marriages could be planned by mother and father with little or no prior consultation or consent of the parties. This is no longer so. Young people now meet and date as they will. This is both a tremendous increase in freedom, which is good, and a considerable increase in danger to the child, which is not good. Parental experience, which was formerly the determining factor in the choice of a life partner, now seldom has any influence at all. In the training of youth, parents can no longer cling to the primacy of obedience that prepared a child for the preplanning of his life, including marriage. In all domains of moral choice and personal action, we are now in a new age: that of freedom of conscience. It is this new freedom children must learn to use in their formative years. This freedom must be real. No longer can parents keep a Victorian control over their teen-agers, checking the company they keep and the use they make of their time. Some control is necessary, but no amount of control will suffice in our days if there has been no proper training in freedom.

Parental overpossessiveness will have ill effects even after marriage. The Gospel clearly says of the young husband: "He will leave his father and mother and cleave to his wife." And so, let us repeat once again: A young couple's allegiance is first and foremost to each other.

Agree to Live on Your Own

Another very important rule: Do not live with your parents or in-laws, except in cases of absolute necessity. To do so is *asking* for the kind of disruptive influence we have just been discussing. If you can do without it, do not accept even financial support from parents or in-laws. Learn to accept hardships and a measure of privation, but be on your own. It is so very easy for the generous parental provider to believe that he or she is entitled to control your life. As much as possible, remain free from any obligations toward anybody, including your own father and mother. This may hurt the older generation. It will hurt *you* much more if you give in, taking the easy way and accepting more help than what you desperately need. Anyway, if you are in desperate need of material help, you should not marry until the crisis passes. If it occurs after marriage, accept only what you need, and keep your self-respect and independence.

As far as actual living conditions are concerned, it is wise never to let *anyone* move in on you or feed on you, emotionally or physically. Never make an arrangement to invite lonesome and deserving Cousin Emily to supper every Thursday evening. The poor thing may soon imagine she has a right to it, and then what? Do not give your neighbors the freedom to drop in at any time. You would be perfectly justified in demanding the courtesy of a forewarning. As soon as a friend, neighbor, or relative shows definite signs of a developing encroachment on your time or privacy, have no scruple whatsoever about throwing the intruder out, politely but firmly. You should tackle the problem well before it gets out of hand. Your home is your castle, and the worst assaults it may have to sustain is from apparently innocent carriers of gifts. The home, the family unit, is made up essentially of father, mother, and children. It is not a community pad. Any constant foreign presence may be disruptive.

In other times and other worlds, it may have been perfectly all right for whole tribes to live within the same compound or under the same roof. The authority of the head of the clan was then absolute, and sons or daughters, married or not, owed him total allegiance. In European families generally, and in many American families, there are gatherings of large groups that live close to each other the whole year round, or spend their vacations together. This may be good. It is quite different from living in the same household permanently.

To summarize: no amount of assistance, financial or other, received from parents, grandparents, or anyone else, will entitle the donors to have the last word in such matters as religion, education, behavior, or even speech and dress. On the other hand, young people should not get into the habit of rejecting a priori everything a member of the older generation proposes. *You* may know better, but it is not that certain. There is a fine distinction to be made between considering a reasonable proposition and knuckling down under a command. Everything a parent suggests is not necessarily wrong and/or outmoded. Before taking a suggestion of help as an unwarranted intrusion, think it over thoroughly; perhaps it is completely disinterested and entirely reasonable. Decision in all such matters must be made with the right proportion of kindness and prudence, that is, with a clear estimate of the risks if there are any strings attached.

A Love Child Should Not Be Postponed Too Long

Let us now consider the immediate problem of your future family. Naturally, at the beginning of a young couple's life, there is a tremendous accumulation of needs, a home, household equipment, furniture, a car, and so on. All this puts an enormous strain on the breadwinner's ambition and energies. Quite often, he needs two jobs to meet expenses. Sometimes the young bride continues to work. But this is not all there is to homemaking. Man and woman are joined in that sacrament by which they are empowered to share in the greatest work of creation: the continuation of the human race. It is so easy to put off indefinitely the coming of a first child just because you absolutely need this or that, and you have to work to pay for it, and therefore could not think of taking care of a baby.

This, again, may be a cause of conflicts. Many a divorce has come about because of an unwholesome friendship that develops at the wife's place of employment. Also, there may be the constant tug of war between the desire for a child and the greed for increased material possessions. This may develop into violent conflicts when there is no clear accord. The ideal would be for the young couple to look forward to the day when the bride will be able to resign her job. And the best reason for such a move would be an early pregnancy. The experience of a love child is something you should not trade for a new car.

Sufficient unto the Day

Each day has its own aches and pains, and also its high points and its rewards. But one day at a time is enough. At the end of each day, put your problems aside, take a look at each other, and remember who you are and where you are going. You are both creatures of love, made for loving and for total fulfillment in Total Love. Even if you have had disagreements, or rather, especially at such times, never go to bed without a kiss of peace. Try to establish a pattern of giving comfort and encouragement to each other at the day's end. There will be times when a simple gesture of peace will be extremely difficult, when tension will make it almost impossible. It is never *completely* impossible to give each other a sign of love.

If you do not develop such mutual giving, your life will soon become a routine. Sex will turn into a stale and self-centered disappointment. Let pass what is passing, the lesser troubles and difficulties. Never let them grow into major obstacles, but nip them in the bud, using simplicity, courage, and humor. This will not guarantee a life as smooth as a lake on a still moonlit night, but it will quite surely prevent tempests in teapots from growing to full-force hurricanes.

There are few differences that a truly loving husband and wife cannot settle in a spirit of tenderness, understanding, and self-sacrifice. The final word in this matter, as in all matters, belongs to Christ: "He who saves his life will lose it. He who loses his life will save it." If you try to "save" your life by carrying a chip on your shoulder and standing up indignantly in defense of every one of your "rights," you will be setting the scene for angry resistance. On the contrary, if you face up to your differences and discuss them maturely, coming to intelligent resolutions and learning to live with harmless idiosyncrasies, you will save your life, your love, and your marriage. By dying to yourself, you may very well "live happily forever after."

PART II

ADVICE TO THOSE PREPARING FOR MARRIAGE

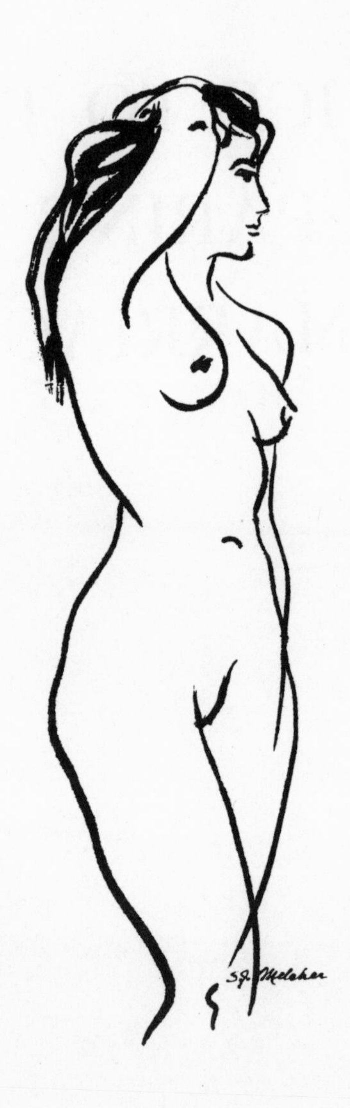

CHAPTER 9

HOW TO FIND PERSONAL FULFILLMENT IN MARRIAGE

What You Do Influences What You Are . . . It Is Essential to Remain Open to the Other . . . True Love Supposes Detachment . . . Openness and Detachment Are Effective . . . Everyone Is Worthy of Love . . . No One Can Have a Total Experience of Love . . . There Are Circumstantial Barriers to Perfect Delight . . . Learn to Be Happy with What You Are and Have

---

The values of a marital and sexual relationship are much more in the order of being than in the order of having. *The success of marriage and the pleasures of sex are more dependent on what you are and what you have to give than on what you do and what you try to get.* The first order of business, then, is not to develop techniques of love, but to cultivate yourself to the point of full flowering.

There is some fundamental truth in the flower child, hidden under an infantile revolt against the Establishment. True lovers will grow only in the natural soil of affection and emotion that is given enough breathing space and freedom to escape from the mold of conformity. There is a right and wrong way of growing "wild." The wrong consists in developing a negative trend that opposes the truly civilized; the right, in developing a positive trend that opposes that which unjustly hampers it. In the education of the young, for instance, there is need for some freedom to be themselves, not against validly established social and moral rules, but against abuses of authoritarianism and encroachments on their personality.

What You Do Influences What You Are

Before attaining that level of "being" that flows naturally into a happy marriage and a happy love relationship, there is necessarily a long period of preparation. In fact, every moment of a young life has some influence on its fulfillment in the adult state. All of us are made of the sum total of what we have received through heredity, and what we have done with it in the interaction of our free will and the objective circumstances of our life. We are in great part what we have made ourselves to be, so that personal fulfillment in marriage is a consequence or follow-through of our general development.

A twenty-four-year-old woman recently called her priest, and with uncontrollable tears tried to express the fear and torment she was experiencing in her marriage. Her husband was a good man: he didn't drink; he wasn't interested in other women; he brought home his whole salary and he loved his children. But he had made one tragic mistake from the viewpoint of his marriage: he had become totally involved in the work of the volunteer fire department. In a few short years, he had become its captain and a qualified instructor in rescue operations, being called upon frequently by the local police to give special classes to the department.

All this had given him a high degree of satisfaction. It had filled him with a sense of importance and put the snap of vitality in his life. As captain, he was in charge of schedules and assignments. Quite frequently, when one of his men could not serve his turn at the night shift, he would fill in.

She was a nervous and immature woman with a very low threshold of tolerance. She never knew when an emergency call would take the captain away from his family. He was now away from home an average of two or three nights a week. But, worse than that, he was enjoying his work so much that she began to feel that he loved it more than he loved her. She nagged and wept, but nothing would budge him: he insisted that his work was important, and was completely blind to what was happening to his marriage. The priest's advice did not affect them in the least.

The final blow occurred when the young woman became sick

one night and appealed to her husband to come home to take care of her. He answered that he would come as soon as he was relieved from duty. He returned four hours later, to find his wife unconscious. She survived the mild heart attack, but never again could she trust him. The marriage ended in divorce.

The problem could have been solved with a little insight and timely advice. The man's deep need for recognition burned within him. In his regular job, he had never achieved a sufficient level of self-esteem. All his energies were concentrated on that one goal, so that he could not see what he was doing to his wife. He failed to realize that in filling his own need, he was saying to her, over and over again, that he loved his work more than he loved her. On the other hand, she had coddled her own feelings of insecurity and failed to allow him the freedom he needed to be himself. Both of them were unable to bear the discomfort of self-surrender.

We are always becoming, whether we are conscious of it or not. The process does not stop when the marriage partner has finally been chosen. Quite the contrary. Young lovers have a lifetime before them to grow in mutual understanding. The beginning of their life together is all-important because it sets a pattern, a tone, a certain quality of living that is irreversible.

The all-important task set before you is to learn to grow together graciously and gracefully, in a manner that is truly "full of grace"—not only the supernatural grace of the Holy Spirit, but the human graces of kindness, consideration, and care. Let us now consider two important conditions of wholesome and gracious development: *openness* and *detachment*.

It Is Essential to Remain Open to the Other

Anything and everything is in a sense marvelous merely by the fact that it exists and offers itself. In an open relationship, subject and object meet as at the dawn of creation: the subject perceives with fresh and sensitive senses, and the object still has its original dew, its peach fuzz, its aura of mystery and depth. In the well-balanced and happy child, openness is a natural quality, the art of possessing unspoiled loveliness. To such a child, everything is surprising and challenging. Experiences occur with a "first-time" impact. No artificial expectation has been developed, so that no excessive or distorted demands are made on people or things, and so there is joy. The preservation of this precious state of mind is essential for the enjoyment of the mystery of sex.

In a conventional society, this openness tends to be lost. The charm of childlikeness and contact with the simple truth tends to be replaced by the ultrasophisticated cynicism of the scoffer who has tried everything and ends up in a state of universal disgust, of total closedness to life. Things become possessions instead of challenges. And since none is perfect, none is found to fit. This occurs not only in the order of things, but most of all in that of persons.

In the realm of marriage, the search for a closed and selfish possession of some predetermined "object" is fatally damaging. If a man seeks for himself a perfect wife, establishing his requirements on the basis of existing models, actresses, or fashion heroines—as he would choose a car from a collection of factory designs—and if he looks forward to her performing in bed with the proficiency of the sexpot, he is living in a never-never land. He is trying to "have" instead of to "be." He is closed, not open, to life. He will miss the most glorious opportunities of meeting real, living, actual women, simply because they do not appear externally to conform to his precast model. He is not open to reality, but imprisoned within his own illusion, his "maya," the vain product of his imagination. Since no real woman can ever match such a fantasy, he will be disappointed in every woman.

By contrast, a man who preserves his openness will be able to observe women as they are, to be himself in their presence, and let them be themselves. Only in this encounter of true persons is there a possibility for sympathy, understanding, correspondence, desire—and finally marriage with the progressive flowering of sexual union.

As applied to preparation for marriage, openness consists in the ability always to see freshly and objectively the beauty and wonder that exist within the prospective partner, and to do away with false images. Within marriage, it is the capacity of ever marveling before the constant revelation of another person.

True Love Supposes Detachment

The second condition of happiness and pleasure is detachment. The detachment of the free and loving is a state of presence, of being, as opposed to one of possession, of having. If you are content to be and to let the other be, there is available to you the possibility of an infinite combination of spontaneous adventures. If you insist on forcing the other into subservience by imposing upon him or her an image or pattern of your own making, the natural consequences will be revolt on the part of the one who is not treated as a person, and disappointment for you because the living reality does not correspond to your predetermined image. And so we come back to openness—detachment being its fundamental requirement.

The idea of owning and possessing the sexual partner is primitive. There may be an illusion of possession because at all times by thought or deed you may exert control over the other's presence or activity. But this is a naïve idea, as naïve, in fact, as trying to catch the ocean by plunging a basket into it. You may hold some of the ocean in your basket, but water is continually flowing in and out of it, and there is at all times immensely more water without than within. Likewise, it is a total fallacy to believe that you can ever fully control your marriage partner. Even the most successful attempt to establish the deepest and most personal relationship of spiritual, emotional, and sensual love will never do more than encompass for a few moments a minute fraction of the other's total being. Much of the beloved is never touched at all. There is some sadness in this, an incompletion of love that will vanish only in the fullness of the beatific vision. Only before God will the mutual knowledge, the being-within-each-other of lovers be complete.

True detachment consists in maintaining a deep reverence that does away with any effort to reduce the other to a mere possession. It does not make marriage a trap, net, or cage for the partner.

Instead of trying to catch the ocean in a basket, come to the ocean of love with empty hands and eyes wide open, offering rather than seeking to take. Instead of wanting to possess the ocean of love, be content to bathe in it, to be yourself, to remain open and expectant before it—then your relationship with the beloved one will be raised to a level of freedom and richness that transforms it into a symbol of that other ocean, God. You will discover in and through your lover that love and God are very much the same. *Love cannot be "had" any more than God, for both are beyond grasping, and both are one, for the love of man and woman is a form of God's life in us.*

If the marriage relationship is ever to serve the whole person, there must be within it sufficient detachment to respect the other's inner freedom. Love is eminently liberating: it seeks to relieve the beloved of the burdens of anxiety, unrest, and emotional strife. It seeks to give life, and does so with abundance: by being both a joyful playfield in which lover and beloved become the persons they were intended to be, and the fruitful union in which life is perpetuated.

The relationship between love and freedom may give you an insight into the apparent detachment of God's love that gave birth to the Death-of-God theology. God is not dead. Dead is the idol, the busybody god who was constantly pushing us around. God loves us, but he leaves us entirely free to either seek or reject him. God could have created a heaven on earth, full of worshiping slaves. But this would have been servitude, not freedom; it would not have been love. Love is given freely. Love flourishes only in an atmosphere of freedom.

Openness and Detachment Are Effective

Some people shine with a very special light. Externally, their lives may be neither prosperous nor spectacular; they may enjoy very few of the twentieth-century status symbols. And yet, there is in them a quiet, glowing quality, a directness that seems to penetrate with ease to the very core of things and to the very heart of human problems. They are the adult persons, those who have developed their personalities, in marriage or out of it, through the practice of openness and detachment. Go to them, and learn that it is through contemplative and restful immersion in love that anxieties disappear, that scales of value are set aright, and that men and women become creatures of joy and peace, open to themselves, to others, and to God with the simpilicity that leads to balance and truth.

You will learn from them that, in both friendship and love, there is need for a considerable amount of inner silence that will give you a chance to receive messages from others; that the constant babble of "I . . . I . . . I . . ." must give way to a state of expectant repose, changing the self from a noisemaker into an instrument receptive to the other's voices, moods, and thoughts. The other is the biblical "neighbor," and your closest neighbor is, of course, your mate.

If you are always seeking what you can get from your neighbor, since you do not know him enough to reach a true level of love, he will generally appear as a vacuous bore, a pauper with nothing to give. But if you try to find out what he needs, if you are sufficiently open to understand him, sufficiently detached to be able to give of your substance, you will discover both his poverty and his deserving inner wealth. In the end you may very well be the one who receives the most.

This is particularly true in the relationship of marriage: there should not be the slightest shame in revealing to each other both your needs and your gifts.

After the Second World War, there was a noticeable rise in the number of foreign war brides. Thousands of men were going back to Europe and even to Japan to find wives. The relatively high percentage of these marriages seems to have been due to the fact that American males had come in contact with a different kind of woman, a woman who was raised from birth to be a loving, serving wife. The American girl has certainly enjoyed great benefits from gaining equality in many ways with her male companion, but she suffers the disadvantage of being now a competitor instead of a complement. Until now, foreign women, by and large, have been trained from infancy to be generous and forgetful of self, to be more concerned with what they can give a man than with what they can receive from him. This is not a position of subordination, but one of openness to the other, and detachment from self that is most appealing as a promise of love and most effective in love realized. American women should take due notice.

Everyone Is Worthy of Love

In one sense, everyone is worthy of your love; but in another, because your deeply personal love is limited, only those closest to you can receive it.

The reason why you should love everyone is not gratitude but metaphysical worth: the inner quality every human being enjoys by the very fact that he or she exists. Everything and everyone that God created is good. Even the most hardened criminal or the most repulsive wretch is worthy of your love, since Christ died for all without exception. And so every man and woman is deserving of your kindness and concern.

Then, there is another degree of worth: that which makes some persons particularly close to you. It is a matter of personal accord and harmony, the very essence of friendship and of true sexual love. Here you are the judge. You are absolutely free to accept or reject personal companionship according to your taste and desires. There is within yourself a domain that is rightly reserved for some very special kind of human contacts that result in mutual enrichment, of mind, heart, and senses. Here, too, before any communication can flow, there is need for inner silence, not the wary and suspicious silence that watches the other as if he were a fly about to be caught in a web, that waits for him to trip himself and show how stupid he is and how right you are to stay aloof. No, this must be a positive silence when the other is speaking, so that you can "read him," so that you can see who he really is.

True love of the other on the high plane of marriage demands silent, attentive listening, followed by sincere self-revealing talk. Then only shall there be conversation, or, to use the word in the old English sense, true intercourse.

In this very special kind of love, then, a good rule seems to be "I give you all I am: you give me whatever you freely want to give." Not only should you be able to give yourself to the beloved in a gesture of unconditional love; you should also be able to receive love, and this may sometimes be the hardest thing. Many people have enclosed themselves within their own defensive fortress. They rush to the wall in order to fight any intrusion from the outer world, including an intrusion of love. They may have been hurt after some earlier attempt at opening the doors; their love may have been spurned and rejected. Out of fear, they close their hearts even to offerings of true love.

If every disappointment, every wound, every rejection, is taken too hard, as further proof either of the world's evil or of your own unworthiness, it may be a sign of immaturity and of a total lack of the indispensable sense of humor. A courageous, normal, healthy attitude would be to take every defeat as a chance to try harder, every wound as an occasion for better love, every rejection as a signal that perhaps all is not well with you. Your failures may be due to your own faults and imperfections.

Many times it has happened that a love of the highest intensity, faithfulness, and delicacy was given to a partner spiritually and emotionally so blunt as to be insensitive to the treasures being offered. There is a great difference between unrequited love and love improperly received. Unwelcome love is a disappointment; it should not be pursued. But the greater tragedy is in love accepted with hardly any appreciation for the gift.

There is no limit to love, to how much you want to love and, correspondingly, how much you hope to receive in return. But *you should never expect a full return for your love, nor should you ever be surprised at being loved much more than you deserve.* It is not for you to judge how much return to expect from your love, but merely to accpet graciously and gratefully whatever human warmth comes your way. By thus limiting your expectation, you will see the smallest gift of love as a miracle, and the largest, as a sign of God's very presence.

No One Can Have a Total Experience of Love

"In the twentieth century we are inclined to feel guilty unless we can respond, with every pore open and every nerve quivering, to each and every opportunity for love. Because those opportunities are infinite we are certain to wind up frustrated, accusing ourselves of heartlessness, nagging at our psyches because emotion won't always come. It is not even love we are after. Love just might consist of knowing and then doing, understanding and acting generously toward what is understood. What we demand of ourselves is the 'sensation' of loving, a ready tingle of the flesh, a tickle at the stomach, a warm and gratifying glow that stirs in the bowels and suffuses the whole body until the body is persuaded that it is totally involved, totally sensitive, all athrob with participation. . . .

"When we feel less than we feel we ought to feel, (you see how complex the matter is) are we being hard-hearted or are we only harassing ourselves? Above all, what are we focusing on, the figure in need of care or the interior reassurance of caring? It's a puzzle, and a universal pressure. The pressure may in the end create contemporary man's most recognizable stance: a faint cringing in fear of not having felt absolutely everything." [1]

There is in the love relationship an almost automatic desire for the best, the utmost, the highest possible level of pleasurable ecstasy. Much premarital daydreaming seems to be devoted to imagining the realization of bliss, embroidering its details, and prefiguring a way of life that resembles what a perfectly developed Adam and Eve would do together on some remote South Sea island. Married life is often anticipated by the very young as a state of constant gratification.

On the other hand, with the current lack of adequate teaching on sex and the artificial taboos and fears transmitted by generations of prudes, there may be quite the opposite anticipation, particularly on the part of the girl. There may be a very real fear of being hurt, wounded, disgraced by sexual relations that are seen as the loathsome outcome of male aggressiveness and lust. Married life is then considered by some unfortunate females as the sacrifice of virginity on the altar of matrimonial duty.

Both views are obviously wrong. Neither one corresponds to the true development of personality available in marriage. And yet many of their characteristics are found in the current attitudes of young people preparing for marriage. Let us, then, try to straighten out some of these ideas.

No human couple has the *physical perfection* attributed to Adam and Eve before the fall. All are more or less defective in

[1] Walter Kerr, in the Sunday Edition of *The New York Times*, February 4, 1968.

their constitution. Imperfection may take many forms, for instance, the lack of physical beauty. Few people actually correspond to the ideals proposed by the fashion plate, the cover girl, or the movie star. Even these much-admired idols are frequently padded and painted so heavily that they would be hardly recognizable in the state of nature.

What, then, of physical beauty? As we all know, there are some outstandingly handsome men and beautiful women who approach the ideals of physical perfection. They have received a great gift and a great power, but they suffer from a correspondingly great temptation: to abuse their gift by selling it out, taking undue advantage of it, or concentrating on it in narcissistic adoration. Physical beauty can also go hand in hand with great stupidity. It would also be an incentive to intellectual laziness. Often, the more handsome a man and the more beautiful a woman, the less they seem to understand the need to love. The love-me-because-I-am-beautiful approach is obviously not the answer to personal fulfillment.

Girls should learn what it is to be a real woman. It has nothing to do with the heaving breasts and parted lips of the movie close-up. Natural womanliness is indescribable. Yet, even limited talents may be developed by observing some truly womanly women in the act of living. What they stand for is presence, compassion, total and joyful and healing gift of self.

The art of marriage, the art of love, and the art of sex all require considerable dedication, intelligent research, and persevering effort. But since most men and women's natural talents are not of the highest order, and their effort toward improvement is of mediocre quality and intensity, marriage, love, and sex will never attain for them the level of total perfection. In fact, such a level is unattainable for anyone on earth. And so it would be folly for any couple to expect to duplicate the romantic heights of Romeo and Juliet, the passion of Abélard and Héloïse, or the sexual prowesses of paperback heroes and heroines.

There Are Circumstantial Barriers to Perfect Delight

Besides limitations brought about by natural defects, there are others brought about by the circumstances of life. The mere fatigue of survival in our high-pressure world, anxieties related to earning the daily hamburger, general anguish about possible thermonuclear destruction, petty, exhausting, and ever-recurring miseries of child care and housekeeping—all these work against the enjoyment of perfect delight in the relations between man and wife.

Sound realism will consist in not expecting more than is actually possible under the circumstances. There is a French proverb that says: "The most beautiful girl in the world can give no more than what she has." And no girl is so beautiful and perfect that she has the power to convey total bliss. To expect total happiness from marriage, and particularly from sex in marriage or out of it, is a dangerous delusion. Even in those rarest of circumstances when all seems to be well, there is only this very human relationship between two very human beings, meeting in the most earthy of their human contacts. There is the meeting of a man hampered by anxiety and worries with a woman dragged down by drudgery and sorrows. In fact, it is a near-miracle, and it should be taken as a happy surprise, that the slightest ecstasy ever does occur.

Is there any reason to be defeatist about marriage, and to believe that true and enduring happiness, including sexual pleasure, cannot be found in it? Not in the least. What is beyond reach is Utopia, that is, the Land of Nowhere, the impossible, Never-Never Land. It is nonexistent because it would have to be the Kingdom of the Flawless Ones—and who is without sin? Even the Unknockables, those who put up an appearance of flawlessness, are found out soon enough when approached with total objectivity.

No husband or wife is flawless. They may be lacking in some talent or ability, or equality: and yet a successful marriage may still be maintained through the patient cooperation of imperfect partners. It is within the complex of human fallibility that the common life of any couple must be built. Happiness is the reward of mutual help, forgiveness, and understanding.

This is true on all three levels: of the mind, the heart, and the senses. If one partner is an intellectual, an avid reader, and the other is not, there can be loving compromise: the bookworm may try not to get involved too often in his paper paradise, while the other may try to increase his or her interest in the treasures of the intellect. If one is warm and gushing and the other has a tendency to express emotions with the eloquence of a dead fish, mutual understanding and help may again lead to a working agreement. Finally, in the sexual relationship, a difference in the degree of information may be corrected easily enough, prejudices may be explained away gently, and even if there is considerable disparity in the intensity and frequency of desire, some healthy compromise is always possible through reasonable mutual sacrifice.

Learn to Be Happy with What You Are and Have

Such is the stuff happiness is made of: realism, peacefulness, kindly acceptance of the inevitable, gentle and persevering effort to improve yourself and your partner, and a joyful development of the fields of common understanding. All this is not the work of a single day. Many good people are aware that if only they were more peaceful about their spouse's faults, the degree of tension and the amount of bickering would be lowered. And yet, they are unable to yield.

Our powers of humility, concession, forgiveness, and love are severely limited by our own imperfection. If we are honest enough to admit this, especially before we marry, there is a good chance that such awareness will keep us out of deep trouble. The best thing to do, then, is to pray for the gift of love, to pray for it with absolute trust, to pray for a lavish, abundant power of endurance that will carry us along, in sickness and in health, in joy and in sorrow. The God of Love is glorified by such a request, and it will not go unanswered.

The way of personal fulfillment in marriage is the same as that of personal fulfillment in any other state, with the specific difference that it is to be lived together with another human being on a unique level of personal intimacy. *The way of personal fulfillment is paradoxically that of personal sacrifice.* The more you give of yourself, the more you will receive. The more you forget yourself, the more you will be remembered. Not only according to the promise in the afterlife of heaven, but right here and now, in the unique state of personal union of a man and woman in love.

CHAPTER 10

HAPPINESS IN LOVE BEGINS WITH SELF-ACCEPTANCE

Your Body Is Sacred . . . The Sexual Drive Is Good and Holy . . . False Shame Is Harmful . . . Learn to Live with Sexual Tension . . . Do Not Be Afraid of Your Humanness . . . Chastity Is the Virtue That Regulates Love . . . Spiritual Values Contribute to Sexual Balance . . . Proper Balance Does Not Exclude Passion . . . Masturbation Is Not Always a Sin . . . Your Capacity to Love Depends on Self-Acceptance . . . Four Rules for Achieving Self-Acceptance

Self-understanding is the key to self-acceptance and the foundation of true love. Some people never seem to reach this goal, while others attain it in the fullness of joy. Generally speaking, there are three different levels of development as regards the proper maturation of love: the childish, the adolescent, and the adult.

The lowest level, childishness, is found in those who are unable to cross the great divide between childhood fantasy and real life. Some fully grown men and women behave like ten-year-olds, with fits and tantrums at every disappointment, crushing breakdowns at every defeat, and uncontrolled elation at every victory. No sane life and marriage can be built on such an immature emotional foundation.

The level of adolescence represents the state of those who are partly established in adulthood, and yet always ready to flee when faced with challenges that seem excessive. All is well as long as there are no problems. But trials and difficulties are met with consternation, because of false expectations of perfect victory and success. The emotionally adolescent comprise people of all ages who behave as if the world owed them a constantly pleasant and successful living without requiring any sustained effort on their part.

The highest level is that of adulthood. It consists in the successful crossing of the divide, with both feet planted in the land of reality; and the full facing of responsibilities, with the strength of character, as Kipling says, to meet "triumph and disaster, and treat those two impostors just the same." This is the way of the full-grown man and woman, the way of sanity, love, and peace.

If maturity comes through self-understanding and self-acceptance, that is the point where you must begin. Consider what and who you are by investigating your body, your emotions, your attitudes toward sex, your strengths and your weaknesses—all for the purpose of helping you develop a keener insight into yourself. With this supporting awareness, you will find it easier to accept yourself, and eventually to accept others properly so as to grow in love.

Your Body Is Sacred

The first condition for a proper attitude toward marriage is the realization of the dignity of your body and of its functions. It is not enough for you to know that there is nothing dirty or evil about the human body. The physical complex of organs, functions, and sensations is good. Your body, like all the wonders of nature, is good—meaning, beautifully designed, integrated in its operations, useful, well conformed, but it is good in a much more profound order. For man is more than a tree or an animal, and the very essence of this higher order is the fact that he is an Heir to the Kingdom, a Child of the Promise. Your body is that to which resurrection has been assured. Furthermore, this same body is the means of perpetuation of the human race. Every saint, past, present, and future, is the fruit of the sexual love of a man and a woman. Everything beautiful that man has ever done or ever will do comes to pass only because he receives life through the ecstatic union of a male and a female in the act of love.

The Sexual Drive Is Good and Holy

The organs of sex are properly called in Latin *verenda* and *pudenda,* "those things to be revered" and "those things to be protected by modesty." In true Christian theology, never are the organs of sex considered as unclean or shameful: it is only in decadent societies in which the use of sex degenerated to criminal depths that shame appeared in relation to the genitals. There is nothing to be ashamed of except sin. Now, sin is not at all automatically involved in every sexual desire or act, as a number of pessimists have tended to believe throughout the ages. Even in the teachings of theologians and in some quite recent manuals of moral theology, there is a failure to mention the distinction between *concupiscence,* the disordered passion of the senses, and the *inclination of nature,* the natural and good passion that leads man to woman, and woman to man, for the consummation of their love in the sexual union.

Did you hear the story about the two little boys who find a hole in the fence of a nudist colony?

"Hey, there's a whole lot of people walking around in there."

"Yeah? Are they boys or girls?"

"I don't know; they don't have any clothes on."

All of us at one time were innocent children, but we allow carefree innocence to be displaced by the dark and ominous feelings of guilt and shame. This is something that can be healed, but it requires a reeducation of the emotions. It would be well to go back to the beginning to examine the origin of man.

False Shame Is Harmful

What of the biblical story of Adam and Eve? Were they not ashamed when they saw they were naked? Are we not told that they covered themselves up? Did not God himself confirm their shame by making clothes for them? There is no need here for an extensive discussion of the historicity of the Bible. What should be said, however, is that the *origin* of man and of sexuality is immensely more remote from us than the writing of Genesis. In the present state of paleontology, it is believed that man began to exist more than two million years ago, and he has kept developing steadily in accordance with the providential plan. Much of the Bible, though inspired by God and rich in poetical and symbolical meaning, cannot be seen as factual recording. The standards of contemporary historical criticism cannot be applied to it, particularly in its chronology. Also, the Bible is marked with the social and personal ideas of those very human authors who composed it. The attitude of Adam and Eve toward sexuality may be seen as reflecting, not the shamefulness of sex as such, but the shame felt by the biblical writer because of the sexual abuses of his time.

There are other passages of Genesis where the sexual difference and function appear as fundamentally good; and yet many religious groups throughout history have relied unduly on the negative interpretation, and taught that there was in sex and passion something intrinsically evil. The Manichaeans, the Cathars, the Jansenists, and early Puritans broadcast pessimistic teachings in matters of sex that are still damaging many minds and spoiling many lives. Most of these teachings were based on the belief that original sin, and therefore all the evil that has befallen man, began with some sexual abuse, when in fact we know from both tradition and the Bible that original sin was essentially an act of pride: man rising against God's authority in order to be like him.

Can this sense of shame that men feel in sexual matters be brushed off merely as a misinterpretation of biblical theology? No. It is an everyday fact that because of uncontrolled desires, passions, lusts, the lives of many men and women are degraded by sexual abuse.

A young girl told the heartbreaking story of her misguided love. She went out with a boy who constantly made sexual demands upon her. His thoughts and actions were often crude, but she felt sorry for him because he seemed to be all alone in the world. On the night he finally triumphed over her, in his selfish haste he caused her great physical pain. She contained her suffering, and cried quietly. When he was through taking his pleasure, he pulled away from her, totally oblivious of her feelings, and stunned her with the words, "All you ever think about is sex!" She related the story tearfully, without comprehending why he acted as he did.

This unfortunate lad was projecting his own guilt feeling on her, blaming her for his own preoccupation. Clearly, then, what is shameful is the abuse of sex, and not sex as such.

Among early theologians, and more particularly some of the Fathers of the Church, Basil, Chrysostom, Jerome, Augustine, and many Scholastics, the reasoning seems to have been that since sex gives rise to such constant abuse, there must be something fundamentally wrong with it. For instance, in the thirteenth century, William of Auvergne, and others with him, went so far as to say: "To God, all carnal pleasure is an abomination!" But a thing is not bad because it can be misused or even because it is generally misused. For as long as there is a possibility of using it well, it is a potential good. And so we should constantly keep in mind the notion that sex may be one of the highest and most rewarding human functions and joys—but also, because of its very power and our own weakness, that it may easily become an occasion of serious disorder.

Learn to Live with Sexual Tension

There is in us an almost constant striving between the instinctive desire for emotional and physiological fulfillment and the moral and rational ideals of perfection. They are not contradictory, nor is the conflict head on: sexual fulfillment is compatible with the highest summit of virtue. But because of the very power of the drive, because of its vital importance, it is sometimes so overwhelmingly strong that only a firm and constant will can keep it straight. There may be a considerable number of lapses and falls—some more serious and others less—but all liable to damage your self-esteem, and therefore, ultimately, your capacity for a sound man/woman relationship. Because of the possibility of such disorder, many young people seem unable to see the possibility of order. Some surrender to temptations as fast as they come. In this way they inevitably follow the current of permissive morality condoned and encouraged by thoughtless lovers who pursue the short-range goal of pleasure. Others retire within the protective tower of their own desire for decency and purity, and run away from the world of sexual encounter. But escapism is unworthy of a fully human person.

Learn to accept yourself as you are, and understand that your sexual tension is good. It is a powerful incentive to the recognition of another person as valuable and important. It procures a radiance of warmth, a vital interest in the fundamentally human, a participation in the ascent of universal life, an escape from narcissism, a chance for personal renewal and development, an inspiration toward effort and progress in other fields, and a million things besides. It would be difficult to imagine our world without the delightful excitement of the boy/girl relationship; in fact, without human love there would be no such world.

Do Not Be Afraid of Your Humanness

Tension itself, increased vitality, thoughts, desires, hopes of true love are all excellent. There is nothing wrong or sinful about yearning for a future love or in a strong curiosity that searches for detailed documentation on the art of love, even to the point of the frankly sensual and erotic. For sex preparation must go beyond romantic sentimentality if it is to be realistic. There is need for stronger food than pious literature. This searching, like all things, should be kept within the boundaries of reason. Daydreaming should not be obsessive, nor should the reading of sexual material turn into a major hobby, but a certain amount of it is normal during the years of adolescence. And the right kind of literature should be made available to all.

A proper balance needs to be established between the frightened rejection of any sexual thought and the gluttonous greed for as much sex as possible in any form. So numerous are the possible manifestations that it is quite impossible to establish a list of things to do or not to do.

There was a severely scrupulous young college man who had picked up some dreadful piece of "spiritual" reading. After a careful study of the text, he had come to the conclusion that if he really wanted to remain chaste, he would have to avoid touching anyone. Because he was emotionally sick, if someone offered him a handshake, he would recoil in fear and give a sad, feeble excuse. He soon became the butt of many cruel jokes, but his will was strong and he persevered in this folly. It was not very long before he had a nervous breakdown. This is often the case when a person, even in good faith, mistakes frigidity and fear for chastity.

Chastity Is the Virtue That Regulates Love

Chastity is a positive virtue; it is warm, tender, and strong. Chastity has nothing to do with negativism. It does not consist in obeying a long list of don't's. For you, chastity will consist in developing your own rules of life along the broad lines of the happiness and perfection you hope to achieve, and in holding to them. This is a lifetime job: according to your fluctuating intentions and ideals, you are always moving up or down the ladder of perfection, without ever staying on the same rung.

Part of this personal perfection program will be a clear understanding of where you stand in the balance of sexual tension. This understanding will include many an important notion, particularly: that spiritual values contribute to sexual balance, and that balance does not exclude passion.

Spiritual Values Contribute to Sexual Balance

A strong young man or young woman will live with faith, hope, and love as their guides.

Faith, not only in God, but in life, in self, in sex, is a potential source of true happiness. This faith implies a clear vision of the actuality of sin in the world and the possibility of personal misuse of a vital power. It implies also a substantial trust in human nature. After all, God made man and woman, and saw that they were good.

Hope, then, is not vain. Nor should it be exaggerated or unreal, indulging in notions of grandeur or ecstasy beyond any possibility of attainment. The only direction in which hope can be infinite is up: toward the perfection of God's promise to those who follow his commands and counsels and obey them. For no eye has seen nor has ear heard what he keeps in store for them.

Love is both the motor and measure of all reality. Nothing comes into being that will not turn into love in its final form. Love is the measure of perfection of all things. And so here, too, in the problem of sexual tension, love in spirit and in truth will serve as the standard of right or wrong. If you make use of this tension as an occasion to increase your acts of kindness, to become more generous with your own gifts, to seek light and truth more ardently and give them more graciously, then it will become a means of enrichment for yourself and others. It will be good, with the goodness of love.

Proper Balance Does Not Exclude Passion

The power of restraint is present in every good man, and self-restraint is born of deep consideration for the well-being of the beloved. Does this mean that before marriage, and within it, a state of perfect equilibrium and happiness may be attained once for all? Of course not. The human condition is one of dynamic tending. Tending, then, in the form of passion, is one of the ingredients of life, and balance is the measured response we give to it. It is constantly dynamic, for the challenge is always there, different from day to day, so that on earth there is really no total rest, no Seventh Day. And even in the Seventh Day of heaven, no doubt some passion will still be there, full of peace, joy, and love, relieved of its burden of doubt and anguish, but nevertheless full of those very aspirations and exaltations that are found in every human form within the faith, hope, and love of man and woman.

This, then, gives you an idea of the respect you are to have for your own body and for its organs and functions. They are the means to something great, the instruments of the Holy Spirit of Love, the occasions of the most soul-shaking and life-giving emotions. They give life to the lovers who live in and for each other, who find their delights in each other's presence and in the intimacy of each other's body; they give life to children in their act of love.

Masturbation Is Not Always a Sin

There are many areas of tension that may bear deeper thought than is usually given when it comes to the formation of a Christian attitude toward sexual acts. Thomas Aquinas, for instance, teaches that the "unnatural vice," which includes masturbation, is the greatest sin within the species of lust because it is the most completely opposed to "nature." According to this ancient teaching, such a vice is always and everywhere a "mortal sin."

This doctrine has been repeated uncritically by almost every moral theologian until very recent times, and is responsible for the flourishing of neuroses and guilt complexes on the part of many good men and women who have been fighting the "unnatural vice" for years—both desperately and ineffectively. The popular moralizing literature on the subject is incredible in its violence and threats. No possible or impossible damaging consequence seems to have been overlooked. In an abundance of writings, the person with the problem of masturbation has been threatened with sterility, impotency, imbecility, insanity, and everything else imaginable. No doubt an unaccountable number of victims of such teaching did lose their minds, not because they practiced masturbation but rather because of the abject terror that had been instilled in them by counselors of immense good will and total incompetence.

The degree of freedom involved in masturbation varies greatly from person to person. In most cases, there is, at times of severe temptation, a drastic reduction in freedom and a proportionate increase in compulsion. Now, it is a solemn teaching of the Church that an extraordinary grace is required to resist extraordinary temptation. This does not mean that in these matters the burden rests with God, but it does indicate that the Church is aware of human limitations.

The problem may be more emotional than moral

It is also a professed principle that "habit" and "passion" decrease the free willfulness of an act, to the point that intense "habit" or "passion" may in some circumstances make a person virtually unfree at a particular moment in regard to a certain act. There is nothing here to disparage the serious obligation to overcome temptation and to rise above self-gratification. But the fact is that many young people are so deeply caught up in the habit that the acts themselves cannot be performed in full freedom, and therefore cannot be gravely sinful. There may still be serious matter, in the Thomistic sense, but in many cases full consent is so very doubtful that it would be most unwise to label every instance of masturbation as a sin.

If, however, because of habit there is limited responsibility as regards individual acts, one may question the person's responsibility in actually acquiring the habit itself. It could be a serious sin if the habit itself had been willfully and maliciously accepted and developed. In the normal course of events, this is rarely the case: there are usually extenuating circumstances, of ignorance, youthfulness, and social conditions, that make masturbation an emotional rather than a moral problem, in which case there is no sin at all. Quite often, too much fear, shame, and guilt have been attached to what is in fact an almost universal phase of emotional development in the adolescent. The problem should not be ignored, but neither should it be exaggerated out of all proportion.

Psychologists, educators, priests, and others who deal regularly with young people have estimated that upwards of ninety percent of boys and a large percentage of girls go through a period of habitual masturbation. A considerable number of these boys and girls feel that masturbation is sinful, and try seriously but unsuccessfully to stop. It is unthinkable that the God who is Unchanging Love would make a law that the majority of the human race would find impossible to obey. For this reason, many contemporary thinkers in the Church are challenging the traditional theological view of sexuality, and there has been much discussion in recent years as to whether masturbation is sinful at all, particularly if the person is striving through prayer and other good works to overcome the habit.

It is even quite possible that masturbation, with its release of pent-up sexual tension, is far less damaging psychologically than the guilt and shame caused by an unrelieved, prolonged preoccupation with sex.

The emphasis, then, should be on compassion and encouragement for the person who is struggling to integrate his sexuality within a well-ordered life, rather than on the aspects of sin, guilt, and shame.

Considering these more advanced ideas, we may well ask how it could be that earlier condemnations were so severe? One reason is that, in the days of Thomas Aquinas, the biological processes of conception and birth were not properly understood. It was generally believed that the sperm contained fully formed miniature human beings that were implanted in the female womb and made to grow. Any self-induced loss of spermatic fluid was then considered a gross offense against life, and in some circles was even compared with murder. For this same reason, there are proportionately much fewer references to female masturbation in ancient moral literature: the major emphasis and guilt seems to have been placed on the loss of male "seed."

Modern physiology has discovered that in any single ejaculate, there are several hundred million spermatozoa, the male fertilizing element. These are neither fully "human" nor fully "personal": they are merely the physiological building blocks of possible human beings when and if they happen to be combined with a mature female ovum. Apart from the meaningful use of sex for procreation, the male sperm is merely a natural surplus material.

What, then, are some practical consequences of the more informed knowledge as regards recent moral teachings?

1. Masturbation, either male or female, is not automatically a mortal sin.

2. If practiced to excess, that is, at such a rate of frequency as to become physically exhausting, or with such obsessive interest as to be psychologically damaging, or again, if it is preferred to intercourse, it can be a very serious disorder. In such cases, the cause is very often a grave emotional disturbance, and the treatment should be related to psychological therapy. Moral guilt should not be presumed.

3. If practiced without any attempt at self-control, it will amount to surrendering without a fight to what is, at the very least, an imperfection, and at the most, a serious sin, encouraging weakness of character, destroying self-respect and, consequently, self-acceptance.

4. In some circumstances, masturbation may occur without any guilt at all. For instance, in the case of an unpremeditated sudden excitation, a boy or girl may experience a high degree of sexual tension that culminates in orgasm, which may have been obtained, not as an end in itself, nor as a valid substitute for love, but simply

as a means of temporary physical and emotional release. There may even be a conscious "giving in" to the pressure without real sin being present. In such cases, it would be better not to fuss about questions of moral guilt. Even if deep venereal pleasure is experienced, sin is not necessarily present, since one has no control over the automatic effects of the act.

The simplest and healthiest attitude, then, is to do the best you can to avoid the regular practice of masturbation. Should there be a slip in spite of every good intention, your mind should be at ease and you should avoid needless anxiety. It is a good idea to talk to God about it, remembering that God is Unchanging Love: there is in him instant tender forgiveness and total security.

Mutual satisfaction in marriage is vital

The same general principles will apply later in marriage. During periods of long and enforced abstinence, when a couple accustomed to frequent and legitimate intercourse are totally deprived of it for long stretches of time—for instance, during the fertile periods if they are practicing rhythm and the wife's cycle is irregular—the tension may build up to a level of intolerable frustration, leading to ill humor, bickering, and fighting, and perhaps even to the very real temptation to seek compensation elsewhere. Because this would be the worst possible thing, many couples engage in acts of legitimate affection that may result in mutual pleasure without intercourse. Here, again, the release of tension can be the overriding consideration, and the couple should not be overanxious about such incidents, nor should the fear of future slips be allowed to crush the affective life of any marriage. Fundamentally, domestic peace and happiness depend upon affection given and received, and in loving each other, married people should be concerned about pleasing each other.

Purity, as indicated by its Greek etymology, refers to the virtue of fire, to the cleansing fire of love. It is usually those who are most capable of human love who suffer the most from sexual repression. The release of tension by which they may be saved from emotional and physical torture cannot be considered an enemy to love or life—or God, for that matter. Too many good people have fallen into despair over their "unavoidable" state of sin. This has led many to give up the struggle and to fall into deeper and more serious sins, and has turned others away from God entirely in a state of utter hopelessness.

There is, in this regard, one point on which all moralists agree. When, in the course of a marital act, the husband has obtained satisfaction but the wife has not, it is perfectly legitimate for him to continue caressing her until she obtains relief. If the husband fails to do so, she is morally free to seek her own relief. The argument generally used here is that it amounts to the continuation of an act of natural intercourse.

Now, in recent views on the sexual relationship, intercourse is not merely compenetration and ejaculation. It comprises the whole range of sensual expressions of mutual love. If, in the course of legitimate endearments, the sexual urge becomes unbearably strong, there is much reason to pursue the action to the point of relief even if conjunction is not possible. The permissibility of relief is founded on the psychological damage inflicted upon the partner who is left "hanging on a cliff." Why should not the permission be extended to both partners, when both are in this uncomfortable position, not by any premeditated lust, but merely as a consequence of the exuberant and vital need for a sexual expression of their love? It would seem, then, that the principles proposed would most properly apply to the married in those cases where there is a spontaneous and legitimate hunger—and a very serious reason to fear pregnancy. Aside from abstinence and induced relief, the only other solution would be the use of some contraceptive method.

Your Capacity to Love Depends on Self-Acceptance

All things considered, Bishop Symon's opinion contains much wisdom. Self-relief practiced occasionally by a person who is good in other aspects of life is certainly less damaging than a neurotic repression based on fear of sex, for this can lead only to anxiety and sexual obsession, culminating for some in severe aberrations and psychic trauma. Such a wounded self-concept can only prolong and intensify the problem, and lead to self-contempt. There should be no exaggerating of the sense of shame or guilt. A peaceful acceptance of yourself in the humble realization that you are human can enhance your capacity to love.

The proper approach to self-understanding—as a condition of self-respect and a preparation for the gift of self—implies coming to terms with what you are. Adolescents often have a feeling of acute isolation. It is hard for them to communicate with their parents or to live with them on personal terms. It seems that they often come home merely to eat and sleep, and consider their parents as unavoidable nuisances who happen to live in the same house. This lack of openness is sometimes answered by a baffled silence on the part of parents, and this, in turn, is taken for a lack of interest and love—and so the spiral of incomprehension grows to the proportion of complete alienation. The young man and woman feel left out or lost, perhaps even rejected, as if something were wrong with them. If such feeling is allowed to establish itself and grow, it may very well give rise to discontent with self, self-criticism turning into dangerous neurosis. This is a serious handicap, since self-acceptance is a necessary condition of happiness and love.

Four Rules for Achieving Self-Acceptance

There are a few good rules that will help to promote a sane and reasonable attitude toward yourself.

Accept your human limitations

No one is perfect and complete. We are all growing—and youth has a longer way to go, but also a longer and better chance for improvement. There are many ways open to progress in culture, attractiveness, charm, personality, that are particularly available to the young, precisely because they are young and malleable.

Live the highest ideal possible

Each individual may determine the pattern and quality of his own ideal, of the inner beauty he seeks to achieve. The best way to it is honesty and authenticity: the opposite of deceit and sham. Be what you are and what you can be, without pretending to be what you are not and can never be. As the old saying goes, You can fool some of the people some of the time, but you cannot fool all the people all the time. And as soon as anyone is able to see right through your sham, both your reputation and your self-esteem are gone. But reach out and try for the highest limit of perfection attainable for you. You'll find it is surprisingly high.

Believe that you are lovable

Every man and woman is lovable as such, even if they have as yet never experienced personal love. Every human person is a creature of love and joy and peace. Love is his origin and destiny.

It would be a gross injustice to allow yourself to coddle feelings of self-contempt because you are not the perfect man or woman. No one is perfect or even nearly perfect. And so, you must try to see beyond your own imperfection; try to see into the essence of your being, and give yourself the kindness and forgiveness you so richly deserve. Reconcile yourself to yourself. Every man and woman is made in the image of God, and everyone has some aspect of this image to offer in a gesture of love. It is the duty of each person to discover his or her personal beauty, so that the gift of self in love will be seen as a gift of great value.

Learn to delight in love

As soon as love is found, there is a kind of revelation of self in the other, a sudden discovery that there was in you much more than you had actually believed, since it is enough to arouse in the other a feeling of enchantment and delight. One of the great pleasures of lovers is to discover in each other many a hidden treasure—of humor, simplicity, imagination, charm, generosity—the existence of which had never been suspected. All of these traits constitute a "personality," the unique combination of elements that makes a human being irreplaceable and different from any other. Between man and woman, besides these personal differences, there is the specific differentiation of sex that adds a kind of vital dimension, a quality of excitement and magic. Let us now try to see in what it consists.

CHAPTER 11

MAN NEEDS WOMAN AND WOMAN NEEDS MAN

Man Is Made in God's Image . . . Sexuality Is Part of Your Inner World . . . Man and Woman Are Complementary Beings . . . The Male Moves from Attraction to Sex to Love . . . The Female Moves from Attraction to Love to Sex . . . The Differences Spark Mutual Attraction . . . The Male Provides Security and Purpose . . . The Female Gives Comfort and Inspiration . . . The Similarities Cement the Union . . . It Is Not Good for Man to Be Alone . . . Man and Woman Work Together

As already noted, the biblical presentation of the origin of the world and of man cannot be taken as a precise and scientific description of what actually happened. It is much less than that, and much more. It is less, because beginnings are so obscure, so silent. As Teilhard de Chardin pointed out, any original act, the first manifestation of any form of life, is lost in the night of time. Things become perceptible only after they have developed in quality and quantity, so as to become possible objects of observation. It is quite useless, then, to seek in the Bible or, as a matter of fact, in any other book, a precise time chart or an accurate description of man's origin. The Bible is not a book of science, and yet it is more than a scientific book. It presents a visionary, poetical, and inspired view of the meaning and purpose of man in relation to his Creator, seen both as his beginning and his end. The Bible also offers deep insights into man's constitution, his natural needs, and the normal conditions for his happy survival and multiplication.

Man Is Made in God's Image

"God said, 'Let us make mankind in our image and likeness; and let them have dominion over the fish of the sea, the birds of the air, the cattle, over all the wild animals and every creature that crawls on the earth.' God created man in his image. In the image of God he created him. Male and female he created him. Then God blessed them and said to them, 'Be fruitful and multiply; fill the earth and subdue it.' [Genesis 1:26–28]

From the very first, the great dignity of man becomes apparent: man has dominion over all other creatures on the earth; he is the lord of all material creation. Then there comes a very intriguing passage, the first biblical reference to sexual dualism: "In the image of God he created him. Male and female he created him." The link between God's image and the concept of male-female distinction is one of the major signs by which mankind can come to know God as dynamic and creative love. A mutual response corresponding to that of sexuality exists within God—not as a distinction, but as a perfect, constant, and actual relationship of love. God is not one, but two Persons united in a love that is itself a third Person. From the very beginning, then, sex is associated with God, with the Highest, with the Best, with supreme and perfect Life. The difference, the conversation, the communication and exchange between man and woman are an image of God's inner reality.

Sexuality Is Part of Your Inner World

Sexuality is a vital part of your own inner world. It is a function of what you are, an aspect of yourself so closely integrated with your person that inadequate knowledge may be damaging to your very life. A man may be totally ignorant of higher mathematics or astronomy, and yet live a completely sane and satisfying life, for the objects of such sciences are things external to the human being. A man may even get away with rudimentary notions of pharmacology or philology, for although such sciences are directly related to man, they are concerned only with incidentals. Not so with sex, with the science of sex and the virtue of sex, for these imply the proper understanding and the proper use not only of something you have but also of something you are.

Profound interest in the sexual differences and an avid curiosity concerning their possible and proper use are nothing to be ashamed of—on the contrary. There is no need whatsoever to repress such interest and curiosity or to make any violent effort to cast them out as if they were impure. If you are to succeed in accepting yourself fully, you must learn to accept yourself sexually. Your sexual instinct is a healthy, normal part of your body, which should be brought under your control in much the same way one controls one's appetite for food. For the good of the whole person we learn to regulate the bodily appetites.

Man and Woman Are Complementary Beings

How, then, does sexuality differ in the male and in the female? The anatomical and physiological details may be found in any technical manual. They are important and should be considered carefully, but it is not our intent to discuss them here. What seems more urgent and important is to analyze a number of psychological differences, or states of mind, that constitute the specific disparity between male and female. When properly understood, they are the elements of the harmonious union of two complementary beings. Otherwise they may be direct occasions of conflict and of the loss of love.

The personal psychological pattern of each and every human being is unique and immensely complex. Any attempt at a description must then be made in general terms. No manual of counseling can be so exactly tailored to a man or woman's needs as to fit exactly. All that a counselor can hope to do is to give some advice that may be found useful in the majority of cases.

Sexually speaking, man is eager, aggressive, impatient, jealous, protective, and in his sexual desire he experiences a sense of intense urgency.

Woman is more reserved, expectant, offering. She, like man, is also jealous and protective, but, in contrast to him, she is almost unpredictably hot or cold.

Because the man is strong and aggressive, he is by nature the leader, the head of the family. Unfortunately, this is not always the case. There is a not-so-funny story about the henpecked husband who was asked whether he was a man or a mouse. He answered, "I must be a man; my wife is afraid of mice." The reversal of roles between a male and a female is a frequent cause of deep unhappiness in marriage. A woman needs a strong man on whom she can lean. A man, on the other hand, needs to know he is in command. His very manhood may depend on it.

Man and woman are both capable of jealousy. This is part of the exclusivity of love. It is also a corollary of protectivity. A man and woman in love have a deep feeling that they have found their lifelong mate, the personification of their temporal happiness. The very first instinct is to defend this mate, this happiness, against all comers. Hence, the jealousy reaction. Between mates, protectivity takes the forms of tenderness, mutual giving and support, concessions and forgiveness when necessary, and fierce loyalty in the face of external aggression.

There is a sense in which jealousy is good: the Bible speaks of a "jealous God." There is in love an absolute right to exclusivity that resembles in some human way God's exclusive right to worship. The very word "worship" is used in the ceremonial of marriage in the English rite: "With my body I thee worship." It properly renders the symbolic relationship between married love and the love of God. There are other words connecting marriage and religion: devotion, the giving of self to a worthwhile person; and most of all, ecstasy: the act of standing out, of experiencing something superior to the natural limits of the ego, of participating in the transcendental. The word "ecstasy" expresses the mysterious link between a human act and a reality actually perceived as surpassing by far the expected possibilities of the merely human.

The Male Moves from Attraction to Sex to Love

Another psychological difference that will appear again and again in courtship and marriage is the basic approach to sex in the male and the female. The male generally moves from attraction to sex to love, in that order. He sees something that stimulates him—a lovely woman or a picture of a girl in a bikini. This instantly stimulates some degree of sexual desire. There are considerable variations in the intensity of the reaction, depending upon a man's capacity for sexual control, his mood at the moment or his habitual pattern of behavior. But generally speaking, when a man is emotionally aroused, it is through his sexual instinct.

The Female Moves from Attraction to Love to Sex

A woman's approach is entirely different: she grows into sex only after experiencing love. Attraction to a particular male seldom has an immediate sexual basis. A woman generally moves from attraction, to love, to sex. Only after she has been wooed and courted and convinced that she is loved and will be well protected does she surrender to the force of mature sexual desire.

The major motive of the male's sexual instinct is the urgent need to discharge the semen that has been building up pressure from within. There is no corresponding pressure in the female. Once she is awakened to the realization that she is fully loved, she fully loves in return, and surrenders in complete openness and receptivity. Then only does she feel the urge to receive the male totally, to receive his body and his seed.

Insufficient understanding of these differences, by husband or wife, or both, may cause deep dissatisfaction and difficulty in a marriage. For a wife must understand the humanness of the male in his urgency and the husband must exercise great consideration for the wife's inability to respond as automatically as he might like.

The Differences Spark Mutual Attraction

The meaning of the marriage union will be better understood through a closer analysis of the differences and similarities found in the sexes. *The differences actually turn out to be the very reasons for mutual attraction, and the similarities are basically the causes of the seal of permanence.* Let us go back, then, to the male and female differences and to their common characteristics of jealousy and protectivity.

The male, as we have seen, follows a pattern. He is almost constant in his desire. He is eager, vital, wide-awake in his sexual interest and hunger. He is the pursuer, the hunter. He becomes restless the longer he must wait. Under the physiological impulse of his desire for discharge, he is always proposing in the expectation of an answer of consent.

There is a surge of power and a sense of personal worth in the young lady who is able to raise such a hullabaloo in the strong, silent, apparently self-sufficient male. A young girl's dream is not all coyness and perfumed gardens: there is also in it, if she be honest with herself, some desire for more potent and exciting approaches than romantic courting—and who is better suited to offer it than the ardent male? Even his eagerness and impatience are homage to the female, for no one, not even a dumb male, would be panting so loudly after a mere phantom. He is, then, panting after something real in you, after something of you, after you: the Helen of Troy that every woman is.

The Male Provides Security and Purpose

A male's attentions are constant, reliable, secure, single-minded, and purposeful. They convey a sense of solidity, a rocklike quality that underlies every variation of the chase and is so predictable and naïve that it may seem dull. And yet, this very solidity is attractive to the female whose senses are not yet fully awakened, whose imagination stretches out in cloudy dreams, whose thoughts are so often a floating mass of confused doubts and hopes. The male approach, firm and constant, appears as a possible foundation on which to build a life.

The Female Gives Comfort and Inspiration

As for the female, she is reserved, expectant, offering, and unpredictable.

She is reserved. All her education has generally been in the form of dire warnings and preparations for self-defense. This makes her shy at first, guarded and slightly negative. She is easily upset and often disappointed. She never expresses what she anticipates nor does she ask for what she wants, and yet she cringes when she fails to get it. She lures superficially while often refusing in depth. All this drives the logical, simple-minded, and direct male to distraction, frustration, and heightened desire: he takes it all very seriously and sees in it the very heart of mystery.

The female is expectant. There is timid eagerness beneath her apparent bashfulness. There is a silent hope that her defenses will be stormed—by the right man, at the right time. And this expectation of possible surrender is what makes the young lover persevere.

She is also offering him a sisterly, motherly concern about coziness and food and drink. She is the professional nest-maker, always gathering, fluffing, comforting. The young man comes to her straight from the raw competitive world where no one seems to pay the slightest attention to his simpler and more human needs, and here is this young female with her proposition of softness and ease. He may be revolted and return in haste to his Spartan past—or tumble head over heels into the downy feathers of life. Which of the two is better? There is a time for hardship and a time for feather beds—but too much of either one will spoil a man.

Then there is her unpredictability. She may say yes or no, or maybe—meaning yes. Or again, she may say yes or no, or maybe—meaning no. She keeps her man constantly on the run, constantly baffled, and if she is wise, will keep him so even after thirty years of marriage. She never gives him the slightest chance to catch his breath, to establish a dull routine in his relationship with her. There is always in her some new challenge, some unexpected turn, some amazing insight that may appear as signs either of genius or of levity—but the poor male is never quite certain which, and in order to live, he must give her the benefit of the doubt.

Perhaps these descriptions do not fit everyone: they are idealized sketches. They represent the reactions of an ideal type of spontaneous humanity of the kind that has the greatest chance for success and happiness. Such characteristics of male and female are powerful means of mutual attraction. They bring opposites together. They are nature's way of trying once more for the original couple, the new experiment in mating and living and reproducing life, so the chain is kept expanding in the direction of a limit appointed somewhere in the unpredictable future.

Man and woman grow so fond of each other that they can no longer live apart: they are joined in marriage, but never do they simply live happily forever after. That is the ending of all fairy tales, but the beginning of real life.

The Similarities Cement the Union

Differences in the psychological make-up have brought the sexes together. Now they will be held together by their similarities: the good jealousy of exclusive love and protecting tenderness. Within their own world, they will develop a constant exchange of thoughts and desires and deeds of love, amounting to the total and tender gift of each one to the other and of both to their children, in perfect conformity with the trinitarian life of God. And so, what had begun as a happy chase through the forests of natural desire turns into an adventure in eternity.

It Is Not Good for Man to Be Alone

What is it to be a man, and what is it to be a woman? Man is a rock that stands firm; woman, a wave that comes and goes, smoothing his asperities, polishing his surface, bringing to light his natural inner patterns and perfections.

A rock left alone will remain harsh and rough, ill-adapted to the natural forms that surround it. A man left alone will almost unavoidably develop some of the unpleasant traits of bachelorhood, aggressive moodiness, annoying idiosyncrasies, inveterate habits developed almost to the level of sacred rites. The same is true of woman alone—of the sea left to churn upon itself.

However, while celibacy and virginity may well be viewed as imperfections in the order of nature, they can and often do represent a very high level of moral and spiritual perfection. In old-fashioned ecclesiastic writings, they were presented as being absolutely of the highest order, a level beyond the reach of the married, who were to be content with second-rate spiritual citizenship. Contemporary theologians have now become more realistic in that they situate perfection, not in relation to any given state of life, but as a matter of personal sanctity in any state whatsoever. There is then a very definite possibility of moral and spiritual perfection for both the celibate and the married. Even in the states of celibacy and virginity, there is need for a clear and positive recognition of the opposite sex, for a smoothing of the rock and for a settling of the sea on some sound emotional basis. This is procured not only through charismatic grace but also through properly organized human relations implying tenderness, respect, and mutual support among the ordained and the consecrated virgins.

Man in his normal state is a rock, stable, unflinching, constantly oriented toward the same goal. A manly man knows where he is going, and that is where he goes. He will have a tendency to press against obstacles, to crush lesser rocks that stand in his way. He may be too sure of himself, rising high over the sands of the beach, lifting an arrogant peak to the sky. He may become dry and infertile in his pride. His ambition may crush his sensitivity and destroy his power to love.

That is why he needs woman, the wave, nourisher, giver of life. She will cover the stark power of his strength with a changing, shimmering veil of give-and-take. With the infinite variety of her comings and goings as she moves according to wind and moon, she will be both a promise and a dream. Like the sea, she may become indignant at his self-centered scorn, slap him into reality with a burst of spray, and then swish around him like receding waters as soon as harmony is reestablished.

She too has her faults. She may be good, bad, or torrid. No man will ever know when or why. Woman, indeed, is the sea—tropical and warm or polar and cold; ever changing, ever surprising both in her anger and serenity, forever bringing up treasures from the deep. Woman is a restless sea, and the sea is a restless woman. No wonder, then, that man falls in love with either one—or both! Whatever a woman's qualifications, she in turn, needs a man who will be the rock—always there to provide support, consolation, and strength.

Man and Woman Work Together

Now, to tumble down from poetical flight into more sober facts of life: man is leader, husband, father; woman is his equal as sustainer, wife, and mother. Man provides and woman administers; man begets and woman gives birth. A man works at a job; a woman's life is her job. In all this, there are some constant characteristics: man's actions are generally external, separate, a succession of distinct pursuits, of goals established and attained and reported further again to be attained anew. A woman's actions are internal and continuous, a slow maturation. A woman's job is never done: running a household, raising a family entails much more than a mere money-making job. On payday, a man's work is generally completed: he may work to help his wife and children, but his professional activity is over. He can forget about it until Monday morning, and relax. By contrast, a woman's job is endless because she is always looking after her family.

To conclude this short analysis of the psychological differences between man and woman, a final poetical flight may not be out of order:

> As unto the bow the cord is,
> So unto the man is woman;
> Though she bends him,
> She obeys him;
> Though she draws him,
> Yet she follows.
> Useless each without the other!
>
> —LONGFELLOW, *The Song of Hiawatha*

CHAPTER 12

TRUE LOVE AND ITS COUNTERFEITS

Love Has Many Levels . . . Friendship Is a Form of Love . . . Sensual Attraction Awakens Erotic Love . . . Neurotic Love Is a Disorder . . . An Unsound Father Image Can Distort Love . . . An Unsound Mother Image May Be Damaging . . . Neurotic Wounds Can Be Healed . . . Beware of Sadomasochistic Symptoms . . . Possessive Love Crushes Human Dignity . . . The Need for Reassurance Is Universal . . . Eliminate the Obstacles to Love . . . And Love Will Make You Free

---

Once a good degree of self-acceptance has been achieved, you have become mature enough to understand and accept another person. But even when the other is understood and accepted, no static or final stage of human relations has been attained, for there is no complete stability in emotional life.

Five years after their wedding day, a young couple came to visit the priest who had married them. The marriage was in serious trouble and they were planning to separate. They were once happy and well balanced; the first year of their marriage was a joyfully extended honeymoon. They seemed to expect everything to remain eternally happy, but gradually their dreams began to fade.

They had staked their future on feelings of romantic love, and tried to perpetuate these feelings. But feelings change, and so do attitudes. They had agreed to postpone children for a few years, and never seemed to settle down to the idea of a family.

They wanted a beautiful home, and they went deeply into debt to make the dream a reality. While all this effort was expended to surround themselves with comfort and stability, they continued to live two separate lives. She bowled and he golfed; their lives were so filled with outside interests and friendships that they hardly noticed what was happening to them. One day, in the midst of an argument over something petty, they both realized that they were almost strangers. They had not really grown together; they had never really communicated. This sorry fact was bad enough, but they had stubbornly come to the conclusion that the marriage was over. There was nothing that could be done for them; both had lost the desire to be married. One wonders if their earlier romance could truly be called love at all.

Communication between individuals either improves or deteriorates. Many marriages are broken off after a period of cooling. They may fluctuate without ever reaching a point of equilibrium, only to dissolve at a later time. Then of course there are many unions that keep rising to the summit of love, resulting in a warm and enriching friendship. In order to succeed, any love relationship requires a combination of elements: grace, wisdom, effort, and luck.

Grace is always present, provided the relationship is in the order of virtue, that is, if it is humanly good, if its fruits are peace and happiness. Every such relationship is blessed, but its blessing must be sought and received and acknowledged with gratitude so that the love expressed in it may be lifted up to its true perfection.

Wisdom is needed in the choice of the partner and of the means of expression, the basic wisdom of common sense which is able to see people and things as they are, and to produce the greatest amount of good out of communication with them. Such wisdom is seldom fully developed in the young, for it is based in great part on experience. Nor is it an automatic consequence of age: there are many old fools.

Effort is an often overlooked condition of successful love. Even the most assured and stable and certain love relationship cannot survive on its first thrust: there is need of constant renewal of the motive power. Friends and married partners are not ballistic missiles that need only to be launched in order to arrive: they are much more like spaceships that require some form of self-propulsion. Both in friendship and in married love, there is a combination of spontaneity and effort. Without effort, spontaneity lacks a propulsion system; and without spontaneity, effort will result in a succession of duds.

Luck, also, is needed. So many times love is based on a chance encounter. Look around and see how many people would say: "If it had not been for this or that extraordinary circumstance, we would never have met." It is impossible to sort out the element of chance from that of grace. But even God's grace often works through a combination of chance and intuition.

Love Has Many Levels

There are many ways of loving another person. It is good at this point to consider the love of friendship. This love may be deep and enduring between members of the same sex or between man and woman. In the first case, the interpersonal exchange is naturally limited to the intellectual or, at most, the emotional level. It may take different forms, such as working together at a common task, enjoying together some form of recreation or vacation, or simply rejoicing in the social interchange of pleasant conversation. In the friendship between persons of opposite sex, true love is quite possible where there are actual recognition and full awareness of sexual appeal, even without natural indulgence. Satisfactions of a physical order between mutually attracted male and female may be morally forbidden by their station in life: yet, they are still free to love each other fully and chastely.

Friendship Is a Form of Love

There may be here too the closeness of true intellectual harmony, a real coincidence of ideas and ideals in the communication of joy. And this joy may be enhanced by an undercurrent of true awareness of the "difference," so that the whole relationship is enlivened, quickened by the silent understanding: "We both know that we are fully man and woman—and it is delightful!" This is the love of friendship; it does not seek immediate self-satisfaction. A true and noble balance may be maintained through prudence, determination, and prayer, without recourse to sexual license. The "difference" itself may be an occasion for the offering of love in other ways besides the physical. It may lead to the exchange of tenderness, mutual appreciation, recognition, greeting. There are a thousand manners, permissible in friendship, of rendering manly and reverent homage and affection to a woman who deserves it. She, in turn, has a storeful of gifts drawn from the harvest of womanliness that she can offer to a delighted man.

A female begins to develop these amiable arts almost as soon as she is born, and seldom does she fail to learn them well. But she must be told very soon about their power. It is so easy for her to go too far with a companion to whom friendship is all that can be given. Excessive generosity and affection may flow from an innocent heart—not from the perfection of innocence, but from the heart of an uninformed child who should have known better. And few men have the courage to resist.

Young men, too, should know how to control their attentions and their gifts so as not to arouse unjustified hope or excessive attachment in young hearts that may be looking for the fullness of love in marriage, when all that is being proposed is uninvolved friendship or perhaps nothing but a game. To flirt in such a way as to awaken in the other an interest that can never be satisfied is an extremely easy and fascinating game. But it is a cruel thing to conquer a heart only to dash it to the ground as soon as it has been won. Many young men and women discard their latest conquest as easily as yesterday's paper, without any concern for possible pain or the wound their flippancy may produce. That is why, in any friendship between a man and a woman, there has to be a clear-cut understanding as to the final outcome. Both have to be fully aware of what is offered and received: either friendship and nothing more, or friendship with a possibility of development into complete love. If one of the two is playing a game while the other is dead serious, there will be sorrow for the victim, a sorrow the likes of which an inexperienced heart cannot conceive. It often happens that the deceiver does not fully realize what he or she is doing and that the deceived will know only when it is too late how deeply she or he can be hurt.

Sensual Attraction Awakens Erotic Love

When close personal harmony has been achieved between a man and a woman, there is a natural drifting toward deeper and more personal expressions of affection. The familiar friend may take on a surprisingly different aspect, passing suddenly from an object of emotional love to an object of sensual desire. Touching lips ceases to be child's play. Something stirs deeply, warmly, at every physical contact. There arises a growing hunger for much more, for clasping and holding, for everything poetry has described as breathing or drinking the beloved. The state of *erotic love* is born.

What is needed is both reassurance and warning: reassurance that the arousal of powerful sensual attraction has nothing sinful in itself. It is but one phase of normal development. The fact that these desires direct themselves toward a sexual expression that is specifically male in man, and specifically female in woman, has nothing disgusting in it; on the contrary, it is the beautiful awakening of a natural hunger that has been designed by God to find its fulfillment in the total union of love. But there is still need of a warning: nature may take over with such power and speed as to run faster than an imperfectly formed intelligence and will. Many a young fool has rushed headlong into trouble because of instinct let loose before practical wisdom had been sufficiently developed. Practical wisdom may be described as the intelligence to know what is right and the will to do it. The storm of erotic desire may seem irresistible. It is irresistible only to the unwise and unprepared.

Neurotic Love Is a Disorder

Your personal make-up may quite possibly have a certain amount of emotional scar tissue from wounds suffered in your earlier years. These wounds should be healed or at least well on the way toward healing before marriage; otherwise you run the very serious risk of building your life on a foundation of neurotic love, a poor substitute for the real thing.

Much has been made of the Freudian theories concerning the sexual interpretation of almost every psychic disorder. It seems now to be generally admitted that while Sigmund Freud made a valuable contribution to the understanding of human nature by emphasizing the widespread effects of repressed sexuality, he went too far in his attempt to explain every disorder as being sexual in origin. There are, however, a number of disorders that do have that particular origin, and become manifest as neurotic love. The most frequent cases seem to be those related to the father image or mother image.

An Unsound Father Image Can Distort Love

The father image affecting the female may lead to two different distortions of love: an exaggerated attachment to the father may induce a young girl to seek as a husband a man who resembles him closely. This may lead to several complications: if the husband does not, in fact, conform to the predetermined model, he will constantly be blamed for a failure he cannot possibly understand. On the other hand, if he does conform, the young woman cannot escape sentiments of guilt, since sexual relations with such a man will have an overtone of incest.

A young girl married a man who she said was "just like my father." She had always responded warmly and affectionately during courtship, but the attempted sexual contacts he made on the honeymoon had a finality about them. She could not accept her husband in the act of love, nor did she ever accept him, because she had fallen in love with her own father in falling in love with him. She carried the natural inhibition toward incest right to her marriage bed. It may sound "far out," but it happens.

Conversely, severe antagonism between father and daughter prior to marriage can also leave a scar. All hatred is personally damaging. For instance, the girl may try to find a husband who is the exact opposite of her father or, worse, she may tend to reject all males. This may be at the origin of homosexual tendencies.

The father image may also affect a son. An overwhelming and authoritarian father may depress a son's personality to the point of making him unable to stand on his own feet at an age when a young man should. Since he never had been free to make his own decisions, the matter of his own marriage may also be left to his father's will, with possible disaster as a result of this surrender. On the other hand, too fond an attachment to the father may result in a similar inability. An inadequate or unsuccessful father may also breed insecurity into his children.

An Unsound Mother Image May Be Damaging

The mother image may affect a son as much as the father image affects a daughter: exaggerated attachment to the mother will induce a son to look for a wife who is another mother to him. This will inevitably lead to the similar effects of possible sexual trouble and guilt. Total alienation between mother and son will lead to the possible rejection of all females, and the seeking of only male companions.

Likewise, an oversuccessful and overbearing mother may annihilate a daughter's personality and lessen her chances of happy marriage. Excessive ties with the mother will prevent a daughter from going out on her own. And the bad example of a mother whose marriage failed may dissuade a daughter from even trying.

There is also possible damaging influence inflicted by both parents. Bickering, and self-centeredness are signs of weak love that expose the children to a constantly negative and depressing image of married life.

Neurotic Wounds Can Be Healed

None of these influences, however, are so strong as to be insurmountable. To be forewarned is to be forearmed. If you suffer personally from any such detrimental experience (the above list is far from exhaustive), you should know that none of the impressions they left on you are ineradicable. As soon as you spot the cause, healing is at hand. You must, however, set your mind to patient endurance of your personal difficulty as you grow out of it. You must put on the will to bear discomfort. Maturity consists in taking a cool look at yourself and your background and building on your stable qualities while working at the elimination of neurotic wounds.

An ambitious couple raised an only son like a hothouse plant, with grand visions of his earthly success. Both parents worked, the father holding two jobs, to send him to the finest college available. They directed his every movement into the lines they had prepared for him. In college he constantly found himself living beyond his social level and going out with wealthy people to places he could not afford. He was always being pressed into situations he found uncomfortable. By the end of college, he expressed open hatred for his parents. "They never loved me," he would say; "they used me to satisfy their own phony dreams."

This bitterness lingered for a while, but the young man eventually came to his senses. He saw that he was destroying himself and punishing his parents for something they had done without malice, in the false belief they were helping him. Gradually, he managed to divest himself of bitterness. He struck out independently from his parents. He deliberately tried to get rid of his hostilities by concentration on the good qualities in his parents. Eventually, he was able to love them for all they had tried to do, for all they had thought they were doing, but he vowed never to make his own children conform to preconceived plans. He used his experience to advantage, by turning hatred into love. It took time, but time does heal all wounds. The mature person can draw good fruit from unhappy beginnings. Only a fool gives up hope.

Total healing is always possible through a careful personal analysis of the circumstances, and the understanding of the reasons for your neurotic desires, fears, or antagonisms. Healing will be greatly assisted through objective appraisal, wise counseling, and a fresh start, once the bugaboos of the past have been rooted out. If you still feel you have difficulties you cannot solve on your own, it is time to look for professional help. Do not be afraid of asking for it from qualified clergyman, psychologist, or marriage counselor. Outside help, combined with your own calm determination, plus a faithful reliance on God's assistance, can overcome many a neurotic obstacle to love.

Beware of Sadomasochistic Symptoms

Besides these relatively frequent forms of emotional damage, there are others that should be mentioned for the sake of completeness: for instance, sadomasochism. The name comes from two historical personages of dubious fame, the French Marquis de Sade whose jaded sexual taste could be satisfied only by inflicting cruelty on his female partners; and the Austrian Baron von Sacher-Masoch, who could achieve sexual pleasure only by debasing himself and suffering indignities at the hands of his mistress. The two distortions are contradictory, since the one is actively cruel and the other passively enduring, yet they are closely related, and may result in the unhealthy union of two partners of opposing type.

A young couple approached their priest to begin preparations for their wedding. He was a milkman and she was a secretary. He was quiet, self-conscious, and very passive. He usually came to the rectory with a faint odor of alcohol on his breath, but he behaved very well. He gave only one-syllable answers to all questions. She was pleasantly happy and did most of the talking. There was nothing particularly unusual about them. Both sets of parents approved of the marriage, which took place in church and was followed by the usual social festivities. Three weeks later, the girl called the priest. She cried hysterically: "He is mad; he is an alcoholic. He beat me; he abused me." She had been deceived and betrayed. After she had calmed down, the facts were unraveled. It was learned for the first time that the boy had had an extensive psychiatric history that he and his parents had concealed. He was a drinker, and he relied heavily on sedatives for his nerves. Incredible as it may seem, she had overlooked all the signs of his emotional disturbance before the marriage. During their honeymoon, her quiet lover turned into a beast. The first night, he bent her arm behind her back until she felt severe pain. "Now I've got you right where I want you and you're never going to get away!" Beatings and ridicule had been his way of showing affection, and he gave no sign of letting up. She left him, and in time the marriage was annulled. It was proved that the boy lacked the capacity to enter into and sustain a marriage union. He was mentally sick.

A counselor must warn prospective brides against the sadistic he-man whose tendency is to push his girl around. He is generally afraid of impotency and is trying to prove his maleness. He must also warn the prospective husband against the tigress who seeks pleasure by punishing her lover, which may be a similar form of compensation. Likewise, the masochistic groveling of man before woman, or of woman before man, is a self-punishment imposed as a confirmation of personal inadequacy. Here again we have a lack of self-love and self-acceptance.

Possessive Love Crushes Human Dignity

Possessive love consists essentially in treating the partner, not as a person, but as a thing. In a possessive love relationship, man or wife clings to the other with the desperate grasp of insecurity. The only proof they have of their sexual success is the actual holding of their beloved as an exclusive belonging, as an object. What is lacking here is respect for the dignity of the other.

Every man or woman has a right to a certain amount of independence and freedom. In fact, the only restriction to this freedom is their promise of mutual faithfulness: they have vowed not to seek venereal satisfaction outside marriage. This leaves to both partners considerable areas of liberty, particularly in the most personal domain, and most of all in that innermost stronghold where every human being must be alone with his God. There should always be a minimum of prying and spying, of suspicion and investigation. There should be a minimum of accounting for time and money. If not reduced to a very low level of intensity, any kind of control frequently leads the "possessed" party to do the very things he or she is suspected of doing, but was quite innocent of at the time suspicion arose. "If I have the name, I'll play the game."

A beautiful marriage broken by jealousy is a heartbreaking sight. A lovely young bride who came for advice explained that she had been forced by her husband to report in detail everything she did during the day. She had even been compelled to get a job at the place where he worked, so that he could watch her at all times. His fears were born of mistrust, and his mistrust crushed her feelings of love. Without love, she became obsessed with her unhappiness, and she fell in love with the first man she had a chance to meet alone. The exhilaration of freedom attracted her as much as the new love. The other man was just a normal male, but in comparing him to her husband, she thought he was a saint.

The Need for Reassurance Is Universal

Even in a true and deep marriage there is need at times of certain proofs of affection. This need is quite normal even though on the surface it may seem possessive. It may also be misunderstood because it takes different forms of expression in man and woman.

A woman needs constantly to be told that she is loved. The typical male reaction will be: "Now, listen, honey! I've told you a hundred times that I love you. And I meant it. Don't you believe me? Do I have to repeat it over and over again?" Well, sir, you may as well face the truth: you certainly do! A woman simply needs to be reassured, but so does a man.

A man needs constantly to feel that he is sexually desired. Even if he knows perfectly well that he is loved, he will crave those subtle flashes of erotic understanding that a wife may grant so sparingly. Her reaction will be: "Do I have to do those silly things?" Yes, lady! You do! In the evening, try making up your face and wearing your jewelry, just for him; or putting on that utterly ridiculous and flimsy "thing" he gave you for your birthday.

These two forms of reassurance, the desire of a woman to be told she is loved and that of a man to see and feel his success as a desirable male, are not neurotic signs of possessive love, but the natural result of differences in the male and female psychologies.

Eliminate the Obstacles to Love

As we have seen, the power to love another may be affected adversely by temporary circumstances of life that bring about neurotic attitudes. What we need to do now is to see how this power can be disengaged from the many obstacles that impede its growth. The power to love grows like a tree. If vines and parasites are not eliminated in time, the young tree will be unable to grow straight. It will be crooked and weak, and its crown will never break out of the underbrush to seek the open sky. The clearing away of entangling vines should consist in a systematic elimination of the irrational, the neurotic, and the overly sensual elements that seem to grow naturally with love.

The false dreams of life

The irrational desires of men and women are those unreal, foolishly ambitious castles in Spain, dreams of star marriages, of heiresses and supermen. Take at least one good look at who you are, throwing out all artificial glamour and keeping but the substance. At first, this may be discouraging, for you discover that you may not be superiorly intelligent, handsome, rich, or sexy. But if you look deep enough into yourselves, the view is much more reassuring. Because you do not need the conventional signs of worldly glamour and success when you have the substantial signs of true value: uniqueness, honesty, faith, hope and love. It is when your power to love another has been unburdened by the conventional notions of success that it really becomes strong, for only then can it be real. You have something more to offer than an artificial dream: you have the reality of your immortal self and an infinite capacity for love.

Neurotic self-centeredness

In men and women, the neurotic element is another form of unreality. It consists in taking accidentals for the constitutive elements of your life; making mountains out of molehills. The best remedy, aside from counseling, is a declaration of independence of self. Yes, I may have had a painful childhood; yes, my mother was overbearingly possessive; yes, I got a rotten deal—in the past. But the future is mine, all mine, if I can take it in its full novelty, if I can make for it a new and glamorous dress out of my personal will instead of clothing it with the tatters of a depressing past. Even personal dispositions induced by earlier neuroses may be tackled and rendered harmless.

Overly sensual attitudes

The overly sensual attitudes of men and women may have produced exaggerated and obsessive concern for the erotic as such; as if it were possible to fulfill human desires perfectly, with nothing more than sexual gratification. The remedy here is not a negative concentration on the elimination of erotic desire, but a positive concentration on the other aspects of love, the spiritual, personal, and emotional, so that the erotic, instead of being lost, returns to its proper place within the general context as soon as the right partner is found. Concentration on the erotic alone will prevent the flowering of true love, and at the same time make it impossible to practice the very thing that is being sought. But the practice of spiritual, personal, and emotional love will eventually allow the full satisfaction of erotic desires.

And Love Will Make You Free

Grace flows only when the obstacles to grace have been removed. That is to say, God's life, which is Love Itself, flourishes only when it is not restricted by egoism, selfishness, and sin. God's Love is always offered to you, but you are not always able to receive it. As long as you are distorted and obsessed with past wounds or excessive greed, there is little freedom left for love.

Love will make you free; but first you must make yourself free for love.

Inevitably, some faults will remain—in yourself and others. But this is no reason to give up fighting those imperfections that can be overcome with persevering effort: selfishness, pettiness, jealousy, anger, possessive greed. Perhaps you were not responsible for their origin; but you certainly can check their growth, and eventually eliminate them. What is left, then, is virtue: the power of being properly, freely, responsibly a man or a woman; the power to love yourself and others, with objectivity and generosity. And what too few people realize is that such virtue and such power are the conditions of survival not only for our own selves, for our own private family lives, but also for mankind as a whole.

CHAPTER 13

WHO WILL BE THE RIGHT PARTNER FOR YOU?

To Love Is to Choose Freely . . . Mature Love Requires Mature Judgment . . . Emotional Involvement Is Not the Same as True Love . . . It Is Important to Keep the Right Kind of Company . . . The Mind and Body Are Designed for Happiness . . . Human Nature Is Informed with the Presence of God . . . Patience Is a Necessary Virtue . . . Genuine Love Involves the Cross

In earlier days, and at present still in several countries of the Middle East and Far East, marriage was seen as being more important for the family group than for individuals. The social position, the financial future, the disposition of the clan's real estate had to be considered over and above any personal inclination. The choice of a bride belonged, not to the young man himself, but to the family matchmaker. There are a number of advantages to this system, but also some serious drawbacks. It contributes greatly to social stability—supposing such stability to be a good—and provides a measure of safeguard against any rash and imprudent selection of a life partner. In the majority of cases, the parents or elders are in a position to judge the qualities of a potential bride much more objectively and dispassionately than could the male candidate for marriage.

On the other hand, in preplanned marriages of this kind, no attention is given to love as a romantic prerequisite to the union. This may sometimes be detrimental to the perfection and fullness of consent that are absolutely necessary. A young man in such a society would not dream of marrying against his parents' will. He would patiently await the bride to be chosen for him. Quite often, he would not see her face before the wedding day. Generally speaking, there is a good chance that a wise choice will have been made and that love will be able to grow. But there is always the risk of incompatibility, in which case it seems that the husband would have a claim against the validity of the marriage, based on insufficient consent. There is also the risk of the matchmaker being influenced by considerations of material wealth or social convenience rather than by the young people's actual welfare.

To Love Is to Choose Freely

In our society, much more importance is given to the freedom of the individual—at no inconsiderable risk to family and social welfare. Boy and girl find each other without parental help. They still hope to obtain their elders' approval, but it seems to become less and less important. Since it is they who are to spend their lives together, the choice undoubtedly belongs to them. Legally, as long as they are of age—and this varies from state to state —they may dispense completely with their parents' permission.

Freedom is an ideal that can be totally successful only under perfect circumstances, that is, when both parties exercise excellent judgment and choose each other rationally. But even with some danger from possible immaturity, hasty choice or blinding passion, a free choice of marriage partner is still the relatively better system. This remains true as long as it is applied with full awareness of the inherent risks, and when these risks are offset by careful preparation and the acquiring of at least a reasonable amount of wisdom and foresight.

Mature Love Requires Mature Judgment

Without such minimal precautions, a marriage may fail. Young people may fall in love and be overwhelmed with the desire to marry as soon as possible, and they contract a permanent bond only to discover that their partner is someone entirely different from what they had imagined. Weaknesses, faults, and defects all come to the surface after a few days of common life. A true picture of the partner may be seen only after the flames of romantic love have faded. And this picture may turn out to be deadly blank.

There are very good reasons, then, for you to keep close to mature people and to discuss your plans with them. In such matters as these, parents are the natural counselors. Often they provide wise and useful advice, but sometimes they do not. Before rejecting their opinion, however, you should be careful never to underestimate their genuine concern for your happiness, and their ability to discern the character of your proposed mate.

Believe it or not, your own parents, in their day and perhaps right now, knew and still know how to practice those ideals of youthful creativity that keep you going. They may have escaped total fossilizing: the older hearts may still be thumping at the right place and speed, with a most tender interest in your welfare. Some parents, however, do indulge in overguidance, and are surprised when their advice is rejected. Others fall into what may seem to be cold indifference: they are, in fact, lost, baffled, stumped. And rather than be rejected together with their advice, they choose to offer none, to remain cool and seemingly aloof. Give them a chance: you may be surprised at the response you will get.

Young lovers tend to seek an ideal partner, and this is fine. It is a natural expression of the search for the absolute, which is man's greatest glory. But when they find someone who appeals to them, unconsciously they project their ideal on the beloved, and in their wishful thinking create in the other a personification of their highest desire. "Create" is the proper word: they make something out of nothing; they pull an image out of the thin air of their dreams, and imagine it has come true in the other.

Emotional Involvement Is Not the Same as True Love

Boy meets girl and they fall in love. Or does he? Or does she? Is this love? There may be a deep and moving emotional turmoil brought about by the presence of the chosen one, a sense of uniqueness, exclusivity, a feeling of never-before and never-again, a total blindness to everyone and everything else. And if marriage follows, it may be catastrophic. Why? Because emotional involvement is not yet true love. Romantic love in itself is not a sufficient condition for a happy marriage. Romantic love is a total emotional intoxication of a person whereby sexual desire is unconsciously elevated to the noblest level, disguising itself as pure and eternal love. Jacques Maritain has stated this very well:

> "Now, since sexual attraction and satisfaction remain the essential aim, it must be said that romantic love—*l'amour passion*—being but a transcendent human expression of the strongest animal instinct, is, by nature: first, deprived of permanence and liable to fade away; second, unfaithful and liable to shift from one object to another; and third, intrinsically torn between the love for another, which has awakened, and its own basically egoist nature.
>
> "Consequently, to found marriage on romantic love, and to think that marriage must be the perfect fulfillment of romantic love, is, as I submitted, a great illusion." [1]

Julie Christie won an Academy Award for her role in *Darling*, the story of a woman whose career and public image improved throughout her life, while her personal life deteriorated. At the conclusion of the picture she is an internationally known cover girl, the wife of a wealthy Italian aristocrat, while her heart is splitting with pain and misery suffered because of her failure at love. She was originally married to a simple man who loved her, but her head was turned by a sophisticated radio announcer. We are not told the story of how she fell in love with her first husband, but it would not be unrealistic to presume she had genuine romantic feelings for him at one time. This is the very point: romantic feelings do not spell out true love. The sensation of being engulfed in an overpowering attraction is not in itself love. By their fruits you will know them. True love prevails over sorrow and reversal, over sickness and human failure. Only the strong and noble can accept the fact that true love endures all things.

[1] *Reflections on America*, p. 80.

It Is Important to Keep the Right Kind of Company

Love may come as a blinding storm, a burst of flames, a fast furious brushfire that needs to be contained, directed, and calmed down, at least enough to let reason and common sense play their part. The danger is that it can very easily run out of control. Your inexperience is perhaps your greatest enemy: it is so easy to take emotion for love. Since the beginning of an emotional relationship is unpredictable, prudence demands that you keep company only with the right kind of person. Try never to get too closely involved with anyone who would be wrong for you. There are certain major headings under which compatibility can be reviewed: personality, habits, social level, character, age, religion, and marital status.

Personality: Compatibility is deeper than attraction

The movie star, the football hero, the queen of the prom, "Gorgeous" Charlie may have some very attractive features—attractive enough to start a young heart spinning. But how good are they as persons, how successful would they be as life partners, as living and loving human beings? Oddly enough, the qualities most desirable at the stage of courting may be the least valuable in the long run of marriage. A boy or girl may be an attractive social prize, but a deadly, self-centered, cold, and insufferable bore at home. Learn to see through people before getting too closely attached to them. See who they are, how they act under stress and challenge, how they face the realities of life. A particular smile, a manner of dancing, a fine build may set aflame the dormant fires of youth. Beware! It can happen to you! At the very first flicker of interest, take one long, cool, solid look at the reality that underlies the charm, and you will not get burned or be forced to live a whole life of regret.

There is no such thing as fatal love. There is no true love at first sight. There may be great attraction at first sight, but love is founded on much more than that. The first emotional shock may be the prelude to deeper and deeper love. It may also be completely deceiving. Yet there is a time—very short, perhaps, but long enough—in which that nasty, cold, and calculating part of you, your reason and conscience, will tell you to give the whole thing some serious thought before allowing yourself to let go and to get romantically, hopelessly or hopefully, involved.

Physical beauty brings about a danger of a different kind. A very handsome boy or an extremely beautiful girl may be so full of themselves, so completely dependent upon adulation and easy success as to become insufferable. By all means, try for the handsomest boy and the most beautiful girl you are able to persuade to live with you: beauty is a gift and a joy, and it does not always damage and corrupt. But be extremely careful. The worst possible combination is that of a very jealous husband and a beautiful wife. Unless the jealousy can be overcome, they would have done better not to marry.

There may also be a serious danger in overestimating the importance and significance of physical beauty—of taking it for a sure sign of perfection on other levels.

> "Man has trouble distinguishing precisely between physical and moral values. The difficulty comes mostly from the fact that in the case of well-balanced personalities, the exterior is a reflection of the inner life. And so a man would be tempted to see in the physical beauty of a woman the expression of a deeper human value." [2]

The greatest of all prizes is unspoiled beauty—beauty combined with innocence—and it should be sought as the pearl of great worth.

Habits: Defects are revealed in off-guard behavior

There are so many bad habits, more or less deeply ingrained in every one of us. In some people, they may become incurable and deadly: a propensity to vice, crime, cruelty, self-centeredness, pride, alcoholism, drugs. Other bad habits are more lenient and curable: laziness, vanity, anxiety, excessive ambition, arrogance. They appear on the surface only in unguarded moments—and it is a characteristic of social meetings that people are closely

[2] Louis J. M. Sahuc, *Homme et femme* (Bloud et Gay, Paris, 1960), p. 219.

guarded, formal, artificial, conformed to a preplanned image of themselves that may be very far from true. And so, before allowing any emotional storm to take control away from reason, seek some occasion when the other party will no longer be playing a role, when natural, instinctive reactions will betray underlying faults or reveal hidden virtues. This is best done in situations that eliminate the artificial elements of a social gathering and come closest to real life. It may be most instructive, for instance, to observe a boy or a girl in their own family surroundings. In these natural settings, people tend to return to their natural selves. If, in these real-life experiences, you discover a pattern of behavior that is seriously objectionable, remember that you may have to live with it for the rest of your life.

Social level: The husband is the head of the house

A prince may marry a shepherdess, and live happily ever after, but a shepherd would never manage to make a princess happy. This is due to the different natural parts that are played by man and wife. The man is the head of the house. The moral tone of a home may be set by the wife, but very often the cultural and social level is naturally determined by the husband. With sufficient talent and inner strength, he may be fully justified in taking for a wife a pretty, good, unspoiled, and simple girl who is his educational or social inferior. There is every chance that he will be able to add to her original virtues the social graces and refinements that will transform her into his fair lady. And the joy of doing so may be very great.

By contrast, a highly educated girl will hardly ever do well in choosing a husband below her level, for he will always resent her superiority openly or hiddenly—which may be worse and lead to much more cruel treatment. Perhaps he will even insist on maintaining his home in accordance with his own taste, merely as a challenge to refinement and in order to prove that he is perfectly free and as good as anybody else. There is not much chance for improvement. Even if he tries to better himself, there may be endless occasions of embarrassment—for both if he is sensitive, for his wife alone if he is not. Whenever too many of the conventional status lines are crossed in a marriage, there is a corresponding multiplication in the number of possible conflicts. The married state is so delicate a matter, its balance must be so finely maintained, and there are, in the state itself, so many natural hurdles, that only a fool would rush into it with unnecessary burdens, particularly those brought about by an excessive difference in social and educational levels. Of course, there are exceptions to every rule, but the experience of mankind generally points to trouble in this area.

Financial status: The man should be the main provider

The same general rule seems to apply to financial disparity. If the groom is rich and the bride poor, all may go extremely well. If, however, the bride is rich and the groom poor, trouble may be brewing. The bride may believe all her life that she was married for her money. The natural self-confidence and authority of the husband are upset from the start. He may either loaf in the contentment of financial ease or work too hard in order to produce on his own as much as his wife had given him. In both cases, he is risking the loss of his manhood: in the former, by surrendering it; in the latter, by driving himself to an early death. The rich often have ingrained habits that would naturally tend to destroy marital harmony. For instance, a young girl brought up in a state of affluence may expect to be maintained in her customary style. This style may be extravagant to the point of being sinful, but habits are hard to break. The young husband, even with an adequate income, may be driven to distraction in his attempt to pay for his wife's expensive tastes. An imbalance such as this could cause serious conflicts.

Character differences: Harmony requires compromise

Character and cultural differences require some reasonable compromises and adjustments. The field is extremely broad: it encompasses all the disparities in interests and development. If one partner is an outdoor fan, a sporting type, and the other a hothouse flower, they may have to limit their personal encounters to meetings in the draft of the conservatory door! If one is an avid reader and the other is concerned only with physical performance, they will never fight over the book section of the Sunday paper, but neither will they get together on much. If one is a fastidious dresser and the other will wear nothing but shirttails over jeans, there may be cause for endless conflict. If one smokes and the other loathes the smell of stale tobacco, battles may occur and windows may be slammed open and closed all day long. If one loves the refinements of major art and culture and the other is perfectly content to memorize batting averages, the batting average of the home may rise sharply in very little time.

Most of these differences may be smoothed out—but all of them require some positive and patient action on both sides. Generally speaking, when the differences in taste and interest are extreme, the consequences may be disastrous. The reason is that people seldom change. One of the most frustrating activities within marriage is the constant effort of one spouse to overcome the natural inertia of the other, to change the beloved into something else. Forcing someone to change has been the cause of many broken homes. Quite often, it is a misplaced apostolic zeal: an attempt to remake the mate according to an image that is believed to be right, but may be no improvement at all. There is immaturity here because mature love consists in loving the other as the person he or she is, and precisely because he or she is that very person, and not a dream.

Differences in character or temperament, when combined with deep and true love, may become an asset instead of a liability in that they may have a balancing effect on both personalities. The violent may be calmed by the meek, the lazy spurred by the active, the emotional controlled by the coolly objective, the creative brought down to earth by the practical, the adventurous led home by the tender.

It is important that your marriage partner share your interests and your social, cultural, and educational standards. But he or she does not have to be a duplicate of what you are. On the contrary, there is a definite need for a certain amount of personality difference. Such a disparity should result, not in tension which may be destructive and negative, but in tending, that is, in moving toward new directions inspired by the difference itself. Specifically male and female virtues, then, may become a strong element of mutual attraction: for a more active tending will produce a more powerful bond.

Age factor: Disparity may sometimes be good

The question of age is highly personal. There are happy marriages in which the wife is ten years older than her husband, others in which she is ten or even twenty years younger. No fast rule seems possible here. Physiologically, a man is perfectly able to beget healthy, normal children even at an advanced age. A woman, by contrast, must limit her birth-giving to her earlier years. There is, then, no natural objection to a man marrying a girl twenty or more years his junior. But there is definitely an emotional and psychological risk, due to the fact that life is seen in an entirely different light by a young girl and an older man. But once again, this is a matter of personal choice, and some such marriages are highly successful.

With early marriages becoming more and more frequent, the question of comparative age loses its relevance, but another important question arises: "How soon is right?" The answer is in the practical rather than the theoretical order: As soon as the partners are sufficiently mature and have enough financial means to support themselves. Maturity may be attained at eighteen, twenty, forty-five—or never. Financial security is generally attained as soon as the future husband can hold a steady job, which allows earlier marriage for a skilled or unskilled worker than for a man who expects to go through many years of college.

What about pregraduation marriages? Again, this is a matter of maturity and finances. If both know what they are doing and are really ready for marriage, and if they have sufficient funds in the form of grants, scholarships, or personal resources, there may be, in their particular case, little reason to wait. However, there is the problem of children: How will a college couple handle that one? The usual answer is: By postponing the birth of the first child. This involves a moral question that has been considered earlier. (See Chapter 5.)

Religion: Differences do matter

Differences of religion may bring about difficulties of a much deeper order. Any man or woman's true religion may be quite different from what appears on the surface. It is made of an extremely complex assemblage of hopes and fears, doubts and beliefs. Besides what is visible, that is, the formal allegiance to some established church and the more or less regular practice of its ritual requirements, there is in every man an invisible religion, in the depth of his heart and at the very core of his life. This inner religious sense may take the form of a void, an absence, a despair that the superficial onlooker will take for a lack of religion. In some cases it could be a more intense form of disbelief, a proselytizing atheism in the communist style, combined with a pie-on-earth philosophy. Whatever the appearance may be, it could also be a subtle atheism that conceals such high respect, such refined adoration for the Unknown God that it spurns the apparently gross and external forms of worship practiced by the established Churches. Again, this religious sense could appear to be an apparently orthodox practice and belief serving as a mask for a total vacuum of ignorance, superstition, and unconcern. The range is infinite. In many people we do find a deep, personal, involved adoration of God, complying with the rituals of community worship and private prayer, a sincere sorrowing at the wounds inflicted on Christ by those he came to save.

On what level is religious accord important? On that of Church membership, formal allegiance, external practice? Since we are interested in the internal reality, an accord on external signs alone will not be sufficient to ensure harmony in marriage. What counts is this: that a man and a woman have a deep sense of love, a deep hunger for truth and justice, a deep earnestness to find and follow the Living God in spirit and in truth. No matter what a man professes to believe or not to believe, if his heart and soul and love are in the right place, he is a hidden member of the Mystical Body of Christ, an heir to the promise, a child of light. This does not mean that it is perfectly sound to marry someone of a religion different from yours as long as you have an inner communion of faith: it means only that it is not always disastrous to do so. The safest road, of course, is to marry within your faith.

This choice of a partner of the same religious convictions eliminates the liability of disputes over the manner in which your faith will be communicated to your children. It also sets up a rapport on the deepest level of inner beliefs.

Marital status: Risking adultery is seriously wrong

Finally, it is, of course, gravely imprudent to initiate courtship with a married man or woman. Once emotional involvement occurs it is too late. Besides the automatic injustice and damage to any children of the first marriage, there is something intrinsically against order in the breaking up of a pact of human love. Dallying with an unhappily married man or woman is a veiled or preparatory form of adultery. Love, or so-called love, does not justify infidelity. In this matter, beginnings are surprisingly easy. Be on your guard, for in such a situation the unhappiness eventually outweighs the happiness by far, and there may be some wounds that even time will never heal.

And so we reach the end of our list. Much more could be said, and has been said by others, about the conditions of perfect married love. At present, however, within the context of this work, it may be sufficient to summarize the positive aspects of love after having covered its potential hazards.

The Mind and Body Are Designed for Happiness

When boy meets girl and both are eager, pure, and healthy, both desiring to establish a happy home in which love will be expressed in the form of children and joyful mutual support, there are many forces working toward harmony. On the simple material level of physical fitness, the human body is a marvelously self-regulated and self-healing mechanism. When treated reasonably well as regards food, exercise, rest, and fresh air, it develops into a properly balanced whole that procures satisfaction and a feeling of vigor and well-being, even under conditions of strenuous and sustained effort. In fact, effort is a condition of well-being, for an excessively easy life atrophies the vital faculties, kills alertness, perspicacity, and vivacity, turning men and women into slugs or even vegetables.

Besides the automatic mechanisms of physiological self-preservation, there are the instinctive reactions of self-defense and adaptation. In some respects, these powers are less developed in mankind than in the animal world. Perhaps this is because in man instinct is not the last line of defense, as it is in animals. We may be slower and less precise in our reactions, less assured in our footing, and less well developed in our methods of perception: but we can still succeed, because over and above instinct we have intelligence and love.

Intelligence is an immensely valuable tool of personal happiness and development. Its mode of action is twofold: deliberation and implementation. First, we must think out a problem, then bring about the most promising solution. There are, then, two possible failures: wrong thinking and ineffective action. That is why education and training are so important. But it must be education in line with wisdom and truth, and training in line with goodness.

Next to intelligence, there is love, an immense power for happiness and progress. If all situations in life are approached with enlightened and kindly consideration, if the sex partner in particular is seen and treated as a beloved person worthy of attention and care, if this force for happiness and progress is allowed full rein, life can then develop in peace and joy, as it always should.

Human Nature Is Informed with the Presence of God

The highest of man's chances for success has not been discussed. There is for the spiritual man and woman a very special outpouring of grace that comes from the sacramental character of their union. By the fact that the promise of common life has been made before Christ and his Church, the merits of Christ, infinite in both quantity and quality, are showered on the couple that is willing to obey the commandments and follow the counsels.

Each state in life has its own special grace. In the married life, grace may be felt as the sudden surge of courage and power in the most trying difficulties—or as that overflowing sense of happiness and joy when all goes well. Grace may be seen as the light shining beyond the drudgery of housework or behind the back-breaking or brain-racking effort in factory or office. It may be witnessed in the immediate and mysteriously soothing effect of man and wife coming together after a hard day or, again, in their total joy of sharing their moments of greatest intimacy. For as there is a virtue of sex, there is also a grace of sex, that is, the spiritual ability to bring the fullest power of love to the physical encounter.

These are some of the beneficent forces that work to support and sustain the married and to quicken their bond, so that there is no justification for starting out in a state of fear, no excuse for trembling at the threshhold of matrimony as if mortal dangers awaited you at every step. As long as reasonable precautions are taken and sufficient information is obtained, the proper response to life is a joyful and hopeful AMEN—and a headlong plunge into marriage. Any plunge into married life is daring and bold, but as long as lovers understand the true meaning of love before they leap, they will not be jumping into fire.

Patience Is a Necessary Virtue

One of the most difficult things to teach young people is how to be patient. It may also be the most crucial in terms of the future prospects for happiness. Particularly in the case of a young girl who feels that life is passing her by, impatience may be a dangerous enemy. She will become easily depressed about her single state, especially if most of her friends are already married. Yet, she must endure the agony.

There was a young lady in her late twenties who had been a maid-of-honor at three of her friends' weddings, and a bridesmaid at two more. She felt her heart sink when people asked the cruel question "Why aren't you married?" Year after year, she had hoped and prayed for someone to come into her life. She had seen her friends having children and had become desolate in her barrenness. Only one young man had professed love for her. He was handsome and could look forward to inheriting his father's business. But she disliked his general character: he was too fast for her. There was something about him she could not quite accept. Her parents and friends ridiculed her for passing him up, and she was blamed for causing her own misery.

At the age of twenty-nine, she met a successful young lawyer. He was a good man, not particularly good-looking, but kind and tender, and his faith was deep. She married him a year later, and they have been happy ever since. The good-looking boy she had turned down also married. Within three years he was divorced because his wife would not tolerate his repeated infidelities.

This parable of patience is based on real life. Decisions based on impatience often lead to heartache and long-suffering. Perhaps the surest way to ensure your unhappiness is settling for a man you *know* is wrong for you, with the hope that he will change later. You need to love and respect the person you marry, and you should do all in your power to preserve yourself from any union that is not built on this foundation. To do otherwise is to run an incalculable risk.

Genuine Love Involves the Cross

Many young people—and old people too—use the word "love" much too freely. In our country, marriage is based on mutual love: but its foundations are often lacking because they are misunderstood. When people speak of love, they generally mean romantic emotion, which may be good, but is only the beginning of love. They mistake the spark for the fire. Romantic love is an elegant disguise for sexual attraction and sensual passion, but true and enduring love is a properly human and spiritual development of the art of self-giving. One does not take a bride: one gives oneself to her and receives her.

Genuine human love transcends sex without being independent

from sex. It survives temporal or definitive privation of sexual satisfaction. It attains a level of purity that procures true freedom from self, to the point of investing in the beloved everything that one is and has. In true and complete love, each of the partners wills to live for the other's well-being, at any price, at any sacrifice. Genuine human love, therefore, is the opposite of self-centered pleasure-seeking. It frequently leads to the cross, to the burden of shouldering the other's pain and grief. The wise man will know that true and perfect love implies a progressive death to self. He that preserves his life shall lose it, but he that sacrifices his life to true love shall find his life restored and glorified a hundredfold, and quite possibly right here on earth. For life is linked, in a mysterious way, to sacrifice and death, and the perfection of love, to the perfection of self-forgetfulness.

There is still one danger left, one subtle temptation: to admire one's own sacrifice and bask in anticipation of its merits. This is no true sacrifice. It has no merit because it has already received its reward. True sacrificial love is totally unconscious and natural: it comes about with the spontaneity of falling rain, and suddenly there shines in it the sign of the promise, the many-hued rainbow of the Covenant with God. Learn to love well, and to forget your sacrifices, that your joy may be full.

CHAPTER 14

HOW FAR CAN YOUNG LOVERS GO?

There Are No Easy Answers . . . Sacrifice Is Necessarily Painful . . . Indulgence Involves Serious Risks . . . Sincerity Is Not Enough . . . All That Glitters Is Not Love . . . What Kind of Person Do You Want to Be? . . . There Are Five Steps to True Love . . . Each Human Act Is Morally Unique . . . Do Not Be Discouraged if You Are Baffled . . . Your Sex Life Has a Spiritual Dimension . . . All the Answers Must Be Your Own

---

There Are No Easy Answers

The deepest and most anguishing questions related to sex have no easy answers, perhaps no clear answers at all in the present state of physiological, philosophical, and theological knowledge. The same may be said of life, of which sex is but a particular aspect. No man ever lives in a state of complete certainty: there is always a domain open to personal research, personal decision, and the use of free will. Although we are still far from complete understanding of the man-woman relationship, and some of its aspects will always remain unknown and unpredictable, yet we are in a much better position at the present time than were those who established the traditional rules of sexual conduct: much more is known about it, and conclusions may be drawn from much broader and sounder premises.

The Second Vatican Council has reaffirmed the timeless truth that we are a pilgrim Church. As long as we are striving along the way, we must put up with a certain amount of confusion, of painful, groping incertitude. Even an enlightened conscience does not always guarantee a wise and prudent action, and the best of good faith may be a deceiving master, for we easily delude ourselves. While we try to do our best, we are still liable to make mistakes. What we must realize is that such mistakes bear no load of moral guilt, provided we have always tried to conform with the indications of good faith and good will.

And yet, even when we obey to the letter all the rules laid down by our conscience and our Church, and struggle to follow the counsels of the Gospel, there are times in life when we wonder whether we are doing the right thing. Do those rules and counsels apply to individual acts in their traditional literal and restricting sense? Or does their spirit demand a broader and more equitable application in those circumstances where no revealed principle is clearly involved, and the classical interpretation may have been founded on misinformation? How can we resolve a conflict between an enlightened conscience and the letter of an incomplete law regarding premarital chastity?

The positive moral laws of the Church, that is, the present disciplinary rules of conduct, reject as gravely sinful any venereal pleasure procured alone or with a partner outside marriage. The word "venereal" (derived from Venus, the goddess of love in Roman mythology) refers to the specific excitation and release of the nervous tension aroused in the sexual organs by word, thought, or deed.

Sacrifice Is Necessarily Painful

When a young man or woman has a strong vocation to marriage and finds that an early union is impossible, what will happen? If the letter of the law is obeyed, the natural sexual joys of early manhood and early womanhood are generally sacrificed, at least in their final phase. Young people then endure a painful state of frustration, stretched as they are between a strong instinctive, emotional, and rational drive, and the command to stop short before fulfillment is attained. They must say "No!" to life in its most powerful and attractive expression.

A pattern of rejection and excessive control of the physiological function may build up, so that the chaste young man and woman, preserving themselves out of idealism for the sake of some future and more perfect love, may end up by becoming strangers to life. They feel lost, abandoned, alone. They are "out of it," in some region of solitude. In extreme cases, when the possibility of marriage has been delayed too long, they may even have hampered their natural capacity to relax, to melt in the earthy flow of sexual love, even when at long last they have found their mate. They may feel, then, that the earlier discipline, practiced painfully and sorrowfully in all its harshness for the sake of a purer love, has turned out to be, not a help, but a hindrance in the fulfillment of their marriage.

One of those mordant lapel buttons reads: "Virginity Gives Cancer!" This is not entirely a meaningless joke. Of course virginity does not give cancer, but a total lack of sexual experience may produce considerable sorrow and some damage in the emotional order. The important points are to determine whether such effects are tolerable, and what, if anything, can be done ot alleviate them.

Religious authorities and authors of conservative manuals of moral theology frequently deny the depth of this sorrow and damage, or brush them under the rug. They have all too often tended to extinguish the fire of "concupiscence" without offering a clear definition of it—without offering a clear distinction between lustful abuse and the holy and healthy inclination of nature. In so doing, they have made the best young men and women suffer unnecessarily.

Those most eager to do well and most interested in the perfection of every form of life, including their undeniable sexuality, are confused by the abstract irreality of outdated commands and prohibitions. Because of this, at the awakening of sexual desire, there may have been a deep fear, a sense of guilt, a crushing of the most natural and wholesome instincts in the name of purity. Prudish attempts to root out the "evil of sex" may have caused a very real emotional diminishing and impoverishment.

Even if, at first, because of a distorted introduction to "the facts of life," your own sexual awakening has been clouded with feelings of guilt and distress, a more objective look should suffice to convince you that *this awakening is but the stirring of a form of life put into you by the goodness of God.* The sexual instinct is naturally good, while fear and falsely based rejection of sex are naturally evil and therefore unnatural.

Indulgence Involves Serious Risks

But unrestrained premarital sexual enjoyment is also unnatural because it gambles irresponsibly with the forces of life and love, and disregards the dignity of the natural gift, thus reducing one of the most noble and purposeful functions of the human body to something lower than what it should have been. It changes a potential offering of stable love into the impatient and irrational grasping of illegitimate pleasure—illegitimate, not because it is evil in itself, but because any anticipation of sexual love is a scattering and a waste of what should have been concentrated and treasured. Love must be administered with responsibility and care. The love act does not exist in a vacuum: it has a past, a present, and a future. Lovers should approach it in its total dimension; otherwise they have not performed a fully human act, but have merely indulged their animal natures.

Aside from any moral consideration, the main objection to the full consummation of sexual desire before marriage is not only its frequent flippancy and degrading ordinariness but also the extraordinary importance and unpredictability of its consequences, even when it has been used as a fully sincere and mutual expression of affection.

To use a comparison, if your car had no headlights, would you speed at night down a dark and unknown road? Would you drive the car at all if you could not see where you were going? Perhaps you would, but not if you had any sense, only if you enjoyed taking useless risks. Since you do not know the road ahead, its curves and hills, its ruts and holes and obstructions, you should be concerned about your own safety and that of the car. If the road happened to be running along a deep ravine, you would have an even more vivid realization of danger, and would be careful to use every possible precaution to avoid falling off to certain disaster.

Likewise, it takes forethought and sound judgment and great restraint to travel along the road of life without running foolish and dangerous risks. In matters of sex, there is an extraordinary amount of evidence to show that premarital involvements are unpredictable: they may lead to temporal happiness and eternal bliss, but very often they lead to unwanted pregnancy, short-lived affairs ending in deep psychological torture and even despair. You have to suffer this pain to understand its gravity.

Sincerity Is Not Enough

A young girl, attractive and about eight months pregnant, came to a priest for advice on whether or not to give up her child for adoption. She told her story tearfully and with great humility. She had been completing her third year at college and was keeping company with a young man. They had courted for nearly two years. She helped him study, and typed his assignments. During their more romantic encounters, they indulged in heavy petting, but the girl consistently refused intercourse, since she wanted to remain a virgin until marriage. On the night before she was to go home for the summer vacation, she surrendered for the first time in her life. "Father," she explained, "he actually begged me. I couldn't stand to see him cry."

She soon realized that she was pregnant. In a panic, she called the young man before telling her parents. He was afraid, and suggested that she "get rid of it." He offered to pay for an abortion, but she refused. Toward the end of the summer, he came to visit her. He felt guilty, but did not want to marry her. All four parents pressured him so much that plans were made for a private wedding. On the assigned date, he failed to appear, and the girl's heart was completely broken.

The priest helped her to weigh the possible personal and family implications about keeping the child, and recommended that she make the ultimate decision by herself, suggesting that she consider the child and its need for love. She struggled in confusion and indecision until reaching the full term of her pregnancy. After the birth of her son, when a social worker came to her bedside and asked explicitly for her signature releasing the baby to the adoption agency, she finally decided not to give it away. She asked the same priest to baptize the infant, and her parents came. Her sister and brother were godparents, and the young mother wept silently throughout the ceremony. Later, she said, "Father, I'm not crying because I'm afraid of the future, but because the baby's father never even came to see him baptized." To this day, she is still hoping her lover will come back to her.

This story demonstrates the often unforeseen effects of romantic love involving two emotionally immature people. The boy, in particular, really knew nothing of life and was utterly unprepared to face the consequences of his loss of control. The danger for these two people was that their physical development had outgrown their power of rational control. That is why it is so important for the young to listen to reason; and sometimes this means that they must face up to the fact that they have to accept some form of authority. Many of them are silently begging to be "told," to be stopped before it is too late.

Simple logic indicates that total isolation of the sexes cannot be a valid preparation for the sudden and total intimacy of wedded life. As in all human activities, there must be some progressive training and development if the flower and the fruit of love are to be good and healthy. And so, the question remains, how far to go?

Judging from current news reports, modern novels, and contemporary studies of campus life, it seems that many have already answered: "All the way!" With easily available and effective contraceptives, the risk of unwanted pregnancy has been practically eliminated, providing a sense of freedom and irresponsibility, disjoining completely the sexual act from any notion of permanent partnership. "No one waits anymore!" was the slogan proclaimed recently on the cover of a teen-age magazine. This results in unfortunate excesses where the splendor of sex is degraded and reduced to a cheap toy—only to be discarded in many cases in favor of the more novel thrills of drugs. Brainless and heartless sex has been drained of its fun. The playboy philosophy misses the mark because of its crudeness and disrespect for the real values of life. Certainly, then, sexual license is not the answer.

All That Glitters Is Not Love

Girls, beware of the boy who asks you to prove that you are sincere by jumping into bed with him! In older times, young people were frightened away from premature sex by threats of detection, infection, and conception. Nowadays, with motels and automobiles, detection is easily avoided. Infection seems to be controlled with the new drugs. Conception, of course, is no longer a threat because of the availability of practical contraceptives. The ancient arguments, therefore, seem to have been reduced to nothing. But have they been? Are you so certain you will not be found out? Have you ever heard boys discuss their affairs over a few beers? And how about your own conscience? Will you be able to retain your self-respect, your reputation, your bodily integrity? These are valuable possessions, compared to a few anxious moments of erotic excitement.

Maybe the girl will not become pregnant, but is she certain? About 10 per cent of experienced married women who use contraceptives to avoid having children do conceive by sheer accident. Among the inexperienced and unmarried, the rate may be as high as 25 per cent. Unwanted pregnancies may be due to many causes: inadequate timing, forgetfulness, defectives means, or lack of proper information. But make no mistake about it: it does happen.

And what of venereal diseases? United States Government statistics have indicated recently an extraordinary rise in the incidence of infection throughout the country. The figures are naturally based on reported cases only. These are estimated to represent only about 10 per cent of the actual number. Many people are disease-carriers without even knowing it. Genital contact of any kind may be sufficient to communicate the most dangerous forms of this scourge. A companion with low moral standards is more likely to carry dangerous germs than another person. Do you think it wise to risk your future happiness? If a boy asks you to prove your love for him, this is very far from meaning he will be faithful to you. He may, perhaps, believe that he is sincere, but how fickle men can be! Have you ever seen a sincere, loving girl discarded like a squeezed lemon? Are you willing to run such a risk before a boy has done anything to prove his love? Do you know the difference between being needed by a man here and now, and being loved by a man forever? You must know this if you are to make the right choice and succeed in your marriage.

A boy may insist that the "New Morality" teaches that love is the important thing and that as long as you love each other you may go all the way. But how can you determine that you really do love each other to a degree sufficient to justify intercourse? Is it fair to ask for all the benefits of love, without testing the strength of that love? There must obviously be a test of love before any test of sex; otherwise the boy may be asking the girl to take a fantastic gamble, while he is risking nothing. The boy may be unconsciously asking her to risk becoming pregnant, and suffering emotional wounds that would be difficult to heal if his love turned out to be too immature for a responsible marriage. A compulsive gambler, that is, a girl who delights in taking chances, insisting on her own freedom, may want to go ahead anyway. This, of course, is her own business, but it would be like speeding down an unkown highway at night without headlights. To thinking people, it makes no sense.

What Kind of Person Do You Want to Be?

In the midst of the free-for-all, there are many lively, well-informed, and highly motivated young people who refuse to be swept by the backwaters of the sexual revolution. They want to have fun, and ride high on its tide while still preserving their integrity and personal dignity. It is for them that the problem of how far to go is most acute. The others are not concerned: they go all the way and care nothing about it. But such a surrender, such a debacle of personal values, and such a loss of moral sense are not valid solutions for one who seeks to build a life with both meaning and substance.

The standard each one chooses as a personal rule of conduct depends upon the answer he or she gives to two questions: What kind of person do you want to be? What kind of person do you wish to attract as a possible marriage partner? The exact degree of self-imposed discipline will be the outcome of some serious consideration of the possible answers.

The major problem between man and woman is not how to kill sensual love in order to be "pure," but how to bring about conditions under which sensual love can flower as the truly rich and valuable experience it is meant to be. Premarital chastity, the control of the sexual instinct, and the limitation of its specific manifestations within the norm of personal decency prior to marriage are not negations of life, as they have so often been represented by the hedonists. They are actually means by which love and mutual respect may be preserved and nurtured into full development.

Because of the power and urgency of the sexual drive, this nurturing demands some measure of contact and satisfaction, some emotional exchange with the opposite sex, some objective and kindly assertion of its goodness as perceived in some of the living persons we meet. Premarital experimenting may be an expression of deep and sincere love, a healthy curiosity about a possible life partner, a preparatory phase to marriage itself. Romance naturally flows into the exploring of each other, the exciting and breathtaking discovery of sexual otherness, and this may take place long before any actual possibility of marriage.

And so we are faced with the two extremes. Both the total rejection of sex and the total premarital experience are to be condemned. What, then, would be reasonable rules of conduct?

There Are Five Steps to True Love

The closer one gets to matters of individual decision, the more difficult it becomes to establish valid norms of conduct, because norms are universal and people are not. Instead of listing clear-cut rules, which will only be abstract and therefore artificial, it seems far better to seek the conditions of life that lead to love and joy. They will be found in a reasonable compromise between rigid and literal negativism on the one hand, and total disregard for moral values on the other. They will consist in a number of specific attitudes toward yourself and your sexual partner.

Acceptance of yourself

The ability to make the total gift of self presupposes that you accept yourself, that you serenely and lovingly possess yourself; otherwise you will have nothing to give. This was covered in Chapter 10.

Respect for your partner

See your beloved as a full person, and not only as an object of desire. Be tender. Man's major weapon for survival is tenderness. It is infinitely more powerful than violence. The reason why man could prosper amid the threats of wild nature and wild beasts is that he and his wife loved each other and loved their young; and if necessary, to the point of total sacrifice—a sacrifice exalted to infinite value by the death of Christ on the cross. Tenderness, kindness, consideration, outgoing concern for the other's welfare will be the touchstones of a valid and permissible relationship. Whoever thinks only of his own pleasure has missed the essential truth—and the essential pleasure—of loving.

Belief in the natural goodness of sex

Be open to life's invitation. Realize with the utmost clarity that the union of man with woman in love is good, holy, perfectible, exalting, and meritorious, when approached in the right spirit; and that there is in this union a tremendously deep and profoundly religious value: it has something to do very directly with God.

Control of sexual desire

There is no need to repress your sexuality: control is not repression. On the other hand, no blinding passion, no obsessive compulson can ever be called upon to legitimate a sexual relationship that is opposed to moral or social law. Contrary to the thesis of many novels, passionate love does not justify everything. It is no excuse for murder, adultery, or the systematic abuse in any way of the gift of sex. Perhaps these excesses make gripping stories and bloodcurdling plays. In real life, however, they produce nothing but a pitiful mess. What is needed, then, is both self-control and sex control—relatively rare virtues in our days.

Acceptance of responsibility

The man-woman relationship can lead to the highest forms of happiness, but also to the lowest depths of physical, emotional, and mental damage. It is always dynamite, and should be handled with extreme care. A boy and girl without experience have the dangerous power of inflicting upon each other much needless pain if they fail to understand what they can do to each other.

Each Human Act Is Morally Unique

With such clear attitudes in mind—instead of negative imperatives—a young man or woman will be better able to chart his or her own course. You may say: "But this is no answer. How shall I know what I can and what I cannot do?" Are you asking that a counselor be more precise, that he make up a list of rights and wrongs that can be memorized easily? Do you expect to be told, for instance, that holding hands is permissible, kissing lightly is permissible, kissing deeply is a venial sin, petting lightly is a venial sin, petting heavily is a mortal sin, and so on? This would be easy, but would it make any sense? And yet, is not this the very form that written advice has generally assumed?

Categories of actions taken in themselves and out of context are meaningless abstractions that cannot be the object of any significant moral judgment. Try to imagine, for instance, at what precise point sexual license switches from venial to mortal guilt, thus endangering your eternity? Every action is unique, and must be considered in relation to the circumstances in the whole of human life. What if a young man does nothing more than hold hands with a married woman with the positive intent of suggesting adulterous intimacies? Is this not considerably more condemnable than even the deepest sexual involvement of an engaged couple?

No one, then, should be surprised or disappointed if no clear answer is given in terms of a catalogue of instructions. No list of permitted or forbidden acts is practical or desirable. Of course, you may prefer neat solutions to your problems. You would like to have rules of conduct spelled out for you in full detail so that you would not have to use your brains and your will in the performance of a free human act. But this is plain laziness—or at least childishness. And so, if you have come to discover that life has to be faced by you alone, and that it must be answered with self-determined and freely chosen responses, and if you are baffled by it, just consider yourself normal: it is a sure sign that you are growing up. There are no easy solutions to your sexual problems, as there are no easy solutions to life in general. The all-important answers you will have to give must be your own. Your job is to figure out your own way. Set up your own goals and strive for them as best you can.

All of us are basically trying to find happiness, to get somewhere. For some, this goal may be a highly ideal state; for others it may be some lowly set of immediate satisfactions. The highest state results from the full development of the attitudes listed above: self-accptance, tenderness, optimism, self-control, and responsibility.

Do Not Be Discouraged if You Are Baffled

And so we are back again at the point from which we started out—the deepest and most anguishing questions related to sex have no easy answers. This, again, may leave you baffled. But bafflement is a common human condition, a natural consequence of freedom. There are all too often no compelling answers, no automatic solutions, no proved roads, no pretested and safe patterns of living. Those who believe otherwise are sadly mistaken. They build up artificial rules endowed with artificial absolutes, and attempt to ram them down other people's throats. This is the inquisitorial approach of the man who believes that he possesses all the truth and that it gives him authority over everyone else. Surprisingly enough, such a smug state of mind is compatible with immense good faith and good will—which makes it all the more dangerous.

This kind of thinking has been the immediate cause of every religious war. Christ alone possessed all the truth, so that anyone who claims to possess it on his own authority is an impostor.

What needs to be done is to develop one's own self to the point of being able to live both freely and critically. Every human life—and every moment of every human life—is excruciatingly untested, free and new, with a newness that may lead to glory or to a catastrophic failure, depending upon the quality of the response you are constantly called upon to give. Precisely because of this freedom, "It is lovely to be human."[1] It is good to be the man or the woman you actually are. God is most pleased with you when you make a sensible effort to be good, not in the old-fashioned sense, but in the contemporary enlightened way: to be fully yourself, to become progressively and dynamically the person you were meant to be.

Your Sex Life Has a Spiritual Dimension

All the foregoing has been considered on the level of natural reason. There is another and higher level: that of union with Christ's sacrificial and saving intention. The properly developed union of man and wife in holy matrimony, the very consummation of their love in the sexual relationship, may be in themselves expressions of commitment to Christ. Anyone who sees anything objectionable in such an association of thoughts understands little about the dignity of man, and even less about theology.

How can there be a true participation in Christ's offering of himself for the salvation of all? The Christian may see, in the pain and sorrow of postponing sexual satisfaction until marriage, and within marriage, a true sacrificial act that may be offered up not only as a sign of love for God but also as a means of reparation for the countless acts of sexual abuse that are being committed every day. There is profound justification for the all-too real suffering and occasional damaging repression that may be the natural consequence of extended continence. If man's pri-

[1] Catherine de Vinck, *A Time to Gather* (Alleluia Press, Allendale, N.J., 1967), pp. 15, 18.

mordial goal were immediate pleasure, self-control would make no sense. But man's primordial goal is related to the progression of humanity toward the fulfillment of the Promise.

In that perspective, premarital and marital chastity become perfectly logical. This does not mean that you should punish yourself and avoid any feeling of sexual pleasure: it would be impossible. But you can transform unavoidable frustration, sorrow, anguish, and solitude into valuable and meritorious assets. Instead of being crushed by your lack of immediate success, you may be lifted up by the knowledge that you are willingly and peacefully contributing to the mysterious love-creating power of Christ, by sharing with him the burden of redemption. This is one of the greatest paradoxes of the Christian faith, and it is also one of its cornerstones.

There is no way to happiness except through the peace and joy of a good conscience, secure in the knowledge that at the end of life God is awaiting you to bring you to perfection. Christ surrendered to the cross in an act of love, doing everything to please the Father. If you would follow him, you too must take up your cross, for the servant cannot be greater than his master.

All the Answers Must Be Your Own

To conclude this important discussion, remember that all the answers must be your own; that they must be given consistently, in the light of your own chosen style of life; and that there will necessarily be a certain amount of privation and frustration in your sexual experience because man is made for infinite perfection, and sex is neither perfect nor infinite.

While preparing for marriage, you will have to choose your own path, somewhere between total denial of sexuality and unlimited sexual license. You alone can know how far to go, in the light of the principles indicated above. But there is one thing on which religious and nonreligious counselors agree: An amazing amount of human misery has come about because of premature sexual indulgence. There are too many unforeseen liabilities, too many chances for tragedy.

CHAPTER 15

HOW TO PREPARE FOR THE WEDDING

Physical Care May Save You Grief . . . Emotional Control Must Be Learned . . . Spiritual Preparation Implies Several Steps

Preceding chapters have dealt with ideas, principles, reasons why. It is time now to be more immediately practical, since we are coming close to the real thing. What we plan to talk about here is not the externals of the wedding. This is no book of etiquette. Personal preparation is the important thing: what you should do to get ready for a complete change in the pattern of your life.

Supposing now that you have made up your mind, that the great question has been asked, and a favorable answer given: what are the next steps? Can you drift into marriage as into a dream and be content to hope for the best without doing anything about it? Certainly not. There are a number of preliminary measures to be taken on very different levels: physical, emotional, and spiritual or religious.

Physical Care May Save You Grief

Have a medical examination

On the physical level, it is important that you take good stock of your health, that you both have a thorough physical checkup. A premarriage examination seems to be generally recommended. It is an important precaution that may have an effect on your future happiness. It may also help detect in time, and eventually correct, any physical defect that would be detrimental to marriage. In some cases, it may even bring to light some unsuspected condition that would render marriage impossible, at least until correction or improvement. And so you both owe it to each other to have sufficient knowledge of your physical aptness for the state into which you plan to enter. This is a matter of common honesty and decency that anyone will immediately understand.

Some young girls, generally because of unhealthy sex education, are dreadfully embarrassed and afraid at the thought of submitting to a gynecological examination. With a reasonable dose of simple common sense, they will come to see the procedure as completely medical and nonpersonal, and will go through it without any difficulty.

Temper your smoking and drinking

Now, about smoking and drinking: excessive smoking may destroy your senses of smell and taste and be the cause of throat cancer, not to mention the disadvantage of filling the house with the stale odor of tobacco. Because of an artificial need, of a nervous and unhealthy habit, smokers will exhale an unappealing stench that may act as a strong sexual repellent. Perhaps now is the time for you to give up smoking. Think it over. And realize that it is much more modern and original to abstain from a useless and even harmful habit than to indulge in it. If both of you smoke, that is no reason not to stop: instead of only one of you missing out on some of the pleasures of intimacy, you will both be dulled. And that is certainly something worth thinking about!

As for drinking: among the college crowd—not to mention partygoers in general—there is a constant temptation to drink too heavily. There seems to be a silly social mystique that the real he-man can hold large quantities of hard liquor. He can't. The real he-man is the one who knows when to stop. On the other hand, there is as much silliness in the dry-state teetotal philosophy as in the bibber's jolly self-destruction. Alcohol was not invented by the devil, nor is it the door to paradise. It may be used reasonably, and enjoyed, but it has led many to oblivion and slow death. It has ruined brilliant careers and promising marriages. It is worthless as a remedy to sorrow, disappointment, or defeat, for it saps energy at the very moment when energy is most needed. If a man or woman drinks to excess when he or she is up, they will go down. If they do so when they are down, they may very well be killing themselves emotionally, socially, or in real and physical actuality. It may all have started so very simply, with the habit of taking "just one more." Between just one more and one too many there is an extremely short step, and an even shorter one between one too many and inveterate alcoholism.

Some people drink in order to increase their self-assurance. They lack guts in their sober state, so they imagine that "a couple of fast ones" will change them into supermen or superwomen. All it does is to eliminate some of the defense inhibitions and to make them say and do a lot of things they will be ashamed of later. In terms of sex, drinking certainly diminishes restraint. It increases boldness in the male and decreases resistance in the female. On the other hand, alcohol is a depressant, so that, as the saying goes, it enhances the desire but hinders the performance. Anything but light drinking is a stupid way of spoiling the sexual relationship.

It is bad enough for men to drink to excess. For young ladies it is disgraceful, and may be disastrous, for the consequences of letting go may be anything from loss of self-respect to pregnancy. There are few sadder sights than a drunken woman—particularly when she is young. A wise young lady will carefully cultivate a taste for ginger ale. It may have a flavor of soapsuds, but it will keep you clean.

Emotional Control Must Be Learned

Emotionally speaking, there is also need of adjustment before the wedding. Until this day, you had both been free as birds, happy-go-lucky young people with no responsibility besides your immediate studies or your job. The world was your oyster, to love and to cherish—to hate and to curse if your disposition happened to be sour—but there was no limit to the area of your emotional spending.

All that must now be tamed and concentrated. Not that your spouse has to become the only object of your emotional interest, but that in one particular field—the specifically marital—you are no longer free to let your dreams go wild or let your eyes roam inquisitively over every possible mate. The search is over. The sum total of your venereal feelings and desires must be concentrated on the chosen one.

This does not mean that any sexual emotion or joy is necessarily disorderly when it is aroused by someone else, for sexuality extends far beyond those acts that are exclusive to marriage. It is important, however, that you begin to discipline yourself by no longer seeking any sexual excitement outside your future marriage relationship. In the present state of our world, it is impossible to escape from sexual provocation. There is no need to shut your eyes at every attractive person or to be guilt-ridden if you enjoy the presence of an appealing individual of the opposite sex, for such enjoyment is the perfectly natural reaction of the human being; but you can no longer allow such a relationship to become too deep.

There is no obligation whatsoever to give up friendship with members of the opposite sex with whom you have developed a valid and mutually profitable communion in the field of art or sports or cooperation in some valid enterprise. But what is absolutely out from now on is any emotional involvement that is a prelude to sexual indulgence. Be friendly, but keep at a distance from anyone except your own future husband or wife. As soon as you have definitely chosen, as soon as you are "spoken for," you belong to each other exclusively in regard to any form of deep intimacy.

Spiritual Preparation Implies Several Steps

Finally, there is much need for spiritual preparation before marriage. No one would want to enter a state of intimate partnership while his conscience is ridden with guilt. A guilty conscience is even worse than a festering body. No honest person would inflict upon the chosen beloved the company of a lover who is not as honest, balanced, and morally clean as he or she can possibly be. Love can thrive only on perfection, or at least on the good will toward perfection, since perfection is not of this earth. We all know quite well what are the less pleasant traits of our personality, where our weaknesses stand, when and how we have fallen below our own chosen style of life. The time before marriage is the time for a major cleanup.

Marriage is a social sacrament. It may be compared to Holy Orders. It is clearly necessary that there be serious preparation for any life change. Ordination is preceded by years of formal training, the only purpose of which is to prepare young men to become good priests and ministers of Christ. Immediately before ordination, there is generally a very important retreat during which the candidate to the priesthood has the opportunity to consider the whole pattern of his life and confirm freely within his mind the providential fact of his vocation.

By contrast, what happens generally before marriage? Boy and girl have thought about it more or less practically. They may have built within their minds an image of what married life should be, of what they would like it to be, but this is generally flimsy and often falsely romantic. Then they go out and meet each other—and are swept off their feet by the strongest natural urge. Much of the little they had planned and understood may be lost in the fire of emotions. And they come to the altar with hardly any preparation other than the shreds of a haphazard collection of immature preconceptions. It is common knowledge that many young people come to marriage utterly unprepared for anything more than a lark.

There are, no doubt, many fine people who take marriage seriously. They seek counsel and advice, read books, consider carefully and realistically the manner in which couples are living, study the spiritual and religious implications of the marital relationship, and come joyfully to the altar with no illusions about the risks. As someone said, there is no danger of the human race becoming extinct as long as there are innocent men and maidens who believe that nothing could happen in marriage that could be worse than not being married at all.

What, then, can a couple do to prepare themselves spiritually for marriage? The spiritual preparation of the young people should be both individual and common. As an individual preparation, you should:

Examine your conscience

Review your past life, check your failures and imperfections, make amends for them, develop a firm intent of improving, and obtain absolution in a sincere and complete confession.

Seek advice

Apply to a competent and enlightened counselor or spiritual director who will help you take the right steps and develop the right attitudes toward your future married life. This is a study more important perhaps than anything you have studied before.

Read the right books

There is an abundance of good marriage literature, but some of the material available is dangerously pessimistic, negative, depressing, and downright wrong. Generally speaking, few books of the nineteenth century or early twentieth concerned with marriage counseling will do much good. It is always to your advantage to read up-to-date material, and so we would advise you to concentrate on postconciliar works. On the other hand, a study of a few of the more conservative essays will give you much information on the sufferings and frustrations endured by earlier generations, perhaps as close to you as your own parents. There is still at large a breed of die-hard counselors who hold to crushing, depressing, and negative views on sex. Others hold views so extremely liberal that nothing is left of the moral law. Be careful not to follow either extreme, but to read those books that combine a healthy natural optimism with a deep sense of moral responsibility, and that present sex neither as God's greatest mistake nor as a lustful free-for-all.

Understand the religious meaning of marriage

Try to deepen the realization that your marital happiness is dependent upon your relationship with reality, that is, with God. You are not independent pleasure-seeking beings: you are the children of God, made for much more than pleasure, made for life, light, and joy. See that true religion does not consist in knowing the Catechism by heart and going to church every Sunday. True religion consists in realizing that you are love-in-action and that this love-in-action within you is an expression of the trinitarian activity of God himself: it is the life of the Holy Spirit rendering homage to the Father through the Word within you, that is, through your own words and deeds and thoughts and actions. You will be real only in the measure in which you become yearnings of love, efforts of love, expressions of love, manifestations of love. God alone is real, and so anything of reality must reflect him. You, in turn, will be real only in the measure in which you will spontaneously and vitally express through what you are the divine dialogue of Father and Son resulting in the Spirit of Love and Life. It is the Holy Spirit who is life and love in you, the Son who speaks of life and love in you, the Father who sustains the power of life and love in you.

Your own relationship with your beloved wife is the closest natural symbol—even more, the closest realization within spatio-temporal nature—of God's trinitarian love life.

The most intimate and warmest expression of your sexual love is perfectly spiritual in the measure in which it is perfectly love. At this point, many an ancient moralist made the sad mistake of false dualism, imagining a distinction between the purely spiritual related to the soul and the purely material related to the body. Since the purely spiritual was the source of good, they reasoned that the purely material must be the source of evil—and so they scorned woman, and sex and all its manifestations.

The truth is that man cannot be divided into body and soul: this is an unreal abstraction. Everything man does involves his whole being. Thinking may be seen as a physiological act of cerebration. Sexual intercourse may with equal accuracy be considered as an act of the soul. Both, of course, are acts of indivisible man. That is why there is nothing suspicious or negative in the sexual relationship as such. It may on the contrary become the source of great spiritual exaltation and merit.

Practice spiritual communication

What, now, can you do together to prepare for marriage? First, there must be—and there generally is, quite naturally—a mutual unfolding of each to each that results in talk, talk, talk. Even the habitually silent develop unexpected vocal talents as soon as they are hit with love. It seems that the lid is taken off the pressure cooker, and the long accumulated steam fizzes out! This is good: the more you talk, the more you know of each other. You will never know enough.

This talk naturally centers on each one of you, comparing experiences, hopes, and dreams of your past life, and anticipations of your life together. Perhaps the most important part is anticipation, planning, for it is there that you will gain the most accurate picture of each other, there that your predetermined and freely chosen style of life will be put to the test by being practically applied. Talk about the future will concern your degree of mutual respect and freedom, what you expect of each other, what your plans are for work and play, how you intend to share your future responsibilities, the number of children you wish to have, and their timing, what kind of home or apartment you will live in, and where, your preference for town, country, or suburbs, and even such details as your favorite style of furniture.

Then, of course, you will share what you have learned and discovered of the higher values of the relationship. You will want to be quite sure that both of you understand the deep religious implication of your union, and the fact that any man and woman left to their own weakness will form an extremely fragile pair—but that with good will, mutual love, and deep reliance on God's strength, their union will remain as strong as granite, even in the fluctuating motion of life. There is a beautiful saying in the Church Fathers: "To the horse, God gave swiftness; to the eagle, the power of flight; but to man he gave weakness so that he himself could be his strength."

Meditate on the words of the marriage ceremony

Another useful preparation for marriage is a careful study of the ritual. The actual form of marriage may differ slightly from place to place, but the meaning is essentially the same: it is a public expression of the love you have for each other, and of the permanency of the bond. The commitment is not merely a promise you make to each other, but a solemn and public religious vow. Both parties pledge themselves in the presence of the whole community and before God that they are surrendering their individual lives for the greater life that they are to share in common.

You are asked to join your right hands. And then the groom is asked to repeat the following words: "I, [Robert,] take you, [Linda,] for my lawful wife, to have and to hold, from this day forward, for better, for worse, for richer, for poorer, in sickness and in health, until death do us part." These words are most serious, for you are involving yourself in the solemn obligation to love and cherish this one woman for the rest of your life. And she will make the very same vow before God.

Hereafter, you will be two in one flesh. Imagine what this means. It is not at all maudlin or morose to consider in detail the implications of this promise. You are making a supreme act of self-sacrifice; pledging yourself to faithful, loving, lifelong dedication to the well-being and happiness of another person. You are surrendering your freedom, or so it seems, and only beginning to find the meaning of real freedom in true love. There is no pain, no inconvenience in this joyful surrender: you are in love, you are on top of the world.

But when your shining knight falls from his white stallion and soils his radiant armor, when his pride is wounded, and he has lost his confidence, when his body is sick and his handsome looks have faded—and when your fair lady has lost the fairness of youth—where will you be? You will have pledged eternal love before God, but will you be true to that pledge when the going gets rough?

Call upon God's assistance

If ever there is a time to be humble, it is now, in the realization that you are vowing everything, while knowing full well your limited power to follow through. If ever you should feel the need of God's presence and strength in your life, it is in this realization: you are weak and vulnerable, but because there is grace, you may promise with quiet assurance the breadth and height and furthest reach of love. There is great need for God's strength in such a sublime act of self-giving. You must not be afraid. As long as you do not presume to succeed on your own strength alone, you will be perfectly secure.

A pathetic situation arises over and over again, and no doubt you have heard of it in your own neighborhood. It is expressed in different ways, but always amounts to the same thing.

"How can a man of forty-two be expected to be bound to a promise he made when he was twenty?"

"I married you because my family wanted it. I never really loved you; I'm in love now with another man, and I've never known such happiness."

"When I married her, she was sweet and good, but she's changed. I hardly know her; I realize now that I never really loved her."

"I should have known it wouldn't work. He never showed any ambition; he never wanted to make anything of himself."

"If it had not been for the children, I would have left him long ago. He was never a husband to me; he was more in love with his job."

And so it goes, a litany of tragic statements made only a few short years after two lovers had joined their right hands in marriage. "I, Linda, take you, Robert, for my lawful husband, to have and to hold, from this day forward, for better, for worse, for richer, for poorer, in sickness and in health, until death do us part."

How sad it will be if you allow this deterioration to take place in your life; how foolish if you do not understand your need of God's assistance. Do not be afraid to consider this need out loud, with your loved one. Perhaps you never have talked about it before. Perhaps you never have bothered to pray together. Perhaps you never have stopped to think that you too may grow cold in your love and that without a deep and abiding awareness of the Eternal Word, your own spoken promise may be retracted in a mood of self-indulgence.

Do not be foolish. Let your heart be young and joyful, untroubled in the delights of love. But let your mind be clear and farseeing in making the marriage vows before God. This is for life, and with God it can be a blessed, happy life, if only you can preserve your faith and fervor in his almighty power to care for you. You must be gentle in leading your beloved to God. The love of God is also freely chosen, but love him yourself, with your whole heart, mind and soul, and that love will illuminate your home and all whom you love.

The blessings after the marriage ceremony are filled with power, and to all men of good will we wish these blessings in abundance.

"May Almighty God bless you and unite you in the enduring bond of pure love."

"May you be blessed in your children and may the love that you lavish on them be returned a hundredfold."

"May the peace of Christ dwell always in your hearts and in your home; may you have true friends to stand by you both in joy and in sorrow."

"May you be ready with help and consolation for all those who come to you in need; and may the blessings promised to the compassionate descend in abundance on your house."

"May you be blessed in your work and enjoy its fruits. May cares never cause you distress, nor the desire for earthly possessions lead you astray, but may your heart's concern be always for the treasures laid up for you in the life of heaven."

"May the Lord grant you fullness of years, so that you may reap the harvest of a good life, and then may he take you up into the eternal dominions in heaven."

"Go in peace and the Lord be with you always. Amen." (From the *Collectio rituum,* Exhortation After Marriage.)

CHAPTER 16

THE MORAL LAW PROMOTES TRUE LOVE

Maturity Is the Power to Accept Responsibility . . . Moral Rules Must Be Justified . . . The Moral Law Has a Threefold External Origin . . . Your Inner Conscience Is the Final Judge . . . To Be Is to Be Loved . . . The Sexual Revolution Is Good and Bad . . . "New Morality" Often Means No Morality . . . Situation Ethics Is a Subjective Morality . . . Virtue Is Its Own Reward

---

Maturity and responsibility are independent notions. A mature individual knows what he is doing. He is one who has reached that level of human balance that corresponds to the full fruition of his gifts. He has attained full ripeness of character. A responsible individual is one who is willing and able to face the consequences of his acts and to follow through until they are completed.

Maturity Is the Power to Accept Responsibility

Maturity has a clear prerequisite: the ability to know what we are doing, and why.

In the daily lives of people around us, and often in our own lives, there are a thousand signs of irresponsibiilty, for instance in some of the classical answers given by children who could not have known better, or, sadly enough, by people not so young, after they have managed to get themselves into trouble. "He made me do it!" This is passing the buck. "I didn't realize what I was doing!" This is probably culpable ignorance. "I didn't do it: I was only watching!" This is cowardice.

"He made me do it!" What this actually means is: "I knew perfectly well that it was wrong, but since I was tempted and too weak to stand up for what is right, I let him push me into doing it." This is the reaction of the undisciplined will, the attitude of the poltroon who would rather surrender than fight. It may also result from the state of mind of the pleasure-seeker who would take his fun and burden his conscience—or even kill his conscience completely—rather than sacrifice anything for the sake of moral truth.

"I didn't realize what I was doing!" This is quite often a lie or at least a lame excuse. You knew perfectly well what you were doing, but pretended you did not, in order to claim ignorance as an excuse. Even if this answer is not a lie, it cannot serve as a moral justification, for if ignorance may excuse the act, there is no excuse for not knowing the difference between right and wrong. No one can claim independence from moral duty, particularly as regards one's state of life. Anyone who says, "I didn't realize what I was doing" is culpably ignorant of his moral responsibility, for it is his business to know what he is doing.

There may be valid cases of ignorance, in difficult matters or in matters related to possibilities and probabilities. A doubtful law does not bind. Yet, it is a fact that some of the clearest and most obvious principles of human decency are often overlooked. People act as they please, before thinking, before consulting their consciences. In such cases, the claim of ignorance is certainly invalid.

"It is not my fault: I was only watching!" Do you have any obligation to interfere and stop something you know to be wrong? Can you participate indirectly in an evil act through passive witnessing, and not incur some of the guilt? Can you, for instance, remain silent when you see your companions engaging in foolish and dangerous relationships, playing with sexual fire, degrading themselves and their partners through lust, greed, ambition, curiosity, or sheer stupidity? Can you remain passive when excessive drinking is going on, or experimenting with hallucinogens, or driving a car at deadly speed? The answer, as in all moral questions, must be qualified.

No positive participation can be condoned, no approving smile, no tolerant "Go ahead and have your fun!" Perhaps the best course of action will be your own good example of restraint, self-control, and respect for others. But sometimes this is not enough: you must act or talk up, perhaps at a serious risk to your superficial popularity. This may be very hard, and yet it must be done. If you seem to fail and are unable to stop the foolish deed, you may still have strongly influenced the weak and undecided witnesses. Even if you have failed completely, no one can blame you for not having tried. Your conscience may then be the only one to approve, but this solitary approval may be far better than the remorse that may come later from not having tried at all.

"Am I my brother's keeper?" To a certain extent, yes. As a French writer said, "A Christian is a man to whom Jesus Christ has entrusted all men." You are responsible for your neighbor to the limit of your ability to influence him. You are not responsible for his ultimate decision or for his final salvation, for they are matters reserved for the individual person and his God. All you are called upon to do is to exert a positive influence whenever you can.

On the other hand, you do not want to be butting into other people's business: the Do-Goodnik is a pain in the neck. A reasonable rule of conduct seems to be to make a careful estimate of your chances of success. If you are absolutely certain that no word or action of yours has the slightest chance of doing any good, but that, on the contrary, anything you say or do is bound to result in antagonism and perhaps even increased evil, the only possible attitude is one of prayerful silence. But do pray. And do not forget that a peaceful word may have some effect, now or later, even if the immediate chances seem to be nil.

Moral Rules Must Be Justified

You probably learned about your moral obligations through a series of "Do's" and "Don't's" handed down to you by different agencies in the course of your development and education: from parental instructions to postgraduate studies. The process will continue until the last day of your life, for learning is an all-time and never-ending job.

Now, moral rules may have been handed down to you properly or improperly. In other words, your teaching authorities, parents, priests, and school instructors, may have been well informed and capable of transmitting the moral truth. They may also have been completely incompetent. Your teaching authorities' qualifications were probably somewhere in between, some better, others less good, so that they guided you partly in the direction of truth and partly in that of prejudice and error. That is why it is so important for every one of you not to swallow any doctrine whole, but to appraise anything critically before accepting it as a rule of life. It is mostly this critical appraisal of right and wrong that is a lifetime job. It will have to serve not only as a guide to yourselves but also as a guide to your future charges, children or students.

The Moral Law Has a Threefold External Origin

Revelation

The rules and laws of morality may have a different origin and a different degree of obligation. Basically, however, they are only roadsigns: they supply directions as you travel along the highway of life. They merely tell you at what point you run the risk of disaster.

For the Judeo-Christian, the primary external source of the moral law is the Bible, with, first of all, its Ten Commandments. Although addressed specifically to the Children of the Promise, these are universal rules that apply to all mankind because all men are essentially the same. No man or woman can ever hope to reach a decent level of human dignity while disregarding them. These roadsigns, then, apply to all men and women, everywhere and always, provided the circumstances are such that some higher rule does not supersede them. For instance, the commandment "Thou shalt not kill" bears the exception of self-defense founded on a superior justice: the victim of unjust aggression has such a clear right to his life that he may defend it even if, as a last resort, he must take the aggressor's life.

The basic moral law of revelation, however, is the law of love exposed by Christ in the Gospels: Love is the greatest commandment of all. It is not only a roadsign; it is a way of life, life itself, the expression of the Spirit of Life and Love within us.

Religious authority

These high, universal, and absolute moral laws require a proper interpretation by qualified authorities. The conditions of application of the Ten Commandments, the actual practice of love, must be studied by professional moralists. The official doctrine must be formulated and promulgated by the magisterium of the Church. Now, the Church in its teaching has two basic areas of concern: faith and morals. Faith is related to those matters we find expressed in the Creed. They are final, fixed, and absolute, not in their expression, but in their essence, because they are firmly based on divine revelation. We can trust this revelation because God, by his solemn covenant, has promised to protect his people and to lead them into light. There may be some development in our understanding of certain aspects of a mystery, as expressed in a theological formula, but the basic reality behind it will never change. Jesus Christ, for instance, is truly a man and truly the Second Person of the Trinity. We may differ from Christians of the sixth century in the understanding of the meaning of his manhood, but we do not differ from them in our essential faith: Jesus Christ is the God-man.

In moral matters, too, certain things are final, fixed, and absolute because they are founded on divine revelation. For instance, the commandment "Thou shalt not commit adultery" is not subject to eventual reconsideration by a papal commission. In other areas of moral teaching, the precepts and commands rest, not on revelation, but on the wisdom of the Church at a given moment of history. They are mostly disciplinary rules. Within these areas, developments occur slowly, gradually, and at times, embarrassingly—for instance, when an excessively strong dogmatic position had been taken on the basis of data that later discoveries and social evolution proved to be incorrect or irrelevant.

Galileo (1564–1642), the Italian astronomer, was severely condemned by the Church, and forced to retract his teaching that the earth revolved around the sun. All earlier cosmologies had been founded on the notion that the earth was the center of creation and that the universe consisted in a number of concentric spheres, the highest one being the empyrean heaven, the dwelling of God and of the elect, and the lowest, hell, coinciding with the center of the earth. Theologians of the time were unable to see that this was pure imagination and that the relative motion of earth and sun had nothing to do with faith. The confirmation of Galileo's discovery was most embarrassing to Church authorities, and one wonders whether any official apology was ever made.

Again, in past ages, when the economy was purely agrarian, usury, or the taking of interest on a loan, was a crime. There truly was no justification for it, besides greed and the exploitation of the poor. The Church condemned it roundly for over a thousand years. But the times have certainly changed: the Vatican itself is now one of the heaviest investors in Italian stocks.

Once more, at the time when the world was insufficiently populated, the limitation of births was a crime—all the more so since a high rate of infant mortality and the general inability to cope with disease regularly reduced the number of the living. The Christian ideal of generous family love was then interpreted as meaning that every couple was called upon to have as many children as possible. But now the Second Vatican Council has endorsed the principle of responsible parenthood: the limitation of the number of births and the planning of the number of desired children have become modern expressions of Christian generosity in family love. By now a better understanding of human sexuality has liberated many good people from fear and shame, enabling them to raise happier, holier, and healthier families, while enjoying their intimate relationship without inhibitions.

In all three instances given above, one of the most uninspiring aspects of churchmen in authority lies in the clear record of their reluctance to admit uncertainty and error, and to make up for the damage inflicted by these falterings. In more recent times, there have been faint but encouraging signs of reversing this practice of triumphalistic claims of perfection. In his ecumenic statements, Pope Paul has had the humility and honesty to ask God's forgiveness for any sins and errors committed by the Roman Catholic Church that may have aggravated divisions in Christendom. In the past, the Church canonized Joan of Arc, but no ecclesiastic seems ever to have apologized for having burned her at the stake.

The social nature of man

Besides moral obligations founded on religion and the commands of God and the Church, there are commands of society: civil laws, disciplinary measures such as traffic regulations, and the conventions of social life. They cannot be ignored by a responsible person. They may not be perfect—no human law is perfect—but they have been worked out with the common good as a goal. They are the basic conditions for a working social group, nation, state, town, club, or family, and as such they have a right to your compliance.

Apart from these valid commands, there are an immense number of national, tribal, local, or personal compulsions or taboos, many of which are obsolete, useless, or even damaging. Some of them border on the superstitious, and like old wives' tales, their degree of obligation is about the same as that of the childish rhyme: "Step on the crack and break your mother's back." In his book *The Status Seekers,* Vance Packard has listed a considerable number of these social superstitions that transform life into a battle for conformism and absorb much energy in the fruitless task of keeping up with the Joneses. We may laugh at some of the compulsions of savage tribes: our own constraints are quite as laughable, even if more sophisticated. What we need is to be freed from them. "The truth shall make you free."

Once again, let us repeat it: Not everything handed down to you by adults, parents, priests, or teachers should be swallowed whole. A rational individual will make fun of all worthless conventions and feel completely liberated from them. Yet, some social habits are so strongly ingrained, even though useless, that as a matter of prudence it may be better to conform outwardly than to risk antagonism and unpleasantness—provided, of course, no damage is done to reason, justice, or common sense. There is wisdom in the axiom "When in Rome, do as the Romans do." If you must work on Wall Street, it will be better to dress like Wall Street, even if you prefer the more flamboyant style of Southern California.

Your Inner Conscience Is the Final Judge

Aside from the moral rules imposed from without, there is ultimately one control, one meaningful principle of personal discipline: your inner conscience, your own individual code of honor. As we have seen, each man or woman sets his or her own standards, high or low, depending upon the level of social or religious ideal. There is a direct, formal, and strict obligation first to think out your own way of life, then to keep developing it according to your personal experience of life, and, finally, to act accordingly. All this is a matter of personal logic, unity, and coherence. Without such an advance view, your person is not creatively individualized. Without a carefully laid-out plan, you are but a collection of loose ends. Once again, remember that the important question is: What kind of person do you want to be? The guidelines for thinking this out are fairly objective: they are based on the common goal of human nature. But your selection of how the general principles of moral conduct are to apply to you will depend upon the degree of your idealism balanced against realistic factors imposed by the particular circumstances of your life. How high are you aiming? How high can you reach?

It is extremely easy to take the low road and drift into moral mediocrity. All it requires is nothing—no thinking, research, effort. Simply vegetating, drifting, being pushed around by your animal appetites, going along passively with every twist and turn of circumstances. For a man, the results are bad enough. For a woman, they may be frightful. No one has any real interest in protecting an unchaste woman—except perhaps in taking precautions so that she does not become pregnant. Even that is done, not to protect the female, but to protect the male against eventual responsibility. Furthermore, unchastity in both man and woman frequently leads to moral and psychological decay. A life of sexual irresponsibility is guaranteed ultimately to impoverish the spirit and to end up in shame and loneliness through lack of true love.

To Be Is to Be Loved

You are called upon to do something positive with your life, by seeing it as a possible answer to a proposition of love: love of God, and of other human beings, love of animals and plants and all creation, for everything created is an object of love, or else it would not have been made, since all that is originates in love and is destined to return to it. To be is to be loved; to be is to be chosen. Everyone of us is an elect.

Normal young men and women avoid unchastity because unchastity is the opposite of love. They want an ethic that confirms their longing for perfection, rules, and principles that will guide them to a completely human fulfillment. College opinion polls show that in spite of changing sexual mores, students still believe in fidelity. They still want a marriage that has depth, meaning, profound joy and peace. They know that enduring love presupposes trust, faithfulness, and respect. This is incompatible with the playboy philosophy that becomes a pattern of irresponsible love tending to perpetuate itself after marriage.

Young people want a life with vitality and lasting happiness. The principles that justify fidelity and integrity in marriage are basically the very same principles that justify premarital chastity. But many still lack the maturity and experience that would enable them to accept the discipline involved in living out these principles. Many are still driving recklessly through life because they have not grown up—and some will not grow up before they have had an accident. Learning by trial and error is doing things the hard way. Much pain could have been avoided with a little intelligent foresight and rational investigation.

As we have seen, the sources of morality, the rules of right and wrong, are found in revelation, in authoritative teaching, and in the laws of society based on the nature of man. But what about the present changes? What about the sexual revolution? What about the "New Morality"? What about situation ethics? Are the old moral laws still binding in our enlightened days?

The Sexual Revolution Is Good and Bad

Recent developments in the understanding and use of human sexuality are good in one sense and bad in another. From the viewpoint of traditional beliefs, and even of Church teachings from the Fathers of the Church to nineteenth-century moral theologians, there is a complete revolution, a complete reversal, in that some attitudes formerly condemned are now accepted and even considered morally good and meritorious. There have been particularly important changes as regards the attitude toward women. The following statements would have been unacceptable under earlier and stricter disciplines dominated by male asceticism:

1. A woman has sexual rights equal to those of her husband.
2. There is nothing sinful, unwomanly, or imperfect in the slightest degree if a wife seeks full erotic release and the perfection of orgastic pleasure in her marital relations.
3. A woman is as free as a man in her choice of a career or a mate, or in determining the number of her children.

The main point recently made in the light of a better understanding of sexuality is that sexual pleasure may be sought as a means of mutual love even with the formal intent of avoiding procreation. The only point still in suspense is the determination of the means by which sexual relations may be relieved of the fear of unwanted and undesirable pregnancy.

Then there is the newly recognized need of establishing some early contact between young men and women, for instance, in coeducation, as opposed to the older concept of total segregation until marriage. Such contacts will lead inescapably to abuses and premature indulgence, but it is generally believed that the psychological damage done by the previous hush-hush atmosphere of secrecy and separation resulted in much more serious damage.

So far, for the good points of the sexual revolution. It has also an entirely different aspect, represented by a considerable easing of public conscience in matters that other ages had considered sinful: premarital and extramarital sex, and homosexuality. The first two are now rendered much easier because of the development of relatively safe contraceptives and the seemingly improved control over venereal diseases. This, then, corresponding as it does with a general lowering of personal discipline and idealism, results in the present attitudes of indulgence. In many circles, the sexual mores are completely liberalized in the name of freedom and the right to pleasure. This is often accompanied by a wave of flippancy that considers the sexual act as both natural and unimportant. The consequences are the boredom of overindulgence and a loss of a proper sense of values.

In this second sense, the sexual revolution is a fact of our age. It is up to you to decide whether you want to roll with the tide, grasp the fruits of sex before they are ripe, give your consent to a way of life that tends to degrade and cheapen one of the greatest marvels of life. Would you not rather stand on your own feet, perhaps in a state of temporary isolation, but with strong faith and love and hope, in the expectation of the real thing that is to come when the time is right? Just think of the difference when you do meet the right man or woman: think of your first night together, and of the joy of giving yourself wholly for the first time without the nagging memory of guilt-ridden, back-seat fumblings?

"New Morality" Often Means No Morality

Three young college men were talking about their favorite topic with a pretty young freshman girl. The boys agreed in their studied conclusion that sex before marriage was good and even necessary. They were well read in the new theology, and they assured the girl that the more liberal scholars would justify the love act between a boy and a girl if they truly loved each other. The girl became perplexed, and began to wonder whether her resistance to these ideas was not a remnant of prudishness.

She should have realized that boys have been handing out this line for centuries. "New Morality" still means the same old thing: no morality—no restriction at all. Either there is morality or there isn't. No innovation can be concerned with essential principles: it would no longer be an evolution of morality but a destruction of it. But the problem is to find out precisely what, in morality, is essential. Is there any authority, divine or human, sufficiently qualified, informed, and powerful to tell you what to do and what not to do? Does anyone, God or priest or parent, have a right to go to you and say: "If you do this, you are in a state of moral disorder and self-destruction. You are an outlaw, a child of darkness, a sinner?"

As long as man has been in contact with the living God, he has accepted the message of morality. He has been convinced that some forms of action were definitely wrong, damaging to himself and others, and that they could be rightfully forbidden by the Church and society. It is this whole tradition, this whole consensus of generations of teachers and prophets, of wise men and of saints, that the proponents of the "New Morality" are trying to oppose. They are not content to adjust some obsolete disciplinary laws in the light of the discoveries of modern physiology and psychology: they want to do away with the whole system of restraint.

The "New Morality," in its crudest expressions, and particularly as regards sex, is an antihistorical, antirealistic, pleasure-seeking, and the-hell-with-the-consequences attitude that manifests immaturity, irresponsibility, blindness, and childishness. No amount of sincerity can change the basic rules of humanity. If we take a close look at the private lives of the adherents of this new morality, it is easy to see that they sow the wind and reap the storm: a storm of disappointments, separations, divorces, mate-switching, and perpetual search for the ultimate freedom—the death wish, freedom from life itself.

If only girls could be wise enough to remember that young men actually want a loving wife, a faithful wife, one who will lift them above themselves and give them a chance for lasting happiness! In sexual matters, men may be liberals as long as they consider females as their playthings; they may want an impure girl for a good time, but they want a pure girl for a good marriage. As soon as they begin to respect their partner as a person, the level of their morality rises considerably.

Do you understand human nature? Do you know that a woman generally sets the moral tone of a family? While a man brings to it his mind and a certain clarity of direction, he may lack moral sensitivity. It is often true that a man is as good as the woman in his life. He knows that he will have to find someone who is strong and good if he is to be good himself. His body gives him a great deal of difficulty; his eye has a tendency to rove; and many a time he appears weak and inconsistent. What he really longs for is love, the rich and tender love of a woman who accepts him just as he is and who has the patience to lift him above himself. What he really wants is to live according to the true moral law of faith, hope, and love.

Does this mean that we should return to the old ways, without any change or even any questioning? Not in the least. Clearly enough, all is not well with the classical expressions of the moral law as regards the proper handling of sex. Most of the conservative ethics manuals, in their chapters on marriage, are narrow, negative, pessimistic, legalistic, and frankly scornful of sexual pleasure.

By contrast, much needs to be said of the thoroughly good and healthy relationship that implies the intelligent development of the full range of sexual intimacies. Would this be a new morality? No, but an enlightened contemporary view of morality as it should have been. For centuries, its expression had been inadequate because of excessive concern for the possible dangers of sexual abuse. We are now taking a positive look at the whole thing.

Sex has not passed suddenly from something shameful and secret to something good and open to honest investigation. Sex is sex, and it has always been good in itself, willed by God, and used by men through their freedom in a good or a disastrous way. But there has been a definite change in approach: instead of considering sex as something unfortunate but necessary for procreation, we now see it as good and delightful, although loaded with potential danger. What is being changed is not the nature of sex, but the interpretation of rules concerning its proper use.

Situation Ethics Is a Subjective Morality

Situation ethics has something in common with the "New Morality": both have a tendency to deny the existence of an objective moral law. Situation ethics, however, does not go as far as the "New Morality," which, as we have seen, consists essentially in the denial of any moral obligation whatsoever. Situation ethics is still an ethics, that is, a set of rules of moral conduct. But according to it, the decisions as to the moral rating of an act are made to depend upon its subjective conditions. An act will be good or bad, depending upon the situation in which the subject found himself at the time—the word "situation" referring, not to any external commitment, but to a subjective state.

The morality of intercourse between free and consenting adults for whom marriage is a permanent impossibility has not as yet been studied with sufficient attention. This should not be assimilated unqualifiedly with the case of young people who are looking forward to marriage and for whom abstention is merely a question of patience and discipline.

Virtue Is Its Own Reward

There has been a good sexual revolution in that the equality of women and the meritorious goodness of sexual joy have been recognized and proclaimed in opposition to the views of obscurantist and obsolete teachings. The virtue of sex is proclaimed once for all.

There is no real "New Morality," for morality as such cannot be new. However, some of its disciplinary rules may be changed in order to conform with a better understanding of the human complex.

Situation ethics cannot be accepted as a rule of life, because it makes the moral judgment depend exclusively on subjective factors, and overlooks the act in itself. However, it has had a good influence on the study of morality in that it has brought to the fore the subjective circumstances as a counterbalance to the automatic application of the letter of the law.

Situation ethics corresponds to an excess of subjectivism as legalism corresponds to an excess of objectivism. True morality consists in the application of revised principles of traditional morality made more open and optimistic, tempered by taking into consideration the subjective element, not as determinants of right or wrong, but as qualifiers of their degree.

Any sexual act implies moral right or wrong. It will be morally good if it is not against the fundamental purposes of sexuality and is performed within the right personal circumstances. Such a moral law shows a way to sexual fulfillment that is wholesome, uplifting, and delightful. Sex, when used within the limits of right reason, that is, within this moral law, does not restrict your love: on the contrary, it promotes it, by contributing to the love relationship of the partners or to procreation, or both.

The mature fullness of love can come only in the serenity of a safe and secure nest: a home of love. Much patience is needed before it can be found, and no one should minimize or deny the pain of this waiting. But it is up to you to decide what you want to do with your life—you may lose it through overindulgence or save it with a reasonable measure of discipline and expectant love.

CONCLUSION

"Then the Lord said, 'It is not good that man should be alone; I will make him a helper fit for him'" (Genesis 2:18).

Man is made for love. Even at a child's earliest stage of existence, it becomes listless, apathetic, withdrawn, and its development is stunted if it is not loved, if it has no contact with a loving presence.

In his personal growth, man needs a "helper"; he needs the encounter with others, the true, creative communication of love in order to become truly and fully himself. Even if he chooses the solitary life for the sake of the Kingdom, he does so, not as a withdrawal from human contact, but, on the contrary, as a means by which he can plunge deeper into the reality of love and thus become more perfectly one with the human family.

As Christians, we are called to fellowship with one another through Christ, in Christ, with Christ. But this fellowship cannot remain vague and abstract: it must become incarnate in our concrete encounters with others, in the "I-Thou" relationship of love. Our very growth as persons depends upon these encounters, not exclusively, perhaps, but certainly in a great measure. And marriage, as the deepest of these encounters, should be the most fertile ground for personal growth.

Paradoxically, growth is possible only if there is "space" in a marriage, if there is freedom, if the partners do not make the mistake of believing that they must be juxtaposed at all times, that in order to be one, they must lose their personal identity, becoming exact replicas of each other. On the contrary, both husband and wife are called to great reverence before the partner's "otherness." They must give each other sufficient space and freedom to allow personal growth.

But each one is called also to sustain, strengthen, enrich the other so that love may become truly creative and fruitful. In allowing space and freedom for development, in being true helpers for each other, both partners develop personhood, the root of happiness. This is not the same as success, nor is it the inner glow of having achieved security, stability, power. It is rather an accomplishment of life itself, the fact of husband and wife becoming their true selves through each other, and thus becoming one with the human family, with their own depth, with God.

People who are content to live superficially, conforming to an image of their social self, to an ego that needs to be constantly fed, coddled, propped up artificially, often lose contact with their own reality, for the reality of man is more than skin deep. "To thine own self be true" contradicts the shallowness of such lives. In the process of becoming his true self, man must reach out constantly. It is a lifelong process, at times very painful. But man and wife engaged in this search may be helped powerfully by each other's personal love.

And yet, no one but yourself can fully assume the burden and tension of your growth. No one, however great his love, can ever find out for you those inner directions that are strictly your own. But genuine love may serve as sustainment and inspiration. By revealing each one to the other in the intimate "I-Thou" relationship, it also reveals each one to himself, and allows each one to discover within himself untapped sources and resources, unsuspected energies and powers.

When you are in love, it is as if you were given new sight, and certainly new insight into the nature of things. You see the world around you with a new intensity; you begin to understand the harmony of the universe. Where there had been nothing but chaos and meaninglessness, you begin to see order and clarity, to hear "the music of the spheres." New horizons open within, at times so vividly that it seems you have received new modes of understanding, new perception, new light. This is no sentimental inner glow, no mere feeling of warmth and delight, but rather the discovery or rediscovery in your own true self of depths and directions and potentials that were dormant and unexplored.

Ultimately, when you say "Thank you" to the beloved, it is not so much out of gratitude for exterior, visible gifts, however delightful or marvelous they may be. Most of all, it is for the sake of this joyful revelation that was made possible by creative love. When you love, when you are loved, you can say "I am" with more certainty, more clarity of vision and knowledge, and with infinitely more joy.

This should not be seen as the glorification of self, as love sought only for the purpose of finding oneself. Rather, it is mutual self-giving, so total that each one becomes inspired, and following through on this inspiration, becomes more truly, more fully a person made in the likeness of God.

When all is said and done, although the sexual relationship is an important factor of harmony and happiness, it is not the essence or the foundation of a happy marriage. No matter how well adjusted sexually a married couple may be, no matter how delightful their relationship, this is not all. The essence of marriage is creative love, and this same creative love is a condition of enduring sexual harmony. What really counts is that love which is able to say "Yes" to the other, to accept the other, to reveal to the other one's own humanity, one's own personhood; that love which is for the other a principle of strength, of inner growth, of grace. Christian husbands and wives know something essential: that their love is Christ-centered. It can be centered neither on themselves nor on each other. They cannot be folded in upon their own happiness, letting no one else in. Their love is centered, not upon an idea, but upon a living person, Christ. And it is only in the full awareness of Christ that this love can be creative, full of grace, and truly inspired.

Non-Christians certainly attain happiness in marriage. Yet, the conscious Christian has access, not to another asset—for we do not wish to manipulate God or his gifts for our own ends—but to another dimension. He knows that "Love is from God" (John 4:7). He has seen the love God has for him, and he has believed. He knows that he is incorporated to Christ, that he is a "new creation" through the death and resurrection of Christ. He knows that in whatever direction his human efforts are moving, no matter the success or failure of his personal endeavors, no matter his deficiencies and defeats, he is alive with a new life. And it is in this life and with this life that he encounters his beloved, so that ultimately what is central to his person is not his sexuality or his achievements as a social being, but his Christian dimension.

Faith in the power of Christ will radically alter your life. It will make you more open, human, truer to your own self. And finally, more capable of love.

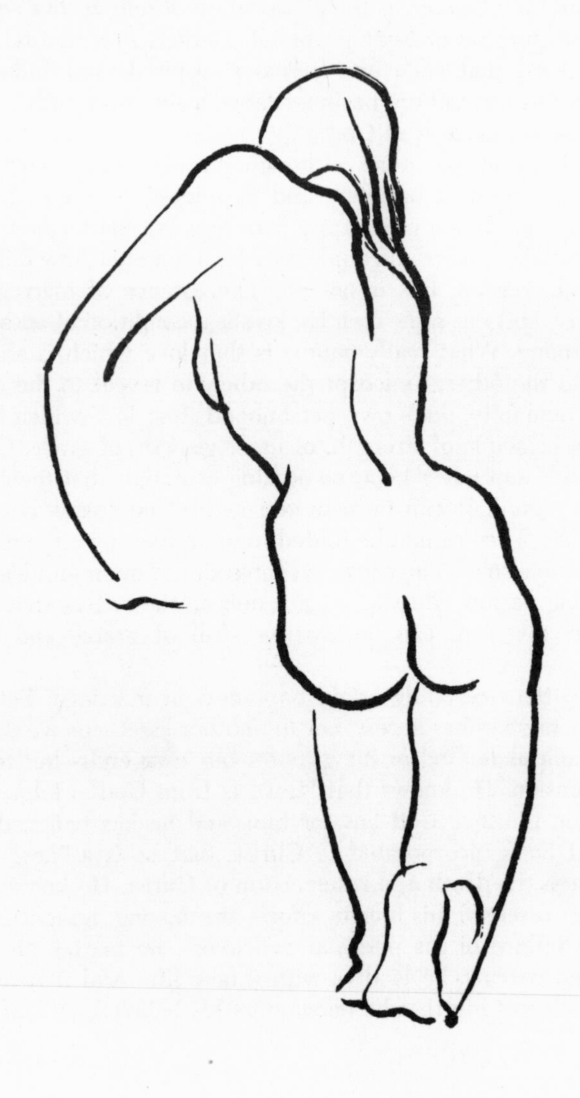

INDEX

IMPRIMATUR: ✠ Lawrence B. Casey
Bishop of Paterson
January 16, 1969

The imprimatur is an official declaration that a book is free from doctrinal or moral error. No implication is contained therein that the one who has granted the imprimatur agrees with the contents, opinions, or statements expressed.